ERIC CLAPTON

THE AUTOBIOGRAPHY

ERIC CLAPTON

THE AUTOBIOGRAPHY

By Eric Clapton

with Christopher Simon Sykes

Century · London

Published by Century 2007

2 4 6 8 10 9 7 5 3 1

First published in Great Britain in 2007 by
Century
Random House, 20 Vauxhall Bridge Road,
London SW1V 2SA

www.rbooks.co.uk

Addresses for companies within The Random House Group Limited can be found at:
www.randomhouse.co.uk/offices.htm

The Random House Group Limited Reg. No. 954009

A CIP catalogue record for this book
is available from the British Library

HB ISBN 9781846051609
TPB ISBN 9781846053092

The Random House Group Limited makes every effort to ensure that the papers used
in its books are made from trees that have been legally sourced from well-managed
and credibly certified forests. Our paper procurement policy can be found at:
www.randomhouse.co.uk/paper.htm

Mixed Sources
Product group from well-managed
forests and other controlled sources
www.fsc.org Cert no. TT-COC-2139
© 1996 Forest Stewardship Council

Typeset by SX Composing DTP, Rayleigh, Essex
Printed and bound in Great Britain by
Clays Ltd, St Ives PLC

The authors and publishers have made all reasonable efforts to contact
copyright holders for permission, and apologise for any omissions or errors
in the form of credits given. Corrections may be made to further printings.

This book is dedicated to my
Grandmother Rose Amelia Clapp,
and to my beloved wife Melia, and
my children Ruth, Julie, Ella and Sophie.

Acknowledgements

For their help in producing this book, I would like to thank Christopher Simon Sykes and Richard Steele, and a special thanks to Nici for all her hard work transcribing the manuscript.

CONTENTS

CHAPTER ONE
GROWING UP

Early in my childhood, when I was about six or seven, I began to get the feeling that there was something different about me. Maybe it was the way people talked about me as if I wasn't in the room. My family lived at 1 The Green, a tiny house in Ripley, Surrey, which opened directly on to the village green. It was part of what had once been almshouses, and was divided into four rooms: two bedrooms upstairs, and a small front room and kitchen downstairs. There was an outside toilet at the bottom of the garden, and no bathroom, just a big zinc bath that hung on the back door. I don't ever remember using it. Twice a week my mum used to fill a smaller tin tub with water and sponge me down, and on Sunday afternoons I used to go and have a bath at my Auntie Audrey's, my dad's sister, who lived in the new flats on the main road. I lived with my mum and dad, who slept in the main bedroom overlooking the green, and my brother, Adrian, who had a room at the back. I slept on a camp bed, sometimes with my parents, sometimes downstairs, depending on who was staying at the time. There was no electricity, and the gas lamps made a constant hissing sound. It amazes me now to think that whole families lived in these little houses.

My mum had six sisters, Nell, Elsie, Renie, Flossie, Cath and Phyllis, and two brothers, Joe and Jack, and on a Sunday it wasn't unusual for two or three of these other families to show up, and they would pass the gossip and get up to date with what was happening with us and with them. In the smallness of this house there were always conversations being carried on in front of me as if I didn't exist, and there were whispers exchanged between the sisters. It was a house full of secrets. But, bit by bit, by carefully listening to these exchanges, I slowly began to put together a picture of what was going on and to understand that the secrets were usually to do with me. One day I heard one of my aunties ask, 'Have you heard from his mum?' and the truth dawned on me, that when Adrian jokingly called me 'a little bastard', he was telling the truth.

The full impact upon me of this realisation was traumatic, because in the time when I was born, in March 1945, in spite of the fact that it had become so common because of the large numbers of overseas soldiers and airmen passing through England, there was still an enormous stigma attached to illegitimacy. Though this was true across the class divide, it was particularly so amongst working-class families such as ours who, living in a small village community, knew little of the luxury of privacy. Because of this, I became intensely confused about my position, and alongside my deep feelings of love for my family there existed a suspicion that in a tiny place like Ripley I might be an embarrassment to them that they always had to explain.

The truth, I eventually discovered, was that Mum and Dad, Rose and Jack Clapp, were in fact my grandparents. Adrian was my uncle, and Patricia, Rose's daughter from an earlier marriage, was my real mother, and had given me the name Clapton. In the mid-twenties, Rose Mitchell, as she was then, had met and fallen in love with Reginald Cecil Clapton, known as Rex, who was the dashing and handsome, Oxford-educated son of an Indian army officer. They had married in February 1927, much against the wishes of his parents, who considered that Rex was marrying beneath him. The wedding took place a few weeks after Rose had given birth to their first child, my Uncle Adrian. They set up home in Woking, but sadly it was a short-lived marriage, as Rex died of consumption in 1932, three years after the birth of their second child, Patricia.

Rose was heartbroken. She returned to Ripley, and it was ten years before she settled down again, after a long courtship, with Jack Clapp. They were married in 1942 and Jack, who as a child had badly injured his leg, and had therefore been exempt from call-up, found himself stepfather to Adrian and Patricia. In 1944, like many other towns in the South of England, Ripley found itself inundated with troops from the USA and Canada, and at some point Pat, aged fifteen, enjoyed a brief affair with Edward Fryer, a Canadian airman stationed nearby. They had met at a dance where he was playing the piano in the band. He turned out to be married, so when she found out she was pregnant, she had to cope on her own. Rose and Jack protected her, and I was born secretly in the upstairs back bedroom of their house on 30 March, 1945. As soon as it was practical, when I was in my second year, Pat left Ripley, and my grandparents brought me up as their own child. I was named Eric, but Rick was what they all called me.

Rose was petite with dark hair and sharp delicate features, with a characteristic pointed nose, 'the Mitchell nose' as it was known in the family and which was inherited from her father, Jack Mitchell. Photographs of her as a young woman show her to have been very pretty, quite the beauty amongst her sisters, but at some point at the outset of the war, aged barely thirty, she had undergone surgery for a serious problem with her palate. During the operation there was a power cut and the surgery had to be abandoned, as a result of which she had a massive scar underneath her left cheekbone, which gave the impression that a piece of her cheek had been hollowed out. This left her with a certain amount of self-consciousness. In his song 'Not Dark Yet', Dylan wrote 'Behind every beautiful face there's been some kind of pain.' Her suffering made her a very warm person with a deep compassion for other people's dilemmas. She was the focus of my life for much of my upbringing.

Jack, who was the love of her life, was four years younger than Rose. A shy, handsome man, over six feet tall with strong features and very well built, he had a look of Lee Marvin about him, and used to smoke his own roll-ups, made from a strong, dark tobacco called Black Beauty. He was authoritarian, as fathers were in those days, but he was kind, and very affectionate to me in his way, especially in my infant years. We didn't have a very tactile relationship; all the men in our family found it hard to express feelings of affection or warmth. Perhaps it was considered a sign of weakness. Jack made his living as a master plasterer, working for a local building contractor. He was a master carpenter and a master bricklayer too, so he could actually build an entire house on his own. He was an extremely conscientious man with a very strong work ethic, and he brought in a steady wage, which didn't fluctuate for the whole time I was growing up, so although we could have been considered poor, there was rarely a shortage of money. When things occasionally did get tight, Rose would go out and clean other people's houses, or she would work part-time at Stansfields, a bottling company with a factory on the outskirts of the village which produced fizzy drinks such as lemonade, orangeade and cream soda. When I was older, I used to do holiday jobs there to earn pocket money, sticking on labels and helping with the deliveries. It was like something out of Dickens. You went in there and it resembled a workhouse, with rats running around and a fierce bull terrier, which used to have to be kept locked up in case it attacked visitors.

Ripley, which is more like a suburb today, was in deep country when I was born. It was a typical small rural community, with most of the residents being agricultural workers, and if you weren't careful about what you said, then everybody knew your business. So it was important to be polite. Guildford was the main shopping town, which you could get to by bus, but Ripley had its own shops too. There were two butchers, Conisbees and Russes, and two bakeries, Wellers and Collins, a grocer, Jack Richardson, Green's the paper shop, Noakes the ironmonger, a fish and chip shop and five pubs. King and Olliers was the haberdashers where I got my first pair of long trousers, and which doubled as a post office, and there was a blacksmith, where all the local farm horses came in for shoes. Every village had a sweet shop; ours was run by two old-fashioned sisters, the Miss Farrs. We would go in there and the bell would go ding-a-ling-a-ling, and one of them would take so long coming from the back of the shop that we could fill our pockets up before a movement of the curtain told us she was about to appear. I would buy two Sherbert Dabs or a few Flying Saucers, using the family ration book, and walk out with a pocketful of Horlicks or Ovaltine tablets, which had become my first addiction.

In spite of the fact that Ripley was, all in all, a happy place to grow up in, life was soured by what I had found out about my origins, and the result was that I began to withdraw into myself. There seemed to have been some definite choices made within my family regarding how to deal with my circumstances, and I was not made privy to any of them. I observed the code of secrecy which existed in the house – 'We don't talk about what went on' – and attached myself to the family dog, a black Labrador called Prince. I also created a character for myself, whose name was Johnny Malingo. Johnny was a suave, devil-may-care, man/boy of the world, who rode roughshod over anyone who got in his way. I would escape into Johnny when things got too much for me, and stay there until the storm had passed. I also invented a fantasy friend called Bushbranch, who was a small horse, and went with me everywhere. Sometimes Johnny would magically become a cowboy, climb on to Bushbranch, and together they would ride off into the sunset. At the same time, I started to draw quite obsessively. My first fascination was with pies. There was a man who used to come to the village green pushing a barrow, which was a container for hot pies. I had always loved pies – Rose was an excellent cook – and I began to produce hundreds of drawings of them and of the pie man. Then I turned to copying from comics.

Because I was illegitimate, Rose and Jack tended to spoil me. Jack actually made my toys for me. I remember, for example, a beautiful sword and shield that he made me by hand. It was the envy of all the other kids. Rose bought me all the comics I wanted. I seemed to get a different one every day, always the *Topper*, the *Dandy*, the *Eagle* and the *Beano*. I particularly loved the Bash Street Kids, and I always used to notice when the artists would change and Lord Snooty's top hat would be different in some way. Over the years I copied countless drawings from these comics – cowboys and Indians, Romans, gladiators and knights in armour. Sometimes at school I did no class work at all, and it became quite normal to see my school books full of nothing but drawings.

School for me began when I was five, at Ripley Church of England Primary School, which was situated in a flint building next to the village church. Opposite was the village hall, where I attended Sunday school, and where I first heard a lot of the old beautiful English hymns, my favourite of which was 'Jesus Bids Us Shine'. To begin with I was quite happy going to school. Most of the kids that lived on the green next to us started at the same time, but as the months went by and it dawned on me that this was it for the long haul, I began to panic. The feelings of insecurity I had about my home life made me hate school. All I wanted to be was anonymous, which kept me from entering any kind of competitive event. I hated anything which would single me out and get me unwanted attention. I also felt sending me to school was just a way of getting me out of the house, and I became very resentful. There was one master, quite a young guy, called Mr Porter, who seemed to have a real interest in unearthing the children's gifts or skills, and becoming acquainted with us in general. Whenever he tried this with me, I would become extremely resentful. I would stare at him with as much hatred as I could muster, until he eventually caned me for what he called 'dumb insolence'. I don't blame him now, anyone in a position of authority got that kind of treatment from me. Art was the only subject that I really enjoyed, although I did win an award for playing 'Greensleeves' on the recorder, the first instrument I ever learned to play.

The headmaster was a Scotsman called Mr Dickson, and he had a shock of red hair. I had very little to do with him until I was nine years old, when I was called up before him for making a lewd suggestion to one of the girls in my class. While playing on the green, I had come across a piece of home-made pornography lying in the grass. It was a kind of book, made of pieces of paper crudely stapled together with rather amateurish drawings of genitalia and a typed text full of words I had never heard of. My curiosity was aroused because I hadn't had any kind of sex education, and I had certainly never seen a woman's genitalia. In fact I wasn't even certain if boys were different from girls until I saw this book.

Once I had recovered from the shock of seeing these drawings, I was determined to find out about girls. I was too shy to ask any of the girls I knew at school, but there was this new girl in the class, and because she was new, there was open season on her. As luck would have it, she was put at the desk directly in front of me in the classroom, so one morning I plucked up courage and asked her, without any idea of what the words meant, 'Do you fancy a shag?' She looked at me with a bemused expression, because she obviously didn't have a clue what I was talking about, but at playtime she went and told another girl what I'd said, and asked what it meant. After lunch, I was summoned to the headmaster's office where, after being quizzed as to exactly what I had said to her, and being made to promise to apologise, I was bent over and given six of the best. I left in tears, and the whole episode had a dreadful effect on me as from that point on I tended to associate sex with punishment, shame and embarrassment, feelings which coloured my sexual life for years.

In one respect, I was a very lucky child. As much as there was fairly confusing stuff going on at home, and dynamics that were difficult to understand, outside there was another whole world of fantasy and the countryside, which I lived in with my pals. Guy, Stuart and Gordon were my best friends, and we all lived in the same row of houses on the green. I don't know if they knew the truth about my origins, and I don't suppose it would have meant anything if they did. To them I was 'El Capitain', sometimes shortened to El, but mostly I was known as Rick. Once school was over, we would be outside all the time on our bikes. My first bike was a James and it was given to me by Jack after I'd pestered him to give me a Triumph Palm Beach, like the one he had, which was scarlet and cream and was as far as I was concerned the ultimate bike. Because it was a proper grown-up bike, however, they didn't make them for kids, so he bought me the James instead. Though it was basically the same colour scheme, it wasn't the real thing, and however hard I tried to be grateful, I was really disappointed, and I think I probably showed it. I didn't let it get me down though, because by taking one of the brakes off, removing the mudguards, stripping it down and giving it different tyres, the kind that are for riding over mud, I turned it into what we called a 'track' bike.

We'd all meet on the green after school and decide where we were going to go. In the summer we'd mostly go down to the river Wey, just outside the village. Everybody went there, grown-ups too, and there was one particular place that was attractive to us, because there was a weir. On one side it was seriously deep and you weren't allowed to swim – a couple of kids had drowned in there over the years – but where the weir came down into the shallows, and it looked like a kind of waterfall, there were little ledges and pools on either side where it was safe to swim and play around in the mud. Just beyond that, it would pan out and deepen up again and it would turn into good fishing water, and that's where I learned to fish. Rose bought me a rod from a catalogue. It was a cheap, very basic bamboo rod, painted green, with a cork handle and a proper fixed reel, but I really loved it from day one. This was the start of my life as a kit junkie. I used to love just to look at it, and I probably played with it as much as I fished with it. We mostly fished using bread as bait, and because we were fishing near to proper fishermen, we had to be very careful not to get in their way. Normally the best you could hope for was to catch a gudgeon, but one memorable day I caught a fairly big roach, which must have weighed a couple of pounds. Another fisherman who was coming up the bank, a real angler, stopped and said, 'That's a pretty decent fish you've got there,' and I was over the moon.

When we weren't down by the river, we would head off to the 'Fuzzies'. This was the name for the woods behind the green, where we used to play serious games of cowboys and Indians, or Germans and English. We created our own version of the Somme in there, digging trenches that were deep enough for us to stand in and shoot out of. Parts of the woods were so thick with gorse that you could easily get lost and we called this area 'the

Forbidden City' or 'the Lost World'. When I was little, I didn't go into the Lost World without an older boy or a gang, because I really did believe that if you went in on your own, you'd never come out. I had my first encounter with a snake in there. I was in the middle of a game, and I heard a hissing noise. I looked down, standing with my legs slightly apart, and an adder went between them, a big one about two feet long. I went absolutely rigid. I'd never seen a snake before, but Rose was terrified of them and had passed her fear on to me. It scared the shit out of me and I had nightmares about it for ages.

Occasionally, when I was around the age of ten or eleven, we would play games of kiss-chase in the Fuzzies, which was the only time girls were involved in our games. The rules were that the girls were given time to hide, and then we went to look for them, and if we found them the prize would be a kiss. Sometimes we played a higher stakes version of the game in which the discovered girls had to pull their knickers down. But on the whole we were rather frightened of the girls in the village. They seemed aloof and rather powerful, and showed little interest in us, their attentions being reserved for cooler types like Eric Beesley, who always cut a bit of a dash and was the first one in Ripley with a crew cut. My experience with the pornography had certainly left me with the feeling that any advance made towards a girl would produce some kind of retribution, and I had no intention of getting caned every other day.

On Saturday mornings, quite a lot of us used to go to the pictures in Guildford, to the ABC Minors Club, which was a real treat. We would watch incredible cliffhanger serials, like Batman, Flash Gordon and Hoppalong Cassidy, and comedies like the Three Stooges and Charlie Chaplin. There was always an MC and there were competitions, and people were encouraged to get up on stage and sing or do impersonations, which I dreaded and always avoided. We were no angels, however. When the lights went down, we would all bring out our home-made catapults and fire conkers at the screen.

In the early fifties, a typical evening's entertainment for Ripley kids was sitting in the bus shelter watching the traffic, in the vain hope that a sports car would go by, and once every six months we might see an Aston Martin or a Ferrari, which would make our day. We were desperate for excitement, and nothing was quite as exciting as breaking the law . . . within reason. We might go 'scrumping', stealing apples, on the Dunsborough estate which in terms of excitement was huge, because it was owned by a film star called Florence Desmond, and we would sometimes see her famous friends walking on the green. I once got Tyrone Power's autograph. Also the likelihood of getting caught was quite high, as there were usually gamekeepers prowling around.

Other times we would go shoplifting in Cobham or Woking, mostly stealing silly things, like ties or handkerchieves, and there were also occasional bouts of vandalising. For example, we'd get on one of the trains from Guildford which stopped at all the small local stations, choosing an empty compartment – the local trains had no corridors – and in between stations we would completely demolish it. We would smash all the mirrors, tear down the maps on the wall, cut up the luggage rack nets with our penknives, slash all the upholstery to ribbons, and then get out at the next station hooting with laughter. The fact that we knew it was wrong, and yet we could do it and get away with it, gave us a huge adrenalin rush. Of course if we had been caught, it could have meant being sent to Borstal, but miraculously we never were.

Smoking was an important rite of passage in those days, and occasionally we would get our hands on some cigarettes. I remember when I was twelve, getting hold of some du Mauriers, I was particularly intrigued by the packaging. With its dark red flip-top box and silver criss-cross pattern, it was very sophisticated and grown-up looking. Rose found the box in my pocket and said, 'OK, if you want to smoke, then let's have a cigarette together. We'll see if you can really smoke.' She lit up one of these du Mauriers, and I put it in my mouth and had a puff on it. 'No, no, no!' she said. 'Take it down, take it down! That's not smoking.' I didn't know what she meant, until she said, 'You breathe it in, breathe it in.' Then I tried it, and of course I was violently ill, and never smoked again till I was twenty-one.

The one thing I didn't like was fighting, which was a popular pastime amongst a lot of the kids. Pain and violence frightened me. There were two families to avoid in Ripley, the Masters and the Hills, who were both extremely hard. The Masters were my cousins, the children of my Auntie Nell, a memorable lady because she suffered from Tourette's syndrome, though in those days she was just considered a little eccentric. When she spoke, her speech was interspersed with the words 'fuck' and 'Eddie', so she would come to the house and say, 'Hello, Rick, fuck Eddie. Is your mum in fuck Eddie?' I absolutely adored her. Her husband, Charlie, was twice her size and covered in tattoos, and they had fourteen sons, the Masters brothers, who were lethal and usually in some kind of trouble. The Hills were also all boys, about ten in all, and they were the village villains, or so it seemed then. They were my nemesis, I was always afraid of getting beaten up by them, so whenever they would pick on me, I would tell my cousins, hoping to cause a vendetta between the Hills and the Masters. Mostly I tried to stay away from all of them.

From the very earliest days, music played a big role in my life; in the time before TV, it was a very important part of our community experience. On Saturday nights, most of the adults gathered at the British Legion Club to drink and smoke and listen to local entertainers like Sid Perrin, a great pub singer with a powerful voice, who sang in the style of Mario Lanza, and whose singing would drift out on to the street, where we would be sitting with a lemonade and a packet of crisps. Another village musician was Buller Collier, who lived in the end house in our row, and who used to stand outside the front door and play his piano accordion. I loved to watch him, not just for the sound of the squeeze box, but also for its appearance, because it was red and black and it shimmered. I was more used to hearing the piano, because Rose loved to play. My earliest memories are of her playing on a harmonium she kept in the front room, and later she acquired a small piano. She would also sing, mostly standards, such as 'Now Is The Hour', a popular hit by Gracie Fields, 'I Walk Beside You' and 'Bless This House' by Josef Locke, who was very popular in our house, and who was the first singer to captivate me with the sound of his voice. My own initial attempts at singing took place on the stairs leading up to the bedrooms in our house. I found out that there was one place which had an echo, and I used to sit there singing the songs of the day, mostly popular ballads, and to me it sounded like I was singing on a record.

A good proportion of any musical genes that I may have inherited come from Rose's family, the Mitchells. Her dad, Grandad Mitchell, a great big man who was a bit of a drinker and a womaniser, not only played the accordion too, but the violin, and he used to hang out with a celebrated local busker called Jack Townshend, who played guitar, fiddle and spoons, and they'd play traditional music together. He lived in Newark Lane, just round the corner from us, and was an important figure in village life, particularly around harvest time, because he owned a traction engine. He was a little strange and not very friendly, and whenever I went round with my Uncle Adrian to see him, he would usually be sitting in his armchair, more often than not quite drunk. Like Stansfields factory, there was something rather Dickensian about the whole thing. We used to visit him a lot, and it was from watching him play the violin that I got the idea to try and play myself. It just seemed so natural and easy for him. My folks got me an old violin from somewhere, and I think I was supposed to learn by just watching and listening, but I was still only about ten years old, and didn't have the patience. All I could get out of it was a screeching noise. I just couldn't grasp the physics of the instrument at all – I had only played the recorder up till then – and I quickly gave it up.

Uncle Adrian, my mother's brother, who was still living with us when I was small, was an incredible character who was to have a great influence on my life. Because I had been brought up to think of him as my brother, that was the way I always regarded him, even after I found out he was actually my uncle. He was heavily into fashion and fast cars, and later owned a succession of Ford Cortinas, which were usually two-tone, peach and cream or something like that, with their interiors upholstered with fur and fake leopard skin, and adorned with mascots. When he wasn't mucking around with his cars, improving their appearance and performance, he was driving them very fast and sometimes crashing them. He was also an atheist with an obsession for science fiction, and had a cupboard full of paperbacks by Isaac Asimov and Kurt Vonnegut, and other really good stuff.

Adrian was also an inventor, but most of his inventions were concentrated in the domestic sphere, such as his unique vinegar dispenser. He had a passion for vinegar, which he would put on everything, even custard. This was frowned on and finally forbidden by Rose, so he designed a secret vinegar dispenser, which basically consisted of a Fairy Liquid bottle, hidden under his armpit, with a tube coming out of it that went down his sleeve. He could then pass his hand over whatever he was eating, and, by secretly squeezing the bottle by lowering his arm, vinegar would invisibly spray over the plate.

He was very musical too. He played chromatic harmonica, and was a great dancer. He loved to jitterbug, and was very good at it. It was an amazing sight to see, because he had extremely long hair which he kept greased down with tons of Brylcreem. Once he got going, his hair would fall down and cover his face, making him look like a creature from under the sea. He had a record player in his room, and used to play me the jazz records he liked, things by Stan Kenton, the Dorsey Brothers and Benny Goodman. It seemed like outlaw music at the time, and I felt the message coming through.

Most of the music I was introduced to from an early age came from the radio, which was permanently switched on in the house. I feel blessed to have been born in that period; musically it was very rich in its diversity. The programme that everybody listened to without fail was *Two Way Family Favourites*, a live show which linked the British forces serving in Germany with their families at home. It went out at twelve o'clock on Sundays, just when we were sitting down to lunch. Rose always cooked a really good Sunday lunch of roast beef, gravy and Yorkshire pudding, with potatoes, peas and carrots, followed by something like spotted dick and custard, and, with this incredible music playing, it was a real feast of the senses. You would hear the whole spectrum of music; opera, classical, rock 'n' roll, jazz and pop, so, typically, there might be something like Guy Mitchell singing 'She Wears Red Feathers', then a big-band piece by someone like Stan Kenton, a dance tune by Victor Sylvester, maybe a pop song by David Whitfield, an aria from a Puccini opera like *La Bohème* and, if I was lucky, Handel's *Water Music*, which was one of my favourites. I loved any music that was a powerful expression of emotion.

On Saturday mornings I listened to *Children's Favourites* introduced by the incredible Uncle Mac. I would be sitting by the radio at nine o'clock waiting for the pips, then the announcement,

'Nine o'clock on Saturday morning means *Children's Favourites*', followed by the signature tune, a high-pitched orchestral piece called *Puffing Billy* and then Uncle Mac himself saying, 'Hello children everywhere, this is Uncle Mac. Good morning to you all.' Then he would play a quite extraordinary selection of music, mixing children's songs like 'Teddy Bear's Picnic' or 'Nellie The Elephant' with novelty songs like 'The Runaway Train' and folk songs such as 'The Big Rock Candy Mountain', and occasionally something at the far end of the spectrum, like Chuck Berry singing 'Memphis Tennessee' which hit me like a thunderbolt when I heard it. One particular Saturday he put on a song by Sonny Terry and Brownie McGhee called 'Whooping And Hollering'. It had Sonny Terry playing the harmonica, then alternately whooping in falsetto, so fast, and with perfect timing, while Brownie played fast guitar accompaniment. I guess it was the novelty element that made Uncle Mac play it, but it cut through me like a knife, and after that I never missed *Children's Favourites*, just in case he played it again, and he did, like on a rotation, over and over.

Music became a healer for me, and I learned to listen with all my being. I found that it could wipe away all the emotions of fear and confusion relating to my family. These became even more acute in 1954, when I was nine, and my mother suddenly turned up in my life. By this time she was married to a Canadian soldier called Frank McDonald, and she brought with her two young children, my half-brother and half-sister, Brian who was six, and Cheryl who was one. I was told we were going to meet my sister off the boat at Southampton, and down the gangplank came this very glamorous, charismatic woman, with her auburn hair up high in the fashion of the day. She was very good-looking, though there was a coldness to her looks, a sharpness. She came off the boat laden with expensive gifts which her husband Frank had sent over from Korea, where he had been stationed during the war. We were all given silk jackets with dragons embroidered on them, and lacquered boxes and things like that.

Even though I knew the truth about her by now, and Rose and Jack were aware of this, nobody said anything when we got home, till one evening, when we were all sitting in the front room of our tiny little house, I suddenly blurted out to Pat, 'Can I call you Mummy now?' There was an awful moment of embarrassment, and the tension in the room was unbearable. The unspoken truth was finally out. Then she said, in a very kindly way, 'I think it's best, after all they've done for you, that you go on calling your grandparents Mum and Dad.' In that moment I felt totally rejected.

Though I tried to accept and understand what she was saying to me, it was beyond my grasp. I had expected that she would sweep me up in her arms and take me away to wherever she had come from. My disappointment was unbearable, and almost immediately turned into hatred and anger. Things quickly became very difficult for everybody, I became surly and with-drawn, rejecting everyone's affection. Only my Auntie Audrey, Jack's sister, was able to get through. I was her favourite, and she would come and see me once a week bringing me toys and sweets, gently trying to reach me. I would often abuse her and be openly cruel to her, but deep down inside, I was deeply grateful for her love and attention.

Things were not made any easier by the fact that Pat, who was now referred to in public as my sister, in order to avoid complicated and embarrassing explanations, stayed on for the better part of a year. Because they'd come from abroad, and the kids had Canadian accents, they were treated like stars in the village, and were given special treatment. I felt shoved aside. I even resented my little half-brother, Brian, who looked up to me and always wanted to come out and play with my pals. One day I was having a tantrum, and I stormed out of the house on to the green. Pat came after me and I just turned on her and shouted, 'I wish you'd never come here! I wish you'd go away!' and in that single moment I remembered just how idyllic my life had really been up until that day. It had been so simple, there was just me and my parents, and even though I knew now they were really my grandparents, I was getting all the attention and there was at least love and harmony in the house.

These events at home had a drastic effect on my school life. In those days, when you were eleven, you had to take an exam called the eleven-plus, which decided where you were going to go next, either to a grammar school, for those with the top results, or a secondary modern school for those with lower grades. You took the exam in another school, which meant that we were all piled into buses and driven to a strange place, where we took exam after exam over the course of a whole day. I blanked on everything. I was so frightened by my surroundings and so insecure and scared that I just couldn't respond, and the result was that I failed miserably. I didn't particularly care because going to either Guildford or Woking grammar schools would have meant being separated from my mates, none of whom were academics. They all excelled in the physical sports and had a certain amount of scorn for schooling. As for Jack and Rose, if they were at all disappointed, they didn't really show it.

So I ended up going to St Bede's Secondary Modern School in the neighbouring village of Send, which is where I really began to make discoveries. It was the summer of 1956, and Elvis was top of the charts. I met a boy at school who was a newcomer to Ripley; his name was John Constantine. He came from a well off middle-class family who lived on the outskirts of the village, and we became friends because we were so different from everybody else, neither of us fitted in. While everybody else at the school was into cricket and football, we were into clothes and buying 78 rpm records, for which we were scorned and ridiculed. We were known as 'the Loonies'. I used to go to his house a lot, and his parents had a radiogram, which was a combination of a radio and a gramophone. It was the first one I had seen. John had a copy of 'Hound Dog', Elvis' number one, and we played it over and over. There was something about the music that made it totally irresistible to us, plus it was being made by someone not much older than us, who was like us, but appeared to be in control of his own destiny, something we could not even imagine.

I got my first record player the following year. It was a Dansette, and the first single I ever bought was 'When', a number-one hit for the Kalin Twins, that I'd heard on the radio. Then I bought my first album, *The Chirping Crickets*, by Buddy Holly and the Crickets, followed by the soundtrack album of *High Society*. The Constantines were also the only people I knew in Ripley who had a TV, and we used to watch *Sunday Night at the London Palladium*, which was the first TV show to have American performers on, who were so far ahead on every level. I had just won a prize at school, for of all things neatness and tidiness, of a book on America, so I was particularly obsessed with it. One night they had Buddy Holly on the show, and I thought I'd died and gone to heaven; that was when I saw my first Fender guitar. It was like seeing an instrument from outer space and I said to myself: 'That's the future – that's what I want.' Suddenly I realised I was in a village that was never going to change, yet there on TV was something out of the future. And I wanted to go there.

There was one teacher at St Bede's, Mr Swan, an art teacher, who seemed to recognise that there was something in me that was worthwhile, that I had artistic skills, and he went out of his way to try to help me. He also taught handwriting and one of the first things he taught me was to write with an italic pen. I was a little afraid of him, because he was known to be a strong disciplinarian and he was very austere, but he was extremely kind to me, which got through to me on some level. So when it came to the time for me to take the thirteen-plus, an exam designed for people who missed passing the eleven-plus, I decided that I would try really hard because I owed him something for his kindness, and the result was that, with some misgivings, as I knew it would mean leaving all my friends at St Bede's, I passed, aged thirteen, into Hollyfield School, Surbiton.

Hollyfield meant big changes for me. I was given a bus pass and every day I had to travel on my own up to Surbiton from Ripley on the Green Line, a half-hour journey, to go to school with people I'd never met. It was very tough to begin with, and hard to know what to do about my old friendships, because I knew quite a few of them would peter out. At the same time it was very exciting, because at last I was out in the big wide world. Hollyfield was different in that, though it was a regular secondary school, it also contained the junior art department of Kingston School of Art, so while we would study normal things like history, English and Maths, on a couple of days a week we would do nothing but art, figure drawing, still lifes, working with paint and clay. For the first time in my life I actually started shining, and I felt like I was hitting my stride in every way.

As far as my old friends were concerned, I had moved up in the world, and though they knew to a certain extent that this was OK, they still couldn't help but have a go at me about it. I knew I was on the move. Hollyfield changed my perspective on life. It was a much wilder environment with more exciting people. It was on the edge of London, so we were skiving off a lot, going to pubs, and going into Kingston to buy records at Bentalls, the department store. I was hearing so many new things all at the same time. I became aware of folk music, New Orleans jazz and rock 'n' roll, and it mesmerised me. People always say that they remember exactly where they were the night that President Kennedy was assassinated. I don't, but I do remember walking into the school playground on the day that Buddy Holly died, and the feeling that was there. The place was like a graveyard, no one could speak, we were in such shock. Of all the music heroes of the time, he was the most accessible, and he was the real thing. He wasn't a glamour puss, he had no act as such, he clearly was a real guitar player, and to top it all off, he wore glasses. He was like one of us. It was amazing the effect his death had on us. After that, some say the music died. For me it really seemed to burst open.

The art annexe at Hollyfield School was a short distance away up Surbiton Hill Road, and on the days when we were doing art we would walk up to this building where our teacher would put us to work doing still life, sculpture or drawing. On the way up we would pass Bell's Music Store, a shop that had made its name selling piano accordions when they were all the rage. Then, when the skiffle boom took off, made popular in the mid-fifties by Lonnie Donegan with songs like 'Rock Island Line' and 'The Grand Coulee Dam', Bell's changed tack and became a guitar store, and I would always stop and look at the instruments in the window. Since most of the music I liked best was guitar music, I decided that I would like to learn to play, so I badgered Rose and Jack to buy me one. Maybe I harped on about it so much, they did it to keep me quiet, but, whatever the reason, one day they took the bus up there with me and put a deposit on the instrument I had singled out as being the guitar of my dreams.

The instrument I had set my eyes on was a Hoyer, made in Germany and costing about £2. It was an odd instrument, it looked like a Spanish guitar, but instead of nylon, it had steel strings. It was a curious combination, and for a novice, it was really quite painful to play. Of course, it was a case of the cart before the horse, because I couldn't even tune a guitar, let alone play one. There was no one to teach me, so I set about teaching

21

myself, and it was not an easy task. To begin with, I had not expected it to be quite so big, almost the same size as I was. Once I was holding it, I couldn't get my hand round the neck, and I could hardly press the strings down, they were so high. It seemed like it was going to be impossible, and I was overwhelmed by the reality of it. At the same time I was unbelievably excited. The guitar was very shiny and somehow virginal. It was like a piece of equipment from another universe, so glamorous, and as I tried to strum it, I felt like I was really crossing into grown-up territory.

The first song I chose to learn was a folksong, 'Scarlet Ribbons', which had been made popular by Harry Belafonte, but I had also heard a bluesy version by Josh White. I learned it totally by ear, listening and playing along to the record. I had a small portable Grundig tape recorder, my pride and joy, a little reel-to-reel thing that Rose had given me for my birthday, and I would record my attempts and listen to them over and over again, until I thought I'd got it right. It was made more difficult because, as I later discovered, the guitar was not a very good one. On a more expensive instrument, the strings would normally be lower in relation to the fingerboard, to facilitate the movement of the fingers, but on a cheaper or badly made instrument, the strings will be low at the top of the fingerboard, and as they get closer to the bridge they get higher and higher, which makes them hard to press down and painful to play. I got off to a pretty poor start because I almost immediately broke one of the strings, and since I didn't have any others, I had to learn to play with only five, and played that way for quite a while . . .

Going to Hollyfield School did a lot to enhance my consciousness of image. I was meeting some heavyweight characters there who had very definite ideas about art and fashion. It had started for me in Ripley with jeans, which in the early days, when I was about twelve, had to be black and have triple green stitching down the outside, very cutting-edge stuff at the time. Italian-style clothes came next, suits with jackets cut very short, and tapered trousers with winkle-pickers. For us, and for most other families in Ripley, everything was bought from catalogues, like the Littlewoods catalogue, and, in my case, was altered if necessary by Rose. The guitar went with the beatnik look, which came in the middle of my time at Hollyfield. This consisted of skintight jeans from Moffats, taken in down the inside, a black crew-necked pullover, a combat jacket from Millets, complete with ban the bomb signs, and moccasins made up from a kit. One day I was kneeling in front of the mirror miming to a Gene Vincent record, when one of my mates walked past the open window. He stopped and looked at me, and I'll never forget the embarrassment I felt, because the truth is that, driven though I was by the music, I was equally driven by the thought of becoming one of those people I had seen on TV, not English pop stars like Cliff Richard, but the Americans such as Buddy Holly, Jerry Lee Lewis, Little Richard and Gene Vincent. I knew then that something was calling me and I wasn't going to be able to stay in Ripley.

Though I still hadn't quite got to grips with the actual playing of the guitar, I wanted to look like I knew what I was doing, and tried to cultivate the image of what I thought a troubadour should look like. I got a biro and wrote on the top surface of the guitar, in huge letters, the words 'LORD ERIC', because I thought that's what troubadours did. Then I attached a string to the guitar to serve as a strap and imagined myself with a girlfriend, also dressed in beatnik gear, going to play folk music in a coffee bar. The girlfriend materialised in the shape of a very pretty girl called Diane Coleman, who was also attending Hollyfield. She lived in Kingston, and we had a short but intense little fling until sex reared its head, and I panicked. Until then, we had become very fond of one another, and would spend hours listening to records together in her mum's front room. My initial career as a troubadour was just as brief. We went out together to a coffee bar about three times, complete with the Lord Eric guitar, and were both embarrassed, me by being too shy to play and she by witnessing it. Then, just when I thought I'd hit a brick wall, I found another guitar.

There used to be a kind of flea market in Kingston, and I was wandering around one Saturday when I saw a very odd-looking guitar hanging up on one of the stalls. It was acoustic, but it had a very narrow-shaped body, almost like a medieval English guitar, and there was a painting of a naked woman stuck on the back of it. Intuitively I knew it was good. I picked it up, and though I didn't play it, because I didn't want anyone to hear, it felt perfect, like a dream guitar. I bought it there and then for £2 10s.; don't ask me where the money came from, possibly cadged from Rose, or 'borrowed' from her handbag. I was getting a pretty decent amount of pocket money each week, but it wouldn't have been beyond me, I'm ashamed to say, to supplement my spending in any way that was open to me.

By now I had mastered some clawhammer, and tried out a few of the folk pieces I had learned on this new guitar. Compared to the Hoyer, I found it was very easy to play. The body was quite small and slim and it had an unconventionally wide flat fingerboard like a Spanish guitar. The strings were spaced very far apart so you could get your fingers quite easily on to each string without your hand feeling crowded, and it was shallow all the way down, making it delicate and fragile, but at the same time easy to play high on the fingerboard, as well as low. It turned out to be a George Washburn, a vintage American instrument of great value, originally manufactured by a company in Chicago that had been making guitars since 1864. On the back of the rosewood body, someone had stuck that piece of paper painted with a pin-up and then varnished it over. It was difficult to scrape this off without damaging the wood, and it pissed me off that someone had done this to such a beautiful instrument. At last I had a proper guitar, meant for folk music. Now maybe I could become the troubadour that I thought I was meant to be.

CHAPTER TWO

THE YARDBIRDS

By the time I took my art A level, at the age of sixteen, and moved on to Kingston School of Art, on a year's probation, I was becoming quite proficient as a player and was learning new things all the time. There was a coffee bar in Richmond I used to frequent, called L'Auberge. It was on the hill just by the bridge, and across the river in Twickenham was a funky old place called Eel Pie Island. This was an island in the middle of the river, which had a massive dance hall built on it. It was an ancient, creaky wooden gin palace, and on a Saturday night they would have New Orleans jazz bands playing there, people like Ken Colyer, and the Temperance Seven, and we loved it. The routine was to start out at L'Auberge in the early evening, have a couple of coffees, and then wander over the bridge to Eel Pie. I'll never forget the feeling as you got about halfway across the bridge, and you'd suddenly realise you were in the middle of a swelling crowd of people who all looked vaguely the same. There was a tremendous sense of belonging back then. In those pre-hippie, beatnik days, it did seem to be all about the music. Drugs were rare, and even the drinking was fairly moderate.

I used to play there with Dave Brock, who later went on to

found Hawkwind, and I fell in with the crowd of musicians and beatniks who used to hang out there. Sometimes we'd all jump on the train and go up to London to the folk clubs and pubs around Soho, places like the Marquess of Granby, the Duke of York and the Gyre and Gimble coffee bar in Charing Cross. The first time I ever got beaten up was outside 'the Gs'. A bunch of squaddies lured me outside, and gave me a good kicking for absolutely no other reason, as far as I could see, than to let off steam. It was a pretty nasty experience, but in a perverse way I felt like I had made my bones, another rite of passage completed. It did teach me, however, that I was not cut out for fighting. I made no attempt to protect myself, maybe because I intuitively knew that would make matters worse, and from then on, I seemed to develop an alert instinct for potentially violent situations, avoiding them like the plague.

The folk scene had a real following in those days, and in the clubs and pubs I began to meet loads of like-minded people and musicians. Long John Baldry was a regular, and I know Rod Stewart used to sing at the Duke of York, although I never saw him there. There were also two guitarists who played regularly in these places, both of whom had a big influence on me. One was a guy called Buck, who played the first Zemaitis twelve-string I ever saw, and the other was Wiz Jones, another famous troubadour of the time. They'd play Irish ballads and English folk tunes, mixing them up with Leadbelly songs and other stuff, which gave me a unique view of the world of folk music. I'd sit as close to them as possible, which was often difficult as they were so popular, and watch their hands to see the way they played. Then I'd come back home and practise for hours and hours, trying to teach myself to play the music I'd heard. I'd listen carefully to the recording of whatever song I was working on, then copy it and copy it till I could match it. I remember trying to match the bell-like tone achieved by Muddy Waters on his song 'Honey Bee'. It was the first time I ever got three strings together on my guitar. I had no technique, of course, and I just spent hours mimicking it.

The main man for me was Big Bill Broonzy, and I tried to learn his technique, which was to accompany yourself with your thumb, using the thumb to play eighth notes on the bass strings, while you pick out a riff or countermelody with your fingers. This is a staple part of blues playing in one form or another, and can be developed into a folk pattern too, like clawhammer, where you move your thumb rhythmically between the bottom strings alternately, while picking out the melody on the top strings with your first, second and sometimes third fingers. My method of learning was pretty basic. I'd play along with the record I wanted to imitate, and when I thought I'd mastered something, I'd record it on the Grundig and play it back. If it sounded like the record, then I was satisfied. As I slowly began to master the art of finger-style acoustic playing, I learned new songs, for instance, the old Bessie Smith song 'Nobody Knows You When You're Down And Out', 'Railroad Bill', an old bluegrass song, and Big Bill Broonzy's 'Key To The Highway'.

At about that time, I met, and followed around for a while, an American female folk singer called Gina Glaser. She was the first American musician I had been anywhere near, and I was star-struck. To make a little extra money, she posed naked for still-life classes at Kingston School of Art; she had a young child, and a slightly world-weary aura to her. Her speciality was old Civil War songs like 'Pretty Peggyo' and 'Marble Town'. She had a beautiful clear voice and played an immaculate clawhammer style. I was smitten with her, and I think she found me attractive, but she was twice my age, and I was still pretty green around women.

As my playing improved, I started to go to a pub in Kingston called the Crown, where I used to play in a corner by the bar billiards table. This particular pub attracted a suave crowd of beat people, who seemed a cut above the kind of people I'd been used to hanging out with. This was an affluent crowd; the guys wore Chelsea boots, leather jackets, matelot shirts and Levi's 501s, which were incredibly hard to find, and there was a kind of harem of very good-looking girls who moved around with them. Bardot was then the icon for women to follow, so their uniform was tight jumpers, slit skirts and black stockings, with duffel coats and scarves. They were very exotic, very fast and very well educated, a tight group of friends who seemed to have grown up together. They'd usually meet at the pub, then go off to hang out at someone's house, and there always seemed to be a party going on around them. It became my ambition to be accepted by these people, but since I was an outsider from the word go, and working class, the only way I could really get their attention was by playing the guitar.

Hanging out with this bunch, and especially seeing all these beautiful girls, really made me want to belong, but I had no idea how to go about it. When I was still at secondary modern, a friend of mine called Steve, one of the lads from Send, who was into clothes and looking cool, took me out on a blind date. I was obviously elected to divert his girlfriend's mate, who wasn't the most beautiful girl in the world. I wasn't interested in her at all, but I was very horny, and although I wouldn't kiss her, I did try to get my hands on her upper torso. She wasn't amused, and created a bit of a scene. That was as far as I had got with sex until Diane at Hollyfield, and we hadn't got much further. I was terrified of going too far, and then being held responsible in some way. Ever since finding that pornography on the green, I felt compelled to discover for myself what it was all about, but my experience of female rejection, stemming from Mother, left me quaking with fear at the threshold.

At Kingston, I set my sights on a girl who was completely out of my league, I think she was the daughter of a local politician.

Her name was Gail, and she was absolutely gorgeous, dark-skinned, tall and voluptuous, with long dark curly hair. She seemed very aloof when I first saw her, but after I had observed her for a few weeks, I could see that she was also pretty wild. I quickly became totally obsessed with her, and somehow got it into my head that the best way to get her attention was by regularly getting blind drunk, as if that would make me more appealing, or more manly in some way. On any given night in Kingston, I would be drinking up to ten pints of Mackeson's milk stout, followed by rum and blackcurrant, gin and tonic, or gin and orange. I learned to try to drink so I'd just stop short of passing out, but I would invariably end up just getting very ill and throwing up. Needless to say, as a courting tool it failed miserably, Gail was not impressed, but if nothing else, I was learning a lot about the power of alcohol.

Only a short time before this, I had gone with three friends on the train to Beaulieu for the jazz festival. We got there on a Saturday morning, and were planning to stay till Sunday night. We decided to go to the pub for lunch, before going on to the festival. The last thing I remembered that day was dancing on the tables with a guy I'd never met before in my life, who became my absolute brother. I can still recall the way he looked and everything about him, though I'd never seen him before or since. I thought he was just the most funny, charismatic person I'd ever met in my life, and we got legless together. I had gone with some friends and a potential girlfriend, with the intention of camping in the woods near the festival, and the next thing I knew was waking up in the morning on my own, in the middle of nowhere. I had no money, I had shit myself, I had pissed myself, I had puked all over myself, and I had no idea where I was. There were signs, like the remains of a fire, that the others had pitched camp close by, but they'd all gone, and they'd left me there. I was stunned. I had to get home to Ripley in this condition and I

31

caught the train at a little country station nearby. The station-master took pity on me, and gave me a handwritten IOU on a piece of paper, which I dejectedly gave to Rose when I got home. I was heavily disillusioned with my friends, shocked that they could have just left me there in that state, alone and without any money, but the really insane thing was, I couldn't wait to do it all again.

I thought there was something other-worldly about the whole culture of drinking, that being drunk made me a member of some strange mysterious club. It also gave me courage, to play and, finally, to get off with a girl. Saturday nights in Kingston always followed the same routine. We would all meet up at the Crown and I would play. There was one guy who was always there called Dutch Mills, a smooth character who played blues harmonica, and most Saturdays he would have a party at his house. I remember going back there one night with about a dozen people, none of whom I knew very well, and at some point the lights went off and everyone went at it. That's where and when I actually lost my virginity, with a girl called Lucy who was older than me, and whose boyfriend was out of town. I was terrified and fumbly, I still am for that matter, but she patiently helped me through, and although I knew all the others were aware of what was happening, either they didn't care, or were so busy with their own endeavours that they just chose to ignore us. The following morning, we parted company, and although we saw one another around often, it was never spoken of again. With what I knew about relationships and sex, I just assumed that's the way it was done, and went on my way.

Going so suddenly from the odd kind of groping session to full intercourse was very, very strange, and it was all over in the blinking of an eye. There was no protection, of course, as the whole thing was so unexpected, so the next time I thought it was going to happen, I went with a mate of mine to a chemist to buy a packet of Durex. It was incredibly embarrassing. I had been told to ask for a packet of three, which I assumed was some kind of code. I remember the man behind the counter smiling at me and giving me a kind of wink and then asking me questions like, 'Do you want lubricated or non-lubricated?' I didn't have a clue what he was talking about. The next time I had the opportunity to use one of these things, it was at Dutch's house again. He had organised two girls, and we went back to his place in the after-noon. He went in one room and I went in the other and I got this thing out of its packet, with absolutely no idea how to use it. I couldn't quite get it on properly, and it was very slippery and weird and I felt very embarrassed about it. Upon inspection, after the event, I realised it had split, and was filled with a sense of dread. Sure enough, a few weeks later, the girl called me to tell me she thought she was pregnant, and that I had to get some money together for her to have an abortion. It gave me a shock even though such events were very commonplace at the time.

Sex was my only distraction from music, where I was begin-ning to seriously explore the blues. It's very difficult to explain the effect the first blues record I heard had on me, except to say that I recognised it immediately. It was as if I was being reintroduced to something that I already knew, maybe from another, earlier life. For me there is something primitively soothing about this music, and it went straight to my nervous system, making me feel ten feet tall. This was the feeling I had when I first heard the Sonny Terry and Brownie McGhee song on Uncle Mac, and the same thing happened when I first heard Big Bill Broonzy. I saw a clip of him on TV, playing in a nightclub, lit by the light from a single bulb, swinging in its shade from the ceiling, creating an eerie lighting effect. The tune he was playing was a song called 'Hey Hey', and it knocked me out. It's a complicated guitar piece, full of blue notes, which is what you get by splitting a major and a minor note. You usually start with the minor, and then bend the note up to the major, so it's somewhere between the two. Indian and gipsy music, as well as the blues, use this kind of note bending. When I first heard Big Bill, and later, Robert Johnson, I became convinced that all rock 'n' roll, and pop music too, for that matter, had sprung from this root.

Next I set about learning to play like Jimmy Reed, who usually plays a twelve-bar form, and whose style has been copied by countless R&B bands. I discovered that the key ingredient was to make a kind of boogie on the bottom two strings of the guitar, by simply pressing down on the fifth string, at the second fret and the fourth fret to make a basic kind of walking figure, and playing the E string at the same time. Then I'd move it up to the next string to make the next part of the twelve bar, and so on. The final step, and the hardest part really, is to feel it, to play in a relaxed rhythm so that it feels and sounds good. I am someone who can't leave things unfinished, and if I've given myself a task to do in the day, then I can't go to bed until I've done it. It was like this with the twelve-bar blues riff. I worked at it until it felt like it was part of my metabolism.

As I worked to improve my playing, I was meeting more and more people who had the same respect and reverence for the music I loved. A particular blues fanatic was a guy called Clive Blewchamp; we met at Hollyfield and set out together on a fantastic voyage of discovery. He really enjoyed finding the hardcore stuff, the more obscure the better. We were also neck and neck in our dress sense, and spent a lot of time together in and out of school. We would go to the blues clubs too, later on, and really it was only when I started working full-time in bands that we stopped hanging out together. I always felt, actually, that he was a little contemptuous of what I was trying to do musically, as if it wasn't the real thing. Of course he was right, but I was unstoppable by then. He finished his term at Kingston after I was thrown out, got his diploma and finally moved to Canada, where he ran a small R&B magazine. We stayed in touch over the years, until he sadly died, about ten years ago.

It was exciting to find that there existed this fellowship of like-minded souls, and this is one of the things that determined my future path towards becoming a musician. I started to meet people who knew about Muddy Waters and Howlin' Wolf, and they had older friends, record collectors who would hold club nights, which is where I was first introduced to John Lee Hooker, Muddy Waters and Little Walter. These guys would get together in one of their houses, and spend the whole evening listening to one record, like *The Best of Muddy Waters*, and then have excited discussions about what they'd heard. Clive and me would often go up to London to visit record stores, like Imhoff's in New Oxford Street, the whole of whose basement was devoted to jazz, and Dobell's in Shaftesbury Avenue, where they had a whole bin devoted to Folkways, which was the major label for folk, blues and traditional music. If you were lucky, you'd meet a working musician in one of these stores, and if you told them that you liked Muddy Waters, they might say 'Well, then you've got to listen to Lightnin' Hopkins,' and you'd be off in a new direction.

Music began to take up so much of my life that it was no surprise that my work at art school began to suffer. It was my own fault that things went this way, because initially I had been really gripped by the experience of getting involved in a life in the arts. I was quite hooked by painting, and to a certain extent by design. I was a good draughtsman, and when I enrolled at Kingston, they had offered me a place in their graphic department, which I accepted, rather than going into fine art. But once I'd got into the graphic department, I knew that I was in the wrong place, and I dropped out. My motivation died. I'd go into the canteen at lunch and see all the students come in from fine art, long-haired, covered in paint and looking completely detached. They were given almost total freedom, developing their skills as painters or sculptors, while I was set to do projects every day, designing a soap box, or coming up with an advertising campaign for a new product. Apart from a short period when I managed to get into the glass department, where I learned engraving and sandblasting, and became quite interested in contemporary stained glass, I was bored to tears. Music was ten times as exciting, ten times as engaging, and as much as I loved art, I felt that the people who were trying to teach me were coming from an academic direction that I just couldn't identify with. It seemed to me that I was being prepared for a career in advertising, not art, where salesmanship would be just as important as creativity. Consequently, my interest and my output dwindled down to nothing.

I was still shocked, however, when I went for my assessment at the end of the first year, and was told that they had decided not to keep me on. I knew the portfolio was a bit thin, but I really believed that the work I had done was good enough to get me through. To me it was much more creative and imaginative than most of the other students' work. But they were judging by quantity, and they booted me and one other student out, just two of us out of fifty, which was not good. I was totally unprepared for it, but it threw me back on to the only other talent I had.

Being thrown out of art school was another rite of passage for me. I got brought up short by the sudden realisation that all doors weren't going to open up for me for the rest of my life, that the truth was that some of them were going to close. Emotionally and mentally, the shit hit the fan. When I finally found the courage to tell Rose and Jack, they were bitterly disappointed and ashamed, because they found out that I was a liar as well as a failure. Much of the time I had told them I was at school, I was actually playing hooky, just wandering around playing the guitar, or hanging out in the pub drinking. 'You've had your chance, Rick,' Jack said to me, 'and now you've chucked it away.' He made it quite clear that if I intended to stay living with them, then I was expected to work and bring money into the house. If I didn't contribute, then I could get out.

I chose to work, and accepted a job working for Jack as his 'mate' at £15 a week, which was a good wage. Jack was a master plasterer, a master bricklayer and a master carpenter. In layman's terms, this meant he had 'mastered' all of these trades, and was entitled to the wages and respect that this commanded. Working for someone as elevated as this was no laughing matter of course. It meant mixing up lots of plaster, mortar and cement, and getting it to him quickly, so that he could lay bricks and put up plaster without taking his eyes off the job. One of the first big jobs we did together was to help build a primary school in Chobham, and the most demanding work for me was carrying semi-liquid mortar in a hod, up a ladder and on to a scaffold, as quickly as my body would allow, so that Jack could lay a true line of bricks. I got extremely fit, and I really did love the work, probably because I knew it would not last for ever. My grandfather really was brilliant with his hands, and watching him plaster an entire wall in minutes was exhilarating. It turned out to be a valuable experience, even though it seemed he was being extra tough on me, which I'm sure was because he wanted no suspicion of nepotism. I learned that he worked, and lived, from a very strong set of principles, which he tried to pass on to me. In those days, there were two schools of thought on a building site. The first was that you did as little as you could, but got away with it by making the foreman think you were really busy, when you were in fact skiving. This seemed to be the norm. The second, as personified by Jack, was that you worked consistently to a rhythm, and did a good job until you had finished it. He had no time for skivers and so, to a certain extent, like me in later years, he was slightly unpopular and was a bit of an outcast. His legacy to me was that I should always try to do my best, and always finish what I started.

All the time, I was working on my playing, sometimes almost

driving my family mad with the repetitiveness of my practising. I was addicted to music, and by now I also had a record collection. Listening to Chuck Berry, B. B. King and Muddy Waters had turned me on in a big way to electric blues, and somehow I had managed to persuade my grandparents to buy me an electric guitar. This happened after I had been up to London to see Alexis Korner playing at the Marquee in Oxford Street, a jazz club that had the occasional blues nights. Alexis had the first real R&B band in the country, with a fantastic harmonica player called Cyril Davies. Watching him play for the first time made me think that there was no reason why an electric guitar shouldn't be available to me.

There was another good reason why I so desperately needed a new guitar. My Washburn was broken beyond repair. Before I started my job working for Jack, Rose had decided to take me to visit my mum for a few days. She was then living on an airforce base near Bremen in Germany, where her husband Frank, or 'Mac' as I called him, was stationed. She now had three children, a second daughter, Heather, having been born in 1958. Almost as soon as I arrived Mac told me that I would have to have my hair cut before I could go into the mess. I was horrified by this request, since my hair was not even particularly long by the standards of the day, but it seemed that the offensive part was that you couldn't see the top of my ears. I looked to the younger generation, in the form of my three half-siblings, for support, but found none there. One by one they came after me too. I was adamant about not doing it, until Rose also joined their ranks, which broke my heart, because up until then she had always been my staunchest defender. I gave in, but it made me very angry, and it seemed like I no longer had anyone on my side. They gave me a crew cut, and I felt alone and humiliated.

I moped around a lot for the remainder of my stay, but things only got worse. One day I was sitting sulking on my bed in the spare room, when my half-brother Brian came in and sat down on the bed without looking. He sat down right on top of my beloved Washburn guitar, which was lying there, and broke the neck clean in half. I could see immediately it was beyond repair, and I was gutted. He was the sweetest kid, totally in awe of me, and it was an accident, but there and then I vowed internally that Pat and her entire family could go to hell. I didn't lose my temper. I just withdrew. Not only had my identity been ripped away, but my most treasured possession had been destroyed. I went inside of myself and decided that from then on, I would trust nobody.

The electric guitar I chose was one I had my eye on in the window of Bell's, where we had got the Hoyer. It was the same guitar I had seen Alexis Korner playing, a double-cutaway semi-acoustic Kay, which at the time was quite an advanced instrument, although essentially, as I later learned, was still only a copy of the best guitar of the day, which was the Gibson ES335. It was cut away on both sides of the neck to allow easy access to the higher frets. You could play it acoustically, or you could plug it in and play electric. The Gibson would have cost over £100 then I think, well beyond our reach, while the Kay cost only £10, but still seemed quite exotic. It captured my heart, but the only thing that wasn't quite right with it was the colour. Though advertised as 'Sunburst', which would have been a golden orange going to dark red at the edges, it was more yellowy, going to a sort of pink, so as soon as I got it home, I covered it with black Fablon. Much as I loved this guitar, I soon found out that it wasn't that good. It was just as hard to play as the Hoyer, because again, the strings were too high off the fingerboard, and because there was no truss rod, the neck was weak, and after a few months' hard playing, began to bow, something I had to adapt to, not having a second instrument. Something more profound also happened when I got this guitar. As soon as I got it, I suddenly didn't want it any more. This was a phenomenon which was to rear its head throughout my life, and cause many difficulties in the future.

We hadn't bought an amplifier, so I could only play it acoustically, and fantasise what it would sound like, but it didn't matter. I was teaching myself new stuff all the time. Most of the time I was trying to play like Chuck Berry or Jimmy Reed, electric stuff, then I sort of worked backwards into country blues. This was instigated by Clive, when out of the blue, he gave me an album to listen to called *King of the Delta Blues Singers*, which was a collection of seventeen songs, recorded by a man called Robert Johnson in the thirties. I read in the sleeve notes that when Johnson was auditioning for the sessions in a hotel room in San Antonio, he played facing into the corner of the room because he was so shy. Having been paralysed with shyness as a kid, I immediately identified with this. At first the music almost repelled me, it was so intense, and there was no attempt being made by this man to sugar-coat what he was trying to say, or play. It was hardcore, more than anything I had ever heard. After a few listenings, I realised that, on some level, I had found the master, and that following this man's example would be my life's work. I was totally spellbound by the beauty and eloquence of songs like 'Kindhearted Woman', while the raw pain expressed in 'Hellhound On My Trail' seemed to echo things I had always felt.

I tried to copy Johnson, but his style of simultaneously playing a disjointed bass line on the low strings, rhythm on the middle strings and lead on the treble strings while singing at the same time, was impossible to even imagine. I put his album to one side for a while, and began listening again to other players, trying to form a style. I knew I could never reach the standards of the original guys, but I thought that if I kept trying, something would evolve. It was just a question of time and faith. I began to play things I had heard on record, but to add my own touches; I would take the bits that I could copy, from a combination of the electric blues players I liked, like John Lee Hooker, Muddy Waters and

Chuck Berry, and the acoustic players like Big Bill Broonzy, and amalgamate them into one, trying to find a phraseology that would encompass all these different artists. It was an extremely ambitious undertaking, but I was in no hurry, and was convinced I was on the right track, and that eventually it would come.

One night in January 1963, I arranged to meet a guy called Tom McGuinness at the Prince of Wales pub in New Malden. He was playing in a blues band which apparently had originally been formed by Paul Jones, with Brian Jones on guitar. When Paul and Brian left, Tom's girlfriend, Jenny, who had been a fellow student of mine at Kingston School of Art, had recommended me as a possible guitarist. The line-up then consisted of Tom McGuinness on guitar, Robin Benwell Palmer on keyboards, Robin Mason on drums and Terry Brennan on vocals. There was no bass player. Terry was a fantastic guy. He was a genuine, full-blown Teddy boy. He had a pompadour haircut, with a quiff which was about six inches high in front, and wore a fingertip jacket with a velvet collar, drainpipe jeans and brothel creepers, which were suede winkle-picker crepe-soled shoes. Unlike most Teds, however, who had a reputation for being hard men, and who only listened to Bill Hayley and Jerry Lee Lewis, he was incredibly gentle, and he really loved the blues. He had a great voice too, and it was my admiration for him and 'Ben', the keyboard player, which made me want to play with them. I knew Ben would be a big part of my life the minute I heard him play. He was an absolute purist, with a love for the blues that more than matched my own. I played a short audition and they immediately asked me to join the band.

The Roosters were a tiny outfit, with virtually no equipment. Guitar, vocals, keyboard all went through one amplifier. We had no proper transport, just Robin's Morris Oxford convertible into which we had to pile all our equipment as well as ourselves, ownership of the car giving him a certain amount of power in the band. We met for rehearsals in a room above a pub somewhere in Surbiton. I would come up from Ripley and plug my guitar into Tom's amplifier and we would just learn things, mostly blues and R&B covers. We taught ourselves a couple of Chuck Berry songs, 'Short Fat Fanny' by Larry Williams, and some stuff by Muddy Waters. The most significant thing for me was that Tom one day produced a record by a black artist called Freddy King. It was a 45 rpm single, an instrumental called 'Hideaway', and he was mad about it. I'd never heard Freddy King before, and listening to him had an effect on me similar to what I imagine I might feel if I were to meet an alien from outer space. It simply blew my mind.

On the B-side of 'Hideaway' was a song called 'I Love The Woman' that had a guitar solo in the middle of it which took my breath away. It was like listening to modern jazz, expressive and melodic, a unique kind of playing in which he bent the strings, and produced sounds that gave me the shivers. It was absolutely earth-shattering, like a new light for me to move towards. Up until that moment, I had always thought of guitar playing as being little more than an accompaniment to the singing, except in one or two rare cases which I had always noticed and wondered where the players were coming from. A good example of this was the Connie Francis number 'Lipstick On Your Collar', which had an incredible guitar solo by a guy called George Barnes; and Ricky Nelson had a guitarist called James Burton, who would play country blues electric guitar solos. Hearing Freddy play explained where all of this had come from.

The Roosters rehearsed more than we played. Even though we did a gig every now and then, mostly in upstairs rooms in pubs, it was more about the excitement of meeting like-minded people. There was really nobody in Ripley that had any interest in blues. Pop was the order of the day, with the current craze being the Mersey sound. The Beatles were just starting to be popular, and once a week there was a radio show called *Pop Go the Beatles*, which consisted entirely of them playing their own songs, and covers of other people's. They were taking off really quickly, and everybody wanted to be like them. It was the beginnings of Beatlemania. All over the country people were dressing like them, playing like them, sounding like them and looking like them. I thought it was despicable, probably because it showed how sheep-like people were, and how ready they were to elevate these people to the status of gods, when most of the people I admired had died unheard of, sometimes penniless and alone. It also made it look like what we were trying to do was already a lost cause.

The gradual increase in popularity of the Mersey sound forced people like me to almost go underground, as if we were anarchists, plotting to overthrow the music establishment. It seemed that the trad jazz movement was dying, and was taking folk and blues with it. So the thing with the Roosters was that, as much as anything, we needed each other for identification. It was not that we were going anywhere, so we just met up and talked and played, and had a cup of tea, and compared any records we might have heard, and tried to learn some of them. The repertoire was a mixture of blues numbers by John Lee Hooker, Muddy Waters, Freddy King and others, regular numbers being 'Hoochie Coochie Man', 'Boom Boom, Slow Down' and 'I Love The Woman', which gave me the opportunity to show off with the solos I was developing. Altogether we played no more than a dozen gigs, for a few quid and free drinks, and since I was still working on building sites for my grandfather, I would often turn up on stage covered in plaster. Most of our gigs were on the Ricky Tick club circuit, a series of clubs in the Home Counties run by Philip Hayward and John Mansfield, two promoters who were into great music and who at that time had a virtual monopoly on the club scene. We also played a couple of times at the Marquee, as support to Manfred Mann, the band Paul Jones was now singing with. The truth is that although I was having a great time with it, enjoying making my mark as a guitarist and the semi-bohemian lifestyle that went with it, the band was deeply flawed, because it didn't really have the wherewithal, either the commitment or the money, to go anywhere. As a result, we lasted only six months, the final gig being at the Marquee on 25 July, 1963.

Though the Marquee had made its reputation as a jazz club, where quite famous musicians like Tubby Hayes used to come and play, it was beginning to get more and more into the R&B scene. Every week I used to go there on Thursday nights, which was blues night, travelling up on the train to Waterloo, then taking the Tube to Oxford Street. Since I rarely had anywhere to stay, the evening would usually end with me walking the streets till dawn, when I could catch the first train home. It was at the Marquee that I first came across John Mayall, and the saxophonist and keyboard player Graham Bond, playing in a trio with bassist Jack Bruce and drummer Ginger Baker. Everyone on the R&B scene hung out there.

After the demise of the Roosters, Tom McGuinness was approached by a Liverpudlian called Brian Casser to join a new band. There were a lot of guys around playing the Mersey clubs before the Beatles, and he was one of these. In 1959 he had fronted a group called Cass and the Casanovas, before moving down to London to run a nightclub, the Blue Gardenia in Soho. With the enormous success of the Liverpool sound and the rapid rise of bands like Gerry and the Pacemakers, and singers like Billy J. Kramer, he had begun to feel left out, so he set about forming a new group to be called Casey Jones and the Engineers. He recruited Tom, and since I was also at a loose end, Tom recruited me.

The best thing about playing with Casey Jones was the experience it gave me; it was the first time I had done any kind of touring. We played in various clubs up North, mostly round Manchester, including one open-air gig at the Belle Vue

Amusement Park. Casey made us all wear black matching outfits and cardboard Confederate army caps, which both Tom and I hated. Gigs were so different then, because compared to today, the sound systems were so tiny. We would be playing through small amplifiers, like Voxes or Gibsons, and we'd have one each, so most groups would then be comprised of three amps plus the drum kit. Only the most well-off groups had their own PA systems, and even those only had an output of about 100 watts, nothing by modern standards. The repertoire of the Engineers consisted of some rock 'n' roll – Chuck Berry, Little Richard and things like that – but the majority of the material was heavily pop-based, doing top-twenty covers, and I couldn't stand that for very long. I was too much of a purist, and after six weeks both Tom and I left.

Casey Jones and the Engineers played only about seven gigs. In between these I was still working on building sites for my grandfather, and hanging out on the local music scene, which was then blossoming. Alexis Korner had started his own club, the Ealing Club, in a cramped basement room opposite Ealing Broadway station, while another blues enthusiast, Giorgio Gomelsky, had opened the Crawdaddy Club in the old Station Hotel in Richmond, where the resident band on Sunday nights were the newly formed Rolling Stones. I'd known Mick, Keith and Brian throughout their long gestation period when they were playing nothing but R&B. Our first meeting had been at the Marquee. It was only the second time I went to see Alexis play, and they were all there. At some point in the evening they all got up to play with Alexis' rhythm section. I got talking to Mick, and we became friends. He always used to carry a microphone in his pocket, a Reslo, and I borrowed it off him to do a gig in Richmond, which was just me and a drummer doing Chuck Berry songs. There was no stand for the mike, so I had to put two chairs, one on top of the other, and Sellotape the mike to the top of this improvised stand.

Mick, Keith and Brian played wherever they could, at Ken Colyer's 51 Club in Charing Cross Road, at the Marquee and at the Ealing Club. I would occasionally stand in for Mick there when he had a sore throat, and for a time we were all quite close. Then they got the residency at the Crawdaddy and they really took off, going in four weeks from audiences of just a handful of people to several hundred. One night the Beatles came in to see the Stones. They'd just released 'Please Please Me' which was a huge hit, and they walked up and stood right in front of the stage, all of them wearing long black leather overcoats, and identical haircuts. Even then they had tremendous presence and charisma, but to me the weirdest thing was that they appeared to be wearing their stage outfits, and for some reason that bothered me. But they seemed friendly enough, and there was obviously a mutual admiration thing going on between them and the Stones, so I suppose it was only natural that I would be jealous, and think of them as a bunch of wankers.

Giorgio Gomelsky, the proprietor of the Crawdaddy, was a Georgian by birth, who was brought up in France, Switzerland and Italy. A very effusive, charismatic man, who peppered his speech with the word 'baby', he was big and round, with black hair slicked back, and a beard, a bit like Bluto with an Italian accent. Flamboyant, worldly and a *bon vivant*, he also happened to love jazz and the blues and had a fantastic ear for talent. He did an incredible amount of work for the early English R&B scene, and was, I think, the first real champion for the Stones. A few months into their stint at the Crawdaddy, they were signed up right under his nose by Andrew Loog Oldham, who at the time was working as a PR for Brian Epstein, manager of the Beatles. One minute he had the hottest club in London, featuring the hottest band in England, and the next thing he knew, they were out of the club, had put out a single, 'Come On', and were on tour with Bo Diddley. I think it was a disappointment that Giorgio never really got over, but he was a pragmatist, and immediately went looking for a replacement for the Sunday-night slot. He eventually set his eyes on the Yardbirds, an R&B group fronted by a guitarist and singer called Keith Relf. Under his guidance and encouragement, they were soon making their own mark at the Crawdaddy. They had a problem, however. Their lead guitarist, a sixteen-year-old called Anthony Topham, was under severe pressure from his parents to leave the band in order to concentrate on his studies.

One night I was at a party in Kingston listening to Keith and another guitarist called Roger Pearce. They were playing Django Reinhardt stuff together, and really well too, although Roger would speed up a bit when he got excited. Keith told me he was the singer with the Yardbirds and asked if I'd like to come down and listen to them at the Crawdaddy, as their lead guitarist was likely to be quitting and maybe I might be interested in taking over. I went to check them out. They were playing good R&B, songs like 'You Can't Judge A Book' by Bo Diddley, and 'Smokestack Lightning' by Howlin' Wolf and just the fact that they knew these songs was enough for me to enjoy them. Topham's guitar playing was a bit stiff, but they were a good band, if a little rough and ready, and I had nothing better to do at the time. So when Topham finally resigned, and they did eventually ask me, I said yes. I was still a bit wary about joining another group, but I genuinely thought it would be no more than a stopgap. There were five of us: Keith on vocals and harp, Chris Dreja on rhythm guitar, Paul Samwell-Smith on bass, Jim McCarty on drums and myself on lead.

For the first time in my life, I now had a full-time job as a musician, which meant giving up working for my grandfather. My grandmother was delighted, as she knew where my talents lay, while my grandfather was quietly amused, so they gave me their blessing. This time there was a contract, which was signed in

October 1963, in the front room of Keith's house in Ham, with all the parents of the band present. To begin with I lived at home, drawing a weekly wage packet, and commuted to rehearsals and gigs, but after a while Giorgio rented us a flat on the top floor of an old house in Kew, and we all moved in together. This was a great period for me as it was the first time I had lived away from home. In the first few weeks, before his American girlfriend arrived, I shared a room with Chris Dreja, and we became really good friends. He was a quiet guy, shy and kind, and I trusted him completely, a rare thing for me. I liked the fact, too, that unlike the others he was not driven by ambition. He was just enjoying the ride.

Our gigs were all divided between various Home Counties venues such as the Ricky Tick, the Star Club, Croydon, and the Crawdaddy. This was my first experience of playing night after night – in the first three months we played thirty-three gigs – and I lapped it up. What I immediately liked about the Yardbirds was that our entire reason for existence was to honour the tradition of the blues. We didn't write any songs at first, but the covers we chose to do defined our identity, personified in songs like 'Good Morning Little Schoolgirl' by Sonny Boy Williamson, 'Got Love If You Want It' by Slim Harpo, and our most popular number which we'd play most nights, 'Smokestack Lightning' by Howlin' Wolf.

We may have thought that we could play the blues, but there was one man who wasn't so sure. Hardly had we signed the contract when Giorgio told us that he had arranged for us to join Sonny Boy Williamson on his forthcoming tour of England. I wasn't a particular fan of Sonny Boy's, my favourite harmonica player was Little Walter, and it was not a happy experience. I knew for example, in my role as blues expert of Ripley, that he was not the Sonny Boy Williamson who had written 'Good Morning Little Schoolgirl', and had been killed with an ice pick, but that his real name was Rice Miller. So when we were first introduced to him at the Crawdaddy, I couldn't wait to show off, and tried to impress him with my knowledge, asking him, 'Isn't your real name Rice Miller?' at which point he slowly pulled out a small penknife and glared at me. It went downhill from there. But he was a famous bluesman, and to all intents and purposes, the real thing, so we were in awe of him, and followed where he led. At one point in the show, he made us kneel, while he did a sort of blues moonwalk along the stage. It was more than a little strange. But he was little impressed with us too for that matter. He is said to have commented at the time, 'Those English kids want to play the blues so bad, and they play the blues so bad.'

I think Giorgio had an agenda from day one. What he had missed out on with the Rolling Stones, he would make up with on the Yardbirds. He would take us up a notch, make us bigger than the Stones. Early in 1964, he got us signed up to Columbia Records, and into a recording studio, a tiny place in New Malden called R. G. Jones, to record a cover of a song called 'I Wish You Would' by Billy Boy Arnold. It was a simple, very catchy song, but though I thought it was great, I was in two minds about making records. I was developing a very purist attitude towards music, and thought that it really ought to be just live. My theory was that making records, first and foremost, was always going to be a commercial enterprise, and therefore not pure. It was a ridiculously pompous attitude, considering that all the music I was learning from was on record. In truth, I was just embarrassed, because in the studio, my own personal inadequacy was there for all to see. But it wasn't just me, and as exciting as it was to be actually making a record, when we listened back and compared it to the stuff we were supposedly modelling ourselves on, it sounded pretty lame. We just sounded young and white, and even though our second single, a cover of a rock version of 'Good Morning Little Schoolgirl', sounded much better, I still felt that we were falling far short of the mark in some way. This was not something I felt just about the Yardbirds, but about other bands that I admired like Manfred Mann, the Moody Blues and the Animals, all of whom were far better live than they were on record.

We too were much better live, a fact that was borne out by the release of our first LP *Five Live Yardbirds*, which, in the absence of many other live albums, proved quite a groundbreaking record. It had a much rawer sound, which I was happier with. What singled us out from most other bands was the way we were experimenting with band dynamics, a direction we were taken in by Paul Samwell-Smith. We became quite well known for the way in which we improvised, taking the frame of a blues standard, like Bo Diddley's 'I'm A Man', and embellishing it by jamming in the middle, usually with a staccato bass line, which would get louder and louder, rising to a crescendo before coming back down again to the body of the song. While most other bands were playing three-minute songs, we were taking three-minute numbers and stretching them out to five or six minutes, during which time the audience would go crazy, shaking their heads around manically and dancing in various outlandish ways. On my guitar, I used light-gauge strings, with a very thin first string, which made it easier to bend the notes, and it was not uncommon, during the most frenetic bits of playing, for me to break at least one string. During the pause while I was changing my strings, the frenzied audience would often break into a slow handclap, inspiring Giorgio to dream up the nickname of 'Slowhand' Clapton.

Giorgio worked us incredibly hard. With Keith Relf's father, Bill, as our roadie and driver, we were out on the road most nights, touring the Ricky Tick circuit and other venues in the South of England with a trip to Abergavenny and a couple of gigs at the Twisted Wheel in Manchester thrown in for good measure. To add to our earnings, and his, he once even hired us out to an advertising company to promote shirts on TV. We had our photograph taken wearing white business shirts, while a jingle announced 'Raelbrook Toplin, the shirt you don't iron!' Even then, I remember feeling distinctly uncomfortable about promoting something that had nothing to do with the music, but these were the days in which musicians still had little say in what went on in their careers, and did what their managers told them.

By the time we played the fourth Richmond Jazz and Blues Festival on 9 August, 1964, it was our 136th gig of the year. The opening act of the weekend had been the Rolling Stones, and we closed things on Sunday night. Giorgio now pulled a bit of a fast one. He told us that we badly needed a holiday, and we should pack our things as we were off the next day for two glorious weeks in Lugano, the Swiss town near Lake Maggiore where he had once lived. So off we went, in a couple of Transit vans, one of which was filled with a gaggle of female fans, girls who really loved us and would come to the Crawdaddy every week to see us, only to find, that when we finally arrived at the hotel after a hair-raising journey over the Alps, it wasn't even properly built. There was nothing on the floor, just bare concrete, and we were all staying in one room. On the second day Giorgio announced that Bill was on his way with all the equipment and that we were going to play by the pool. It was now quite clear that our 'holiday' was just part of some dubious deal that he had pulled off with the hotel owner to provide cheap entertainment for the non-existent guests, and we ended up playing to a sprinkling of locals and our fans who had come out from England.

By the end of 1964, after playing well over 200 gigs, we were getting a bigger and bigger following and playing on package tours with big American stars like Jerry Lee Lewis and the Ronettes. Ronnie Ronette made a move on me one night. I couldn't believe that out of all the men on the tour she should single out me to seduce, but it was just a momentary flirtation, and she confessed to me later that I reminded her of her husband, Phil Spector! Needless to say, I became besotted, and fell head over heels in love. She was the most sexual creature I had ever laid eyes on, and I was determined to make the most of it. At the end of the tour, I hung around their hotel in London, and was utterly heartbroken when I saw her, and one of the other girls in the group, come out on the arms of Mick and Keith. Unlucky in love again.

At the end of December, we were invited to perform as a support act to the Beatles in their twenty-night series of Christmas shows at the Hammersmith Odeon in London. These were a curious mixture of music, pantomime and comedy in which we shared the support bill with pop groups like Freddie and the Dreamers, solo artists such as Billy J. Kramer and Elkie Brooks, and the R&B band Sounds Incorporated. The Beatles appeared in a comedy sketch with England's best-known DJ, Jimmy Savile, and generally hammed it up throughout, before playing a half-hour set at the end. Giorgio decided that we needed a uniform for the gigs. Knowing how important my image was to me, and that I would fight tooth and nail to wear exactly what I wanted, he gave me the job of designing it. What I came up with were black suits, with jackets that had, instead of a standard lapel, something that was more like a shirt lapel, and which buttoned almost up to the top. We had them made up, in black and beige mohair, in a workshop somewhere in Berwick Street, Soho. They were actually really nice.

Even though we were quite low on the bill, playing these shows was fine for us. It was fairly local, and all our followers from the Crawdaddy would come and see us, so we had our own fans to play to, and they actually listened to our music. It was different for the Beatles. One night I went to the back of the auditorium to watch them, and you couldn't hear the music at all because of the screaming. Most of their fans were young girls around the age of twelve to fifteen, who had no intention of listening. I felt sorry for the band, and I think they were already quite sick of it too. In some respects, it was funny, but I imagine it had become pretty soul destroying for them.

Hanging out backstage at the Odeon was where I had my first meeting with the Beatles. Paul played the ambassador, coming out to meet us and saying hello. I remember him playing us the tune of 'Yesterday', which was half written and asking everyone what they thought. He didn't have the words. He was calling it 'Scrambled Eggs', and singing, 'Scrambled Eggs . . . Everybody calls me scrambled eggs.' George and I hit it off right away. He seemed to like what I did, and we talked shop a lot. He showed me his collection of Gretsch guitars, and I showed him my light-gauge strings which I always bought from a shop called Clifford Essex in Earlham Street. I gave him some, and this was the start of what was to eventually become a long friendship; though not for a while, since the Beatles were then in another world to us. They were stars who were climbing fast.

My meeting with John was a little different. One night I was on the Tube, travelling to Hammersmith for one of the shows, and I got talking to an elderly American woman. She was lost and was asking me for directions. She asked me what I did and where I was going, and I told her I was going to play guitar in a concert with the Beatles. 'The Beatles?' she said, astonished, and asked, 'Can I come along?' 'If you want to, I'll try and get you in,' I replied. When we arrived at the Odeon, I told the stage manager she was a friend of mine, and took her off to the Beatles' dressing room, which was on the same level as the stage. They were getting ready to go on, but they took a moment and were really friendly and polite to her. But when we got to John, and I introduced her, he made a face of mock boredom and started doing wanking movements inside his coat. I was really shocked, and quite offended, because I felt responsible for this harmless little old lady, and in a sense of course, he was insulting me. I got to know

John quite well later in our lives, and we were friends I suppose, but I was always aware that he was capable of doing some pretty weird stuff.

Though the Yardbirds weren't yet in the big-money league, we were making enough for me to buy my first really serious guitar, a cherry red Gibson ES335, which was the instrument of my dreams, of which the Kay had been but a poor imitation. Throughout my life I chose a lot of my guitars because of the other people who played them, and this was like the one Freddy King played. It was the first of a new era of guitars, which were thin and semi-acoustic. They were both a rock guitar and a blues guitar, which you could play, if necessary, without amplification and still hear them. I had seen the Gibson in a shop in either Charing Cross Road or Denmark Street, where there were several music stores that had electric guitars in the windows. To me they were just like sweet shops. I would stand outside staring at these things for hours on end, especially at night when the windows would remain lit up, and after a trip to the Marquee I would walk around all night looking and dreaming. When I finally bought the Gibson, I just couldn't believe how shiny and beautiful it was. At last, I felt like a real musician.

The truth is, I was starting to take myself far too seriously, and was very critical and judgemental of anybody in music who wasn't playing just pure blues. This attitude was part of my intellectual phase. I was reading translations of Baudelaire, and discovering the American underground writers like Kerouac and Allen Ginsberg, while simultaneously watching as much French and Japanese cinema as I could. I began to develop a real contempt for pop music in general, and to feel genuinely uncomfortable about being in the Yardbirds. No longer were we going in the direction I wanted, mainly because, seeing the runaway success of the Beatles, Giorgio and some of the guys had become obsessed with getting on TV and having a number-one record. It's quite possible that Giorgio was still smarting from having lost the Stones, but what was clear was that we weren't moving upwards fast enough, so each of us was told to go out there and find a hit song. Actually I had no problem with having a hit, as long as it was a song we could be proud of. Funnily enough, Giorgio had played me a song by Otis Redding called 'Your One And Only Man' several months before. It was a catchy song which I felt we could do a version of without selling ourselves short. Then Paul Samwell-Smith came up with a song called 'For Your Love' by Graham Gouldman, later of 10CC, which was clearly a number one. I baulked, but the others all loved it, and that was that.

When the Yardbirds decided to record 'For Your Love', I knew it was the beginning of the end for me; I didn't see how we could make a record like that and stay as we were. It felt to me that we had completely sold out. I played on it, though my contribution was limited to a very short blues riff in the middle-eight section, and as a consolation, they gave me the B-side, an instrumental called 'Got To Hurry', which was based on a tune hummed to me by Giorgio, who gave himself the writing credit under the pseudonym, O. Rasputin. By then I was a pretty grizzled and discontent individual. I deliberately made myself as unpopular as I could, by being constantly argumentative and dogmatic about everything that came up. Eventually Giorgio called me to his office in Soho and told me that it was quite clear that I was no longer happy in the band, and that if I wanted to leave, then he wouldn't stand in my way. He didn't exactly fire me. He just invited me to resign. Totally disillusioned, I was at that point ready to quit the music business altogether.

CHAPTER THREE

JOHN MAYALL

Initially I was distraught after leaving the Yardbirds. I felt much as I did when I was thrown out of art school, and the reality finally kicked in. But in a short amount of time my equilibrium came back, and I was able to pat myself on the back for sticking to my principles, even though I wasn't really sure at that moment quite what my principles were. 'For Your Love' was a huge hit, and nobody on the outside could understand why I had chosen such a moment to quit, when the band was on the up. But the truth is that I felt it was a dreadful waste of what had potentially been a good rock/blues band. For a time I returned to live in Ripley, feeling shy, frightened and disheartened by a business in which everyone seemed to me to be on the make and selling out rather than being in it for the music. For a while I stayed with Rose and Jack, who were both very supportive of me. By then I think they knew I was serious about what I was doing, and had decided to stand behind me.

I had a West Indian girlfriend around this time, called Maggie, who was a dancer on *Top of the Pops*, and one night she and I went down to Ronnie Scott's club in Soho to meet up with a friend of mine called Tony Garland. Tony was a fellow music fan I used to hang out with at the Marquee, and in the early days, he was the first person who I ever saw wearing flared trousers. He made them himself by sowing triangular inserts into his Levi's. On that particular night, he was with a great-looking girl called June Child, who was as smart as a whip and very, very funny. She and I got talking and laughing, and taking the mickey out of Tony, who she referred to as 'Wanker Garland'. This was much to the annoyance of Maggie, who was more accustomed to getting all the attention, and the result was that by the end of the evening we had swapped partners. June instantly became one of my best friends, but we did not become lovers. I'm pretty sure she wanted to go down that road, but at that point I hadn't figured out that it was possible to fancy a girl and be friends with her. Sex was still a matter of conquest rather than the result of a loving relationship. The idea simply never occurred to me that you could have an intelligent conversation with a girl and then sleep with her. Retrospectively, I regret that we never got it together; I'm sure we would have had a great time.

June not only became my pal, she also, since I couldn't drive, became my voluntary chauffeur. One day I asked her to take me to Oxford to visit Ben Palmer, the keyboard player with the Roosters. Ben was an incredibly charismatic man, very funny, very intelligent and very worldly wise, with strong, aristocratic features that made him look as if he came from the eighteenth century. He was a creative man of great depth, who could turn his skill in any direction. He was then living in a studio above some stables, where he had taught himself woodcarving, and when we arrived, he was putting the finishing touches on a Tang horse. He said he had given up the piano completely. I tried to talk him into doing something with me, I thought maybe we could produce a guitar and piano blues record, but he steadfastly refused. To begin with I felt very depressed, and for a few weeks Ben looked after me like an older brother, keeping an eye on me and cooking me delicious meals. He also introduced me to *The Lord of the Rings*, which I spent hours reading.

In the meantime, June had given Ben's number to John Mayall, a blues musician with a credible reputation, and leader of his own band, the Bluesbreakers. He called me and asked if I might be interested in joining his outfit. I knew who he was from the Marquee, and I admired him because he was then doing exactly what I always thought we could have done with the Yardbirds. He had found his niche and was staying there, touring good clubs and making the odd record, without ever really going for broke. The fact that I didn't really like the two records he'd made – 'Crawling Up A Hill' and 'Crocodile Walk', which to me were like pop R&B – was immaterial, because what I saw was a frame that I could fit into. I wasn't sure about the way he sang, or the way he presented himself, but I was very grateful that some-one saw my worth, and my thinking was that maybe I would be able to steer the band towards Chicago blues, instead of the sort of jazz blues that the band were currently playing. He seemed happy to go along with this. I think that, until I came along, he had been quite isolated in his musical tastes, and now he'd found someone just as serious about the blues as he was.

I joined the Bluesbreakers in April 1965, and went to live with John in his house in Lee Green, which he shared with his wife, Pamela, and their children. Twelve years older than me, with long curly hair and a beard, which gave him a look not unlike Jesus, he had the air of a favourite schoolmaster, while still managing to be cool. He didn't drink and he was a health-food fanatic and the first proper vegetarian I had ever met. Trained as a graphic artist, John made a good living as an illustrator of things like science-fiction books, as well as working for advertising agencies, but his real passion was music. He played piano, harmonica, organ and guitar, and he had the most incredible collection of records I had ever seen, with rare singles which you would otherwise find only on compilation albums. Many of these were ordered through *Blues Unlimited*, a specialist magazine run by a guy called Mike Leadbetter. I had a tiny little cupboard room at the top of the house, barely big enough for a narrow single bed, and over the better part of a year, when I had any spare time, I would sit in this room listening to records and playing along with them, honing my craft.

Modern Chicago blues became my new Mecca. It was a tough electric sound, spearheaded by people like Howlin' Wolf, Muddy Waters and John Lee Hooker, who had come up from the Delta to record for labels like Chess. The great guitar players of this genre were Otis Rush, Buddy Guy, Elmore James, Hubert Sumlin, Robert Lockwood Jr and Earl Hooker, to name a few. The genre perfectly suited our line-up of guitar, bass, drums and keyboard. On drums we had Hughie Flint, who was to go on to form a band with Tom McGuinness called McGuinness-Flint. I played lead guitar, and the bass player was John McVie, who later formed Fleetwood Mac with Mick Fleetwood. Not only was he a brilliant bass guitarist, but he was an incredibly funny man with a very dark, cynical sense of humour.

At that time, the two Johns and myself were obsessed with the Harold Pinter play *The Caretaker*. I had seen the film, with Donald Pleasence as the tramp, Davies, countless times, and had also bought the script, a lot of which I knew by heart. We would spend hours acting out scenes from the play, swapping roles, so that sometimes I would play the character of Aston, other times Davies or Mick, and although it's not meant to be a comedy, the dark humour of it would make us piss ourselves with laughter.

To begin with, since Mayall was that much older than the rest of us, and was to our minds a respectable middle-class man living with a wife and kids in suburbia, the dynamics of the band were very much 'him and us'. We saw him in the role of schoolmaster, with us as the naughty boys. He was tolerant up to a point, but we knew there was a limit and we did our best to push him to it. We would take the mickey out of him behind his back, tell him he couldn't sing, and giggle when he went out on stage bare to the waist. He was a well-built man, and more than a little vain, and we liked to see just how far we could go before he lost his temper. John didn't like alcohol around when we were working, and unfortunately McVie, who was our self-appointed spokesman, liked to drink quite a bit. This would often lead to some form of confrontation, and one of them would lose it. Loveable though McVie was, there were often times when his drinking made him aggressive, and he would either be left behind or, as on one occasion when we were returning from a gig up North, actually turfed out of the van on to the side of the road.

Less than a month after I joined the Bluesbreakers, John asked me to go down to a studio to play on some tracks he had been asked to work on with Bob Dylan. He was very excited about this, as Dylan, who was over to tour England, had specially asked to meet him after hearing his song 'Crawling Up A Hill'. My feelings about Dylan at the time were rather ambivalent, coloured perhaps by the fact that Paul Samwell-Smith had been a big fan of his, and anything Paul liked, I didn't. So I went down to the studio where the session was taking place, and was introduced to Bob and his producer, Tom Wilson.

Unfortunately, I wasn't open to any of it at the time, I hadn't really listened to any of Bob's stuff, and was developing a healthy prejudice towards him, based, I suppose, on what I thought of the people that did like him. As far as I was concerned at that time, Dylan was a folkie. I couldn't understand all the fuss, and it seemed like everyone around him was patronising him to death, There was, however, one person in his entourage who I did take to instantly. His name was Bobby Neuwirth, and I think he was a painter, or a poet. It seemed like he was Dylan's pal, but he took the time to talk to me, and tried to clue me in on what was going on; I'm not sure it did any good. I was like Mr Jones in 'Ballad Of A Thin Man', but it was the beginning of a lifelong friendship. I don't recall Dylan talking to anybody; maybe he was shy like me. As for the session, I don't remember much about it. I don't think any of the songs got finished, and then Bob suddenly disappeared. When somebody asked where he was, we were told, 'Oh, he's gone to Madrid.' I didn't think much about Bob Dylan for a while, until I heard *Blonde on Blonde* and then, thank goodness, I finally got it.

The moment I said yes to John, I joined a working schedule the likes of which I had never experienced. If there had been eight nights a week, we'd have played them, as well as two shows on a Sunday. Our bookings were handled by two brothers, Rick and Johnny Gunnell, who owned the Flamingo Club in Wardour Street, a tiny basement club which was the most authentic soul-music venue in London. Both edgy and cliquey, it catered to tough, mostly black audiences who were hardcore R&B, blues and jazz followers. The Gunnells represented a lot of the bands who played the London nightlife circuit, people like Georgie Fame, Chris Farlowe, Albert Lee and Geno Washington. Rick and Johnny were a couple of loveable rogues. They enjoyed good relations with the police and they kept their club open till 6.00 a.m. They had their own patch and were treated with respect by gangland figures like the Krays. John, the younger of the two, was very good-looking, although he had a great big scar across his face from where he'd presumably been bottled. His elder brother Rick used to get very drunk and would walk in and demand of the entire club, 'Why aren't the band playing?' Though undoubtedly tough guys, they were music lovers too and were always very kind to me, possibly because they realised how seriously I took the music.

Another club I used to hang out in was the Scene, in Windmill Yard, which was run by Ronan O'Rahilly, who went on to set up Radio Caroline, England's first pirate radio station. I used to watch, and finally made friends with, a small group of guys who hung out there and who had a big influence on how I wanted to look at the time. They wore a hybrid of American Ivy League and the Italian look, as personified by Marcello Mastroianni; on one day they might be wearing sweatshirts with baggy trousers and loafers, on another maybe linen suits. They were an interesting bunch because they seemed to be miles ahead of anyone else in terms of style. I found them fascinating. They were all from the East End. There was Laurie Allen, a jazz drummer, Jimmy West and Dave Foley, who were tailors, and went on to start a business making suits for people like me, called the Workshop, in Berwick Street, and Ralph Berenson, a natural comedian and mimic. I would sometimes play at the Scene, and one night I was approached and asked to go and play a gig at another club called Esmeralda's Barn, which was a nightclub in Mayfair owned by the Kray brothers. It was a weird evening because I played with the resident band and there was no one else in the club except the Krays, sitting at a table right at the back, and I didn't know what the hell I was doing there. It felt like an audition.

We were paid £35 a week to play with the Bluesbreakers, which we used to collect from the Gunnells' office in Soho. It was a set wage no matter how much work you did, and though there may have been ructions from time to time from other members of the band about trying to get an increase, I don't remember really caring about it, because my expenses were very small. I was usually on the cadge, rarely paying for anything and living free. We certainly earned our money. The idea was that you would play a gig, and when you were done, you might have to play again that night. Every Saturday they had an all-nighter at the Flamingo at which we were regulars, which was fine if you had been playing Oxford, or somewhere not too far away, but quite gruelling if the earlier show had been in Birmingham, which necessitated an exhausting trip back down the M1. Travelling to these, what seemed to us then, faraway places was important, as there was only so much work in the Home Counties, and it was essential for bands to play in the better-known clubs in the North in order to get recognition and consolidate their following. To name a few, there was the Twisted Wheel in Manchester, the Club a Go-Go in Newcastle, the Boathouse in Nottingham, the Starlight in Redcar, and the Mojo in Sheffield, where Peter Stringfellow was the DJ. The concept of paying someone to play records in a club until the band came on was then entirely new, and he was one of the original DJs, playing really good sounds, mostly blues and R&B.

It was exciting to go to different parts of the country. There were girls everywhere, which meant that I was having a pretty extraordinary sex life, dating and picking up anyone I could get my hands on. Most of the time it was just innocent groping, and only rarely did it go all the way. In those days, you hardly ever had a dressing room, like bands do today. You just got on and off the stage from the audience. There might be someone I'd met while I was walking about before the show or someone I'd noticed while I was on stage, and I'd just get talking to them and go off with them. I remember there was a particular girl that I'd always meet in Basingstoke. The band would do two sets, with a half-hour interval, and I'd meet this girl after the first set and go off with her somewhere backstage, and come back on stage with the knees of my jeans covered in dust from the floor. This was quite normal, part of the geography of touring being which girls were where; Bishop's Stortford, Sheffield, Windsor, Birmingham . . . for us it wasn't a girl in every port, it was a girl at every gig, and the girls themselves seemed to be quite happy to have that kind of relationship, seeing me only occasionally. I can't say I blame them.

We also loved to travel round England, because we knew that was as far as we were going to get. No one would ever have thought of sending us to Ireland or Scotland, because they weren't going to pay for hotels, so we had to get back after the gig. Though it's difficult to imagine it now, going to Newcastle then was, for me, like going to New York. It seemed like another world. I didn't understand a word people said, and the women were really fast and quite scary. A not untypical night might involve travelling up to Sheffield to play the evening gig at eight o'clock, then heading off to Manchester to play the all-nighter, followed by driving back to London and being dropped off at Charing Cross station at six in the morning.

We travelled in John's Ford Transit. Back in the sixties there was a lot of status attached to the kind of van a band had. A Bedford Dormobile, which was ugly and clunky and had sliding doors, denoted lowly standing, but owning a Transit showed that you were at the top of the pile. They had powerful engines and really zipped along, meaning you could do a fair amount of mileage in them, and they were big inside and comfortable. The multitalented John was also a bit of an inventor, and he had tailor-made the interior of the Transit to his own design. This entailed making a special space to carry his Hammond B3 organ, which was rigged up so it could be carried on two poles, like a sedan chair. Then in the space between the organ and the roof of the van, he had built himself a bunk bed, so on our return trips from faraway places like Manchester or Sheffield, we'd be all sitting in the front of the van on the bench seats, while he'd be in the back, asleep in his bed. Apart from once or twice, we never stayed in a bed and breakfast, or a hotel. The most you could hope for was, if you were playing in Manchester, where John's family came from, he might invite you to stay in one of the family homes. I did this once and it was pretty lugubrious, though it was better than sitting up all night in the van.

It was an incredible life, and at times I didn't believe it was happening to me. One night, for example, Mike Vernon, who owned Blue Horizon Records, asked me to go down to a studio to do some session work, and I found myself playing with Muddy Waters and Otis Spann, two of my all-time heroes. I was absolutely terrified, not because I felt I couldn't carry my weight musically, but because I just didn't know how to behave around these guys. They were incredible. They had these beautiful baggy silk suits on, and were so sharp, and they were men, and here I was, a skinny young white boy. But it was fine. We cut a song called 'Pretty Girls Everywhere I Go', and I played lead over Muddy's rhythm, while Otis sang and played piano. I was in heaven, and they seemed pretty happy with what I did.

At this point people began to talk about me as if I was some kind of genius, and I heard that someone had written the slogan 'Clapton is God' on the wall of Islington Underground station. Then it started to spring up all over London, like graffiti. I was a bit mystified by this, and part of me ran a mile from it; I didn't really want that kind of notoriety, I knew it would bring some kind of trouble. Another part of me really liked the idea, that what I had been fostering all these years was finally getting some recognition. The fact is, of course, that through my playing, people were being exposed to another kind of music, which was new to them, and I was getting all the credit for it, as if I had invented the blues.

As for technique, there were hundreds of guitar players who were better than me. Apart from the famous blues guys, there were a lot of white players too. Reggie Young, for example, a Memphis session player, who was one of the best guitarists I had ever heard. I had seen him playing with the Bill Black Combo on the Ronettes package tour. Don Peake, who I saw play with the Everly Brothers, and James Burton, who played on Ricky Nelson's records, were two others. The English guitarists I had seen who had knocked me out were Bernie Watson and Albert Lee, who both played with Screaming Lord Sutch's band, the Savages. Bernie and Sutch's pianist, Andy Wren, were supreme musicians who were far ahead of anybody at the time. I remember hearing them play 'Worried Life Blues', the Big Maceo song, and Bernie was bending notes, which he had been doing long before anybody. Though I rated Jeff Beck, and also Jimmy Page, their roots were in rockabilly, while mine were in the blues. I loved what they did, and there was no competitiveness between us, we just played different styles.

But there was another part of me that thought the 'Clapton is God' thing was really quite nice. I'd been ousted from the Yardbirds, and they'd brought in Jeff Beck. They immediately had a string of hits, and I was quite put out by that, so any kind of accolade that came from just playing, without selling myself, or promoting myself on TV, was welcome. There's something about word of mouth that you cannot undo. In truth, I felt grateful about it because it gave me status, and it was the kind of status nobody could tamper with. After all, you can't muck around with graffiti. It comes from the street.

By the early summer of 1965, though I was still living in John's house in Lee Green, I was spending a lot of time with a group of friends hanging out in a flat in Long Acre, Covent Garden, owned by a woman called Clarissa, who was the girlfriend of Ted Milton. Ted was the most extraordinary man. A poet and visionary, who I had first met at Ben Palmer's, he was the first person I ever saw physically interpreting music. We were at home at Ben's house, and after dinner he put on a Howlin' Wolf record and began to enact it with his entire being, dancing and employing facial expressions to interpret what he was hearing. Watching him, I understood for the first time how you could really live music, how you could listen to it completely, and make it come alive, so that it was part of your life. It was a real awakening. Ted and Clarissa lived in a second-floor flat, which consisted of several rooms opening off a long corridor and a big kitchen, and it was the centre of our lives for a little while. There was John Bailey, known to us as 'Dapper Dan' for his suave good looks and natty sense of dress, who was studying anthropology; Bernie Greenwood, a doctor with a clinic in Notting Hill, who was also a great saxophone player; Micko Milligan, a jeweller and part-time hairdresser; Peter Jenner and Andrew King, who lived in the flat opposite and were just starting to manage Pink Floyd; and my old friend June Child who now had a job working for them as their secretary. Looking back on it, we had the time of our lives, drinking, smoking massive quantities of dope, thinking everything we were doing was totally original (and sometimes it was), while poor old Clarissa went out to work to pay for it all.

Bit by bit this scene began to take up more and more of my spare time. It was outrageous really. We'd just spend hours and hours listening to music and drinking Mateus Rosé, real headache material, which I absolutely loved. Sometimes we'd get into spontaneous laughing jags, brought on by God knows what, where we'd latch on to a particular word or phrase, or on something we'd seen, and we'd just start laughing hysterically, and it would become unstoppable. We could literally laugh for hours at a time. Laughing was also part of another pastime, where we'd listen to one song over and over for a whole day – a favourite was 'Shotgun' by Junior Walker – before passing out, and then starting again when we came round.

In the middle of the summer of 1965, six of us spontaneously decided to get a band together and drive round the world, financing the trip by playing gigs along the route. We called ourselves the Glands. John Bailey would be the vocalist, Bernie Greenwood on sax, Ted's brother, Jake, played drums, Ben Palmer was lured back to the piano and on bass we had a guy called Bob Rae. Bernie had a car, an MGA, which he traded in for an American Ford Galaxy station wagon to serve as our transport, while I had a few hundred quid in wages saved up and bought an amplifier and a couple of guitars. Considering I was supposedly the draw of the Bluesbreakers, I suppose you could say it was a tad irresponsible of me to be just taking off like this. If I mentioned it to John at all, it was only to say that I was going off for a little while. I really did leave him in the lurch, and he had to trawl through several different guitarists to fill the gap while I was away.

With six of us squashed into the Ford Galaxy, we set off in August, driving through France and Belgium, our plan being to just keep going until we found somewhere to play. We really hadn't a clue what we were doing, trusting that some good fortune would come our way. The trip almost ended as soon as it began. We arrived in Munich at the same time as the famous beer festival was under way, and we were in one of the beer tents, when Bob Rae chose to light his cigarette with a £5 note. This led to a serious altercation between him and another member of the band over the blatant extravagance of such a gesture, a fight which ended with all the gear being unloaded from the car and a general decision to go back home.

The following morning, we all made up, loaded the equipment back into the Ford and set off again on the road. Driving through Yugoslavia, on a cobbled road between Zagreb and Belgrade, the car shook so much that it came apart. The body actually left the chassis. We had to get a piece of rope and tie it round and underneath the car. So there were now six people and all the equipment travelling in a car held together by a piece of rope. It was a shambles. When we finally got as far as Greece, to Thessaloniki, we were so hungry, because we hadn't eaten anything for days, that we ate raw meat at the butcher's! Eventually, when we reached Athens, we got a job playing at a club called the Igloo.

The Igloo Club was so called because it was designed to look like the inside of an igloo, with everything rounded. It had a resident band called the Juniors, and their manager needed another band to support them, because their set started at seven and the club would stay open until two or three in the morning. John Bailey talked this guy into hiring us. We found a place to stay, in a room on the top floor of a house that was run by an old Egyptian colonel. I loved it there, and I was soon having the time of my life. The gig consisted of us playing three sets a night, alongside the Juniors, who were playing songs by the Beatles and the Kinks. Since they didn't know these very well, we were also helping them out a little bit.

Two nights after we got this gig, the Juniors were involved in a car crash, and two of them were killed outright. The following morning, we were having coffee at the club when the manager came in and started screaming the name of Thanos, the keyboard player, who he was apparently in love with, and who was one of the guys who had died. 'Thanos, Thanos, Thanos,' he screamed, and then started throwing glasses at the mirror behind the bar. Someone said we had better get out, so everyone left and he smashed the club to bits. It was closed for two days, and we were advised to stay put because something would be sorted out.

They repaired the club and someone who represented the heartbroken manager approached me and told me that they needed to get things up and running again, and they wanted me to play with the Juniors. So the next thing I knew, I found myself playing a set with them, then a set with my band, another set with them, followed by a set with my band etc., until I had played a six-hour stretch without stopping. After a few days of this, the Juniors suddenly took off. I knew all the songs they wanted to play, and I seemed to have put something into the band that hadn't been there before, and the next thing I knew we were doing gigs in Piraeus playing to 10,000 people. I was thrilled to be able to help the Juniors get to a bigger audience, but it all smacked of the pop world I had tried to put behind me. It was like déjà vu. Meanwhile the Glands had had enough and were itching to move on. When I told the drummer in the Juniors that I was thinking of leaving, he said, 'You'd better not. The manager will come after you if you try to leave, and he'll cut your hands off.' I got the impression he wasn't joking, so we planned to do a runner. Ben secretly organised train tickets, while the band packed up their stuff so they were ready to go. I turned up as usual one afternoon for a Juniors rehearsal, but we had a car waiting on the other side of the building. At a given signal, I said I was going to the toilet and walked out of the front door, got into the car, and went straight to the station where Ben and me caught a train back to London, leaving the Juniors high and dry. The drummer with the Juniors was our inside man, and basically I owe him my hands. Thanks man, I can never repay you enough. I left behind a beautiful Gibson Les Paul, and a Marshall amp. The rest of the boys continued on their way round the world, though God knows what they sounded like without a guitar and a piano.

Returning to England in late October 1965, I found that my place in the Bluesbreakers had been filled by a brilliant guitarist called Peter Green, later of Fleetwood Mac, who had pestered John to employ him, often turning up at gigs and shouting from the audience that he was much better than whoever was playing that night. Though I barely knew him, I got the impression that here was a real Turk, a strong, confident person who knew exactly what he wanted and where he was going, but who played his cards close to his chest. Most importantly, he was a phenomenal player, with a great tone. He was not happy to see me, as it meant rather a sudden end to what had obviously been a good gig for him. One change that didn't particularly surprise me was to find that McVie had finally been given the boot, and had been replaced by Jack Bruce. He stayed for only a few weeks before moving on to join Manfred Mann, during which time we toured the club circuit in the South of England, but doing those few gigs, we had a chance to take stock of one another. Musically he was the most forceful bass player I had ever played with. He approached the gig almost as if the bass was a lead instrument, but not to the point where it got in the way, and his understanding of time was phenomenal. All this was reflected in his personality, fiery and quick-witted. I'm glad to say it seemed like a mutual admiration, and we fitted together brilliantly, a taste of things to come.

1966 turned out to be a momentous year. It got off to a great start when John decided to throw a party for my twenty-first birthday at his house in Lee. This was the first time that he had met any of my new friends from the Long Acre flat, and I was quite proud to show off these extraordinary people, who appeared to me to be the elite of intellectual society. The theme for the party was fancy dress. My costumes were hired from Bermans in Shaftesbury Avenue, the windows of which I used to gaze in on my many post-Marquee night walks, and consisted of one penguin suit, which had a beak you could open with a piece of string so that you could look out of it, and a gorilla suit. I started the evening as a gorilla, but when it got too hot I changed into the penguin suit. For some reason, during the course of the evening, I remembered the saga of my grandmother and the cigarettes, so I got hold of a packet of twenty Benson and Hedges, which came in a gold box and were the trendy cigarette of the day, and lit one after the other till I had all twenty in my mouth simultaneously, and smoked the whole lot. I carried on smoking for another thirty years, finally giving up at the age of forty-eight, by which time I was smoking about sixty a day. Finally, at the end of the night, I wound up in bed with a very pretty Chinese girl, who would later become a very good friend. When the party was over, I considered myself well and truly grown up, a man of the world, a bit rebellious and anarchistic, but most of all, experienced. It felt like my life was really taking off.

Looking back, it felt like I had closed the door on my past, I had little or no contact with my old friends from Ripley, and my family ties felt very weak. It was as if I was starting a brand-new life, where there was no room for any excess baggage. I was very confident of my capabilities, and very aware that this was the key to my future. Hence I was extremely protective of my craft, and ruthless in cutting away anything that stood in my path. It was not a path of ambition, I had no desire for fame or recognition, I just needed to be able to make the best music I could, with the tools that I had.

CHAPTER FOUR
CREAM

Bluesbreakers: John Mayall with Eric Clapton was the breakthrough album that really brought my playing to people's attention. It was made at a time when I really felt I'd found my niche, in a band where I could remain in the background, yet at the same time develop my skills, driving the band in the direction I thought it ought to go. We went into the Decca studios in West Hampstead for three days in April, and played exactly the set we did on stage, with the addition of a horn section on some of the tracks. These songs included 'Parchman Farm', a Mose Allison number on which John performed a harmonica solo, the Ray Charles song 'What'd I Say', featuring a drum solo by Hughie Flint, and 'Ramblin' On My Mind' by Robert Johnson, on which John insisted I did vocals. This was much against my better judgement, since most of the guys I longed to emulate were older and had deep voices, and I felt extremely uncomfortable singing in my high-pitched whine.

Because the album was recorded so quickly, it had a raw edgy quality about it which made it special. It was almost like a live performance. I insisted on having the mike exactly where I wanted it to be during the recording, which was not too close to my amplifier, so that I could play through it and get the same sound as I had on stage. The result was the sound which came to be associated with me. It had really come about accidentally, when I was trying to emulate the sharp, thin sound that Freddy King got out of his Gibson Les Paul, and I ended up with something quite different, a sound which was a lot fatter than Freddy's. The Les Paul has two pickups, one at the end of the neck, giving the guitar a kind of round jazz sound, and the other next to the bridge giving you the treble, most often used for the thin, typically rock 'n' roll sound. What I would do was use the bridge pickup with all of the bass turned up, so the sound was very thick, and on the edge of distortion. I also always used amps that would overload. I would have the amp on full and I would have the volume on the guitar also turned up full, so everything was on full volume and overloading. I would hit a note, hold it and give it some vibrato with my fingers, until it sustained, and then the distortion would turn into feedback. It was all of these things, plus the distortion, that created what I suppose you could call 'my sound'.

On the day we had to have the photograph taken for the cover, I decided to be totally uncooperative, since I hated being photographed. To annoy everybody, I bought a copy of the *Beano* and read it grumpily while the photographer took the pictures. The resulting cover, showing the band sitting against a wall with me reading a comic, led to the album being dubbed *The Beano Album*.

Though I was happy with the Bluesbreakers, I was also beginning to get restless, nurturing somewhere inside me thoughts of being a frontman, an idea that had been evolving ever since I had first seen Buddy Guy playing at the Marquee. Even though he was accompanied by only a bass player and a drummer, he created a huge, powerful sound, and it blew me away. It was almost as if he didn't need anyone else. He could have played the whole set on his own. Visually he was like a dancer with his guitar, playing with his feet, his tongue, and throwing it around the room. He made it look so easy, and as I was watching, I was thinking, 'I can do that,' and now that my confidence was high, I began to really believe that I could make that leap. I was truly inspired. So when Ginger Baker, the drummer from the Graham Bond Organisation, came to see me and talked about forming a new band, I knew exactly what I wanted to do.

The Bluesbreakers were playing a gig in Oxford when Ginger first came to see me. I'd seen him down at the Marquee, and at the Richmond Jazz Festival, but didn't know much about him. Drumming was something about which I knew very little. I presumed he must be pretty good as he was first choice with all the musicians I rated, so I was very flattered that he was interested in me. I was also rather frightened of him because he was an angry-looking guy, with a considerable reputation. He appeared physically very strong although extremely lean, with red hair and a constant expression of disbelief mixed with suspicion. He gave the impression that he was fearless and that he would take anybody on. He would sometimes arch one eyebrow as if to say, 'Who the hell do you think you are?' He also had a very dry sense of humour, which I didn't really see until I got to know him, which was a surprising experience in itself, because in truth, he is a very shy and gentle man, thoughtful and full of compassion.

That night, after the gig, he offered me a lift back to London. He had a new Rover 3000, which he drove like a maniac and while he was driving he told me he was thinking of forming a band, and asked if I'd be interested in joining. I said I'd think about it, but that I'd only be really interested if Jack Bruce was involved. He almost crashed the car. I knew that the two of them had played together with Graham Bond and had heard that there wasn't much love lost between them, but I've never really known what this was all about, or if it was a particularly serious issue. I had actually seen them play together in Alexis Korner's band, and they seemed perfect together, like a well-oiled machine, but that was the music, and sometimes the music isn't enough.

Ginger was initially very reluctant to work with Jack again, and I could see that it was a huge obstacle for him, but when he realised it was the only way I would do it, he agreed to go away and have a think about it. He eventually came back and said that on reflection he would give it a go, but I could tell it was going to be a rough road. In fact the very first time that the three of us got together, in March 1966, in the front room of Ginger's house in Neasden, they started arguing right away. It seemed like they just naturally rubbed one another up the wrong way, both being very headstrong, and both natural leaders. But when we started to play together, it all just turned into magic. Maybe I was the necessary catalyst for them to get along, like a fulcrum. Temporarily it seemed that way. We played through some songs acoustically, including some of Jack's new material, and it sounded great. There was a driving feeling to it that felt really good. We all looked at each other and grinned.

The first time we rehearsed fully electric, however, I began to get mixed feelings, because I suddenly missed the keyboards that I had got used to in the Bluesbreakers. Having had in my mind the ideal of Buddy Guy, who had managed to make the sound of a trio seem so full, I realised that that was because of him, and that, lacking his virtuosity and confidence, I wasn't going to be able to carry off what he did. This would mean that the balance of power would rest much more with Jack and Ginger than it did with me. In truth the band sounded a bit empty to me, as if we needed another player. I had someone in mind from day one, Steve Winwood, who I had seen play at the Twisted Wheel and other clubs, and who had really impressed me with his singing and playing. Most of all, he seemed to know his way round the genre. I think he was only fifteen at the time, but when he sang 'Georgia', if you closed your eyes, you would swear it was Ray Charles. Musically, he was like an old man in a boy's skin. When I touched on the subject with Jack and Ginger, they made it quite clear that they didn't want anyone else in there. They liked the set-up as it was, although whenever we went into the studio to make records, we usually tracked and overdubbed, creating another player, with either Jack playing keyboards, or me playing first rhythm and then lead. We very rarely recorded just as a trio.

Over the next few months we continued to rehearse secretly, wherever and whenever we could, and we had an unspoken agreement that that was the way things should remain till we were ready to go public. After all, we were all contracted to other bands. Then Ginger let the cat out of the bag by giving an interview to Chris Welch of *Melody Maker*, and all hell broke loose. Jack was furious about it and almost came to blows with Ginger, and I had the unenviable task of explaining myself to John Mayall, who had been like a father to me. It was not a happy experience. I told him I was leaving because I had come to a fork in the road and I wanted to form my own band. I was quite surprised by how upset he was, and though he wished me well I was left in no doubt that he was pretty angry. I think he was sad too, because I had sort of helped take the Bluesbreakers to another level. When John had been running the band, it was much more jazz-orientated and more low profile, and I had stirred it up and pushed it in a new direction. Having been rather straight, he was beginning to enjoy this transition, and everything that went with it, the adulation of the girls and the lifestyle, and was beginning to be influenced by it. He was upset, I think, that I was jumping off the train just as it was beginning to gather speed.

Ginger wanted to bring in the manager of the Graham Bond Organisation, Robert Stigwood, to handle us, a suggestion which Jack railed against on the grounds that it would compromise our independence, and that it would be better for us to manage ourselves. He was finally persuaded, and came with us to meet 'Stigboot', as Ginger called him, in his office in New Cavendish Street. By the time we met, the Robert Stigwood Organisation had had some measure of success, but mostly with pop singers like John Leyton, Mike Berry and Mike Sarne.

Robert was an extraordinary character, a flamboyant Australian who liked to pass himself off as a wealthy Englishman. He would usually wear a blazer and grey slacks, with a pale blue shirt and a smattering of gold, and was the epitome of a man of leisure. Seated behind an ornate desk, he launched into a very confident monologue, telling us all the things that he could do for us, and how wonderful our lives were going to be. Although it sounded like a lot of flannel to me, I was struck by his obvious artistic flair and thought he had a pretty unique and interesting vision of life. He also seemed to be genuinely keen on what we were trying to do, and I think in some ways he truly understood us. It took me a while to tumble to the fact that he was partial to good-looking guys, but I had no problem with that, and in fact it made him appear rather vulnerable, and very human to me.

Musically, we didn't really have a plan. In my mind, when I had fantasised about it, I had seen myself as Buddy Guy, heading a blues trio with a very good rhythm section. I didn't know how Ginger and Jack saw it in their heads except that I'm sure it would have been more jazz-orientated. Since Stigwood probably had no idea what we were doing either, it is clear that the whole project was a colossal gamble. The very idea that a guitar, bass and drum trio could make any headway in the era of the pop group was pretty outrageous. Our next step was to think of a name for the band, and I came up with Cream, for the very simple reason that in all our minds we were the cream of the crop, the elite in our respective domains. I defined the music we would play as 'Blues Ancient and Modern'.

In the summer of 1966, the whole of England, bar us, was in the throes of World Cup fever, and it just so happened that our first proper gig, at my old stamping ground, the Twisted Wheel in Manchester, was on 29 July, the night before the final. I had persuaded Ben Palmer to come out of retirement, not to play piano, but to act as our roadie, and he drove us up North in a black Austin Westminster which Stigwood had bought for us. This was a pretty swanky car, a cut above the Transit I was used to. I remember Ben being horrified when we arrived to find out that the word 'roadie' did not just mean driver, and that he was expected to lug all our equipment around. He was on a learning curve just as we were. The club was pretty quiet that night as we were a last-minute, unannounced addition to the bill, replacing Joe Tex, who had called off, but the show, consisting of predominantly blues covers like 'Spoonful', 'Crossroads' and 'I'm So Glad', was merely a warm-up for the real debut that Stigwood had planned for us, two nights later at the sixth National Jazz and Blues Festival at Windsor racecourse.

I wore a special outfit for this gig, a dance-band jacket I bought from Cecil Gee in the Charing Cross Road. It was black, with grain lapels and gold woven thread all over it, like flocked wallpaper. It's funny to think of now, but we were all so nervous. We were an unknown band and we were topping the bill, closing the last night's session. We were used to playing in clubs and now we were performing outside to 15,000 people. We had a tiny amount of equipment, and being only a trio, there didn't seem to be any power. It all sounded so small, especially playing after the group who were then known as the world's loudest rock band, the Who. The weather was abysmal. It poured with rain and we only played three songs before we ran out and Ginger had to make the announcement 'Sorry there are no more numbers.' I think we played a couple of them again, but nobody seemed to care. Then we just jammed, and the audience went crazy. The music press also went crazy, describing us as the first 'Supergroup'.

Cream took a while to really take off. From the huge audience of the Windsor Jazz Festival, we were straight away back on the ballroom and club circuit, starting on 2 August at Klooks Kleek, an R&B club in West Hampstead, London, working hard to persuade audiences that a trio could be every bit as good as a loud four-piece pop group, and we were also still finding our direction. We felt we needed to play material that was recognisable, but that would also push the boundaries of what the audience would approve. In the end, the solution was often just to jam. I never discussed our musical direction with the others because I didn't then know how to verbalise anything, so most of the conversations/ arguments took place between Jack and Ginger, who were both writing their own material, in particular Jack, who was working a lot with the lyricist and poet Peter Brown. Peter had a band called the Battered Ornaments and had a knack of writing quirky song lyrics, which Jack would put music to. Songs with titles like 'She Was Like A Bearded Rainbow' and 'Deserted Cities Of The Heart'. The only way I had to influence the direction of the group was in the way I played, and by suggesting new cover versions of old blues songs like Howlin' Wolf's 'Sitting On Top Of The World', and 'Outside Woman' by Blind Joe Reynolds.

The dynamic of playing in a trio greatly influenced my style, in that I had to think of ways to make more sound. When I was playing in a quartet, with keyboard, bass and drums, I could just ride on top of the band, making musical comments, coming in and out at will. In a trio I had to provide a lot more of the sound, and I found that difficult, because I didn't really enjoy having to play so much. My technique altered quite a lot, in that I started playing a lot more barré chords, and hitting open strings to provide a kind of drone for my lead work.

Naturally Stigwood was keen to get us the hit single that all bands strived for, and we had a few days in August recording at a studio in Chalk Farm, which produced one song, 'Wrapping Paper', written by Jack and Peter, which was eventually to find its way on to the A-side of our first 45 rpm. But it was in September, in Ryemuse Studios, a tiny studio above a chemist's shop in South Molton Street, that we finally recorded a song that gave an indication of our true potential as a band. Another of Jack and Peter's compositions, 'I Feel Free', was a faster, rockier song with a driving beat, recorded on a single Ampex reel-to-reel recorder. Stigwood, assisted by the studio engineer John Timperley, took credit as producer himself, though the truth is that it was an ensemble job. Because Stigwood saw this song as a potential single, he chose to leave it off our first album, *Fresh Cream*, and both were released simultaneously at the end of December.

When I left the Bluesbreakers, it was obvious that I could no longer go on living with John in Lee Green, so in the meantime I had been moving about, sometimes staying in Ripley, other times in Long Acre, or wherever I could find a bed or sofa. I had to find myself somewhere new to live. Salvation came in the form of three American girls who I met after one of our shows. I got talking to one of them – her name was Betsy – and she asked if I'd like to go and stay with them. I ended up moving into the front room of their house in Ladbroke Square. They were all doing internships of one kind and another, and it was an entirely platonic relationship, but it made me feel incredibly grown up. I was living with the opposite sex, unattended. At the same time I bought my first car. It was a 1938 right-hand drive Cadillac Fleetwood that had been made for the London Motor Show and I saw it in a garage in Seven Sisters Road. It was huge, in perfect condition, and cost only £750. Even though I couldn't drive, I bought it anyway. The dealer delivered it and parked it right outside the house. It sat there, getting covered in leaves, and I used to just look at it out of the window. A couple of times Ben

Palmer drove me around in it, but he said it was a nightmare to drive because it was so big, and had no power steering.

Almost exactly two months to the day after our debut at Windsor, on 1 October, we were booked to play at the Central London Polytechnic in Regent Street. I was hanging about backstage with Jack, when Chas Chandler, the bass player with the Animals, appeared accompanied by a young black American guy who he introduced as Jimi Hendrix, informing us that he was a brilliant guitarist and he wanted to sit in with us on a couple of numbers. I thought he looked cool and that he probably knew what he was doing. We got talking about music, and he liked the same people I liked, so I was all for it. Jack was cool about it too, though I seem to remember that Ginger was a little bit hostile.

The song Jimi wanted to play was a Howlin' Wolf song called 'Killing Floor'. I thought it was incredible that he would know how to play this, as it was a tough one to get right. Of course Jimi played it exactly like it ought to be played, and he totally blew me away. I mean if you're jamming with someone for the first time, most musicians will try to hold back, but Jimi just went for it. He played the guitar with his teeth, behind his head, lying on the floor, doing the splits, the whole business. It was amazing, and it was musically great too, not just pyrotechnics. Even though I had already seen Buddy Guy, and knew that a lot of black players could do this kind of stuff, it's still pretty amazing when you're standing right next to it. The audience were completely gob-smacked by what they saw and heard too. They loved it, and I loved it too, but I remember thinking that here was a force to be reckoned with. It scared me, because he was clearly going to be a huge star, and just as we were finding our own speed, here was the real thing.

The single of 'I Feel Free' was released in America on the Atco label, a subsidiary of Atlantic Records, the head of which was the Turkish-born New Yorker Ahmet Ertegun, a legendary figure in the world of black music. He had masterminded the careers of artists such as Ray Charles, the Drifters and Aretha Franklin, as well as producing many of their records. He had taken an interest in me since he was on a trip to London, early in 1966, to see Wilson Pickett, one of his artists, playing at the Astoria Theatre in Finsbury Park. After the show, he had thrown a party at the Scotch of St James's, a fashionable club in Mayfair and had been impressed by my playing during a jam session with Pickett's band. Cream were signed up by Atlantic not long after this, and when our first album *Fresh Cream* was about to be released in the States, Ahmet persuaded Stigwood that it was vital that we came over to promote it.

We were all so excited. To me America was the land of promise. The first thing I did when I knew we were going, was to make a shortlist of all the things I had fantasised about doing if I ever went there. I was going to buy a fringed cowboy jacket, for example, and some cowboy boots. I was going to have a milkshake and a hamburger. Stigwood had booked us into a hotel on West 55th Street called the Gorham, a real fleapit, from which we emerged daily to perform in the show for which we had flown all this way, the *Murray the K Show*.

Murray 'the K' Kaufman was the most successful radio DJ in New York, and he was running a series of shows at the RKO Theater on 58th Street, called 'Music in the Fifth Dimension'. Never having had a hit record, we were at the bottom of the bill of a pretty good line-up, which included Wilson Pickett, the Young Rascals, Simon and Garfunkel, Mitch Ryder and the Who. There were five shows a day, and each artist, except for the headliners, was expected to play for no longer than five minutes. The shows started at 10.30 in the morning and went on till 8.30 at night. Murray's wife, Jackie, was head of the chorus line, and her girls, go-go girls really, would perform a routine called 'Jackie and the K Girls Wild Fashion Show' between the acts. Murray ran the show like a sergeant major, giving strict instructions that on no account were we allowed to leave the theatre between sets, ensuring that boredom soon set in, which led to all manner of pranks like flooded dressing rooms, and flour and smoke bombs. He kept telling us to make our set shorter and shorter, and even when we were doing just one song, which was 'I Feel Free', he said it was still too long. The whole thing was absolutely chaotic.

On the first day, while I was sitting in the theatre during rehearsals, watching the various acts do their turn, a very beautiful blonde girl came and sat next to me. We struck up a conversation, and at some point she asked if I would like to stay with her while I was in town. She was gorgeous and, seeming to sense my shyness with women, did her best to put me at ease. Her name was Kathy, and she took care of me the whole time I was in New York. She had her own apartment, and I moved in with her. She showed me around, taking me to the various places where I could tick off the list of things I wanted to experience. I remember her taking me to various coffee bars in the Village, and we went to one or two music stores, like Manny's on 48th Street. She also took me to a big saddler's called Kauffmans, which sold western gear, where I bought my first cowboy boots, and with this beautiful girl on my arm, I thought I had died and gone to heaven.

Because Murray the K kept us on such a tight leash, there was very little time on this trip to really explore New York, though not all my after-hours time was wasted. I hung out a lot with Al Kooper, the keyboard player and guitarist with the Blues Project, who were also appearing on the show. The music scene in the Village was flourishing at the time, and there were loads of clubs and bars that were really taking off. One night Al took me down to the Café Au Go Go on Bleecker Street to see a new band he had formed called Blood, Sweat and Tears. On another night when we went down there, I met B. B. King for the first time, and the two of us ended up jamming after the show. We just sat on the stage and played with what was left of the house band for a couple of hours. It was fantastic. On return visits to New York, I used to go down to the Village with Jimi Hendrix, and we'd go from one club to another, just the two of us, and we'd play with whoever was on stage that night. We'd get up and jam and just wipe everybody out.

The last day's gig on the *Murray the K Show* took place on Easter Sunday, and coincided with the first ever New York Be-In, a gathering of 20,000 hippies which took place on the Sheep Meadow in Central Park. We managed to slip out of the theatre to join in with these incredible long-haired loons, who were all singing and dancing, smoking joints and dropping acid. Jack ended up having his first trip after eating some spiked popcorn. When we got back to the RKO to play our last show, stoned out of our heads, we devised a plan to pelt Jackie K and her girls with eggs and flour when they went on stage for their fashion show. Unfortunately Murray got wind of what was going on and put an end to it. We threw it all round the dressing rooms instead. We couldn't wait to get out of the place.

On the following day, our last before we returned home, Stigwood had arranged with Ahmet Ertegun that we go to the Atlantic Studios to record some material for a possible new album. To be introduced to Ahmet and his brother Nesuhi, and to be accepted into that particular musical family, was a fantastic piece of good fortune for us. Because our visas were about to expire, we had only one day spare. We laid down one track, a song called 'Lawdy Mama', which I had heard on an album called *Hoodoo Man Blues* by Buddy Guy and Junior Wells. It was the only song we completed before we had to leave, booked to return the following month.

London in 1967 was buzzing. It was an extraordinary melting pot of fashion, music, art and intellect, a movement of young people all concerned in some way or another with the evolution of their art. There was an underground too, where you would get these seminal influences suddenly showing up out of nowhere, like they had come out of the woodwork. The Fool were a good example of this, two Dutch artists, Simon and Marijke, who had come over to London from Amsterdam in 1966 and set up a studio designing clothes, posters and album covers. They painted mystical themes in fantastic vibrant colours and had been taken up by the Beatles, for whom they had created a vast three-storey mural on the wall of their Apple Boutique in Baker Street. I asked them to decorate one of my guitars, a Gibson Les Paul, which they turned into a psychedelic fantasy, painting not just the front and back of the body, but the neck and fretboard too.

I used to hang out a lot at a club called the Speakeasy, in Margaret Street. This was a musicians' club run by Laurie O'Leary, who had previously managed Esmeralda's Barn for the Krays, and his brother Alphi. Everybody went there and jammed with whoever was the resident band that night. It was at the Speakeasy, around this time, that I had my first LSD trip. I was in the club with my girlfriend Charlotte, when the Beatles came in with an acetate of their new album, *Sgt Pepper's Lonely Hearts Club Band*. The Monkees arrived and shortly afterwards someone in the club started handing out these pills, which he said were called STP. I had no idea what that was but somebody explained that it was superstrong acid, which would last for several days. We all took it, except for Charlotte, who we both agreed should stay straight in case of any emergency, and shortly after that, George gave the DJ the acetate to play. Even though I was not overawed in the least by the Beatles, I was aware that this was a very special moment in time for anyone that was there. Their music had been gradually evolving over the years, and this album was expected by everybody to be their masterpiece. It was also supposedly written under the influence of acid, so it was an amazing experience to be listening to it in the condition we were in. They had also begun to explore Indian mysticism, perhaps as a result of George's influence, and at some point the chanting of 'Hare Krishna, Hare Krishna, Krishna Krishna, Hare Hare' began to be heard in the club. The acid gradually took effect, and soon we were all dancing to the sounds of 'Lucy In The Sky' and 'A Day In The Life'. I have to admit I was pretty moved by the whole thing.

At about six in the morning we piled out into the street, where there was a huge gathering of policemen waiting on the other side of the road. There seemed to be hundreds of them. Maybe someone had tipped them off that the Beatles were inside getting stoned, who knows. The point was, they seemed frozen, unable to move. John came out of the Speakeasy with Lulu on his arm and as he did so, his beautiful hand-painted Rolls-Royce came round the corner. It pulled up outside the club, and as he got into it, he gave the police the V-sign, and it was as if there was a force field all around them. They stood there paralysed, and we all just took off. I stayed high for three more days. I couldn't sleep and I was seeing the most extraordinary things; without Charlotte's help and guidance, I probably would have gone mad. Most of my vision seemed to be through a glass screen with hieroglyphics and mathematical equations painted on it, and I remember I couldn't eat meat, because it looked just like the animal. For a time I was a bit concerned about whether it was ever going to wear off.

It was at the Speakeasy, several months before, that I first met Charlotte Martin. I was smitten with her from the very first moment I set eyes on her. She was very beautiful in an austere way, classically French, with long legs and an incredible figure, but it was her eyes that got me. They were slightly oriental with a downward slant, and a little bit sad. We started dating right away, and soon moved in together into a flat in Regent's Park belonging to Stigwood's partner, David Shaw, who was the financial brains behind the organisation. Charlotte was an incredible girl, more interested in films, art and literature than modelling, and we had a great time together. One night, down at 'the Speak', we were sitting with some friends at a table, when we were joined by an Australian friend of hers, an artist called Martin Sharp who had also just started writing verse. When he heard I was a musician, he told me that he had written a poem which he thought would make good lyrics for a song. As it happened I had in my mind at that moment an idea inspired by a favourite song of mine by the Lovin' Spoonful called 'Summer In The City', so I asked him to show me the words. He wrote them down on a napkin and gave them to me. They began:

> You thought the leaden winter would bring you down forever,
> But you rode upon a steamer to the violence of the sun.
> And the colours of the sea blind your eyes with trembling mermaids,
> And you touch the distant beaches with tales of brave Ulysses.

These became the lyrics of the song 'Tales Of Brave Ulysses'. It was the start of a long friendship and a very fruitful collaboration.

The recording of 'Tales Of Brave Ulysses' and the other songs which were to make up the album *Disraeli Gears* took place back in New York at the beginning of May. This was quite a different experience to our previous trip. We stayed at the Drake Hotel on 56th Street, and Ahmet had his top people in the studio to record us: a hot young producer called Felix Pappalardi, and one of his most experienced engineers, Tom Dowd. We recorded the whole album in the space of a week. I was impressed by the way Felix took what we had and polished it into something more saleable. On the very first night he took home with him the tape we had previously recorded of 'Lawdy Mama', which was a standard twelve-bar blues, and came back the next day having transformed it into a kind of McCartneyesque pop song, complete with new lyrics and the title 'Strange Brew'. I didn't particularly like the song, but I respected the fact that he had created a pop song without completely destroying the original groove. In the end he won my approval, by cleverly allowing me to include in it an Albert King-style guitar solo.

To begin with, Tommy Dowd, who was to become a close friend of mine and be very instrumental in my future projects, was thoroughly confused with the way in which we approached recording. We were used to making albums as if they were live, and did not expect to play songs over and over again, or to have to play instruments separately on different tracks. He wasn't quite prepared for the noise levels either, and they used to say we could be heard several blocks away. As for Ahmet, he was under the impression that Cream was my band, and that, as the leader, I, rather than Jack, should be singing, and he kept pushing for me to do so. In the end they both decided to let us get on in our own way. While we were recording, all kinds of famous musicians would drop by the studio to say hello, Booker T and Otis Redding amongst them; the word seemed to be out that something extraordinary was in the making.

I will never forget returning to London after recording *Disraeli Gears*, with all of us excited by the fact that we had made what we considered to be a groundbreaking album, which was a magical combination of blues, rock and jazz. Unfortunately for us, Jimi had just released *Are You Experienced?* and that was all anyone wanted to listen to. He kicked everybody into touch really, and he was the flavour, not just of the month, but of the year. Everywhere you went, it was wall-to-wall Jimi, and I felt really down. I thought we had made our definitive album, only to come home and find that nobody was interested. It was the beginning of a disenchantment with England, where it seemed there wasn't really room for more than one person to be popular at a time.

What I loved about America was that it seemed such a broad breeding ground for different acts and talent, and different forms of music. You could be in a car and tune the radio to a country music station, a jazz station, a rock station, a blues station or an oldies rock station. Even back then the categorisation was so wide, and there seemed to be room for anyone to make a living out of it and be at the forefront of what they were doing. When I came home, it felt as though that if you weren't scoring ten out of ten on the day, you were nowhere.

On the plus side, even if the record wasn't selling as well as I'd hoped, I was having a great time. I had moved from Regent's Park to the King's Road, Chelsea, to share a studio with Martin Sharp, with whom I had become good friends. Martin was a very gentle man, with an insatiable appetite for life and new experiences. At the same time he was very considerate and sensitive to others. An admirer of Max Ernst, who inspired a lot of his work, he was and still is a great painter. Our apartment was on the top floor of the Pheasantry, a historic eighteenth-century building, so called because pheasants had once been reared there for the royal household. We had a large kitchen, two or three bedrooms, and a huge living room with beautiful wooden floors and great views from the dormer windows. I decorated my room in bright red and gilt, a reflection of the times.

There was quite a community of people living in the Pheasantry. Martin and I had two of the rooms which we shared with our respective girlfriends, Eija and Charlotte. The third room was taken by another painter, Philippe Mora and his girl-friend, Freya, and the ground floor was a massive studio owned or leased by a portrait painter named Timothy Widbourne, who was busy painting the Queen's portrait, while we were upstairs, quietly getting out of our skulls. But the most colourful character in our midst, if not the most powerful, was David Litvinoff. Litvinoff was one of the most extraordinary men I've ever met, a fast-talking East End Jew, with a stupendous intellect, who appeared not to give a shit what anyone thought of him, even though I know he really did, and sometimes painfully so. He talked ten to the dozen, usually jumping from one subject to another. He had piercing blue eyes, set in a sharply chiselled face, which had a huge scar right across it. This, he said, was the result of an altercation he had had with the Krays; I never found out the exact reason for this, and I didn't feel comfortable asking him about it, although he seemed to wear the scar with pride.

Litvinoff told me that he had once worked in Fleet Street, helping to put together the William Hickey gossip column on the *Daily Express*, a job which had got him into all kinds of interesting situations, often connected with people not wanting to feature in the column. He had a vast knowledge of music which gave us a lot in common, and he was very funny, with his humour usually directed towards himself. I remember walking with him once in the King's Road and making some comment about the shirt he was wearing. 'Oh this fucking thing?' he said, and ripped it off from under his jacket. We would sit in the local café, the Picasso, and he would character-assassinate everybody who came in. He'd go up to people he'd never met before and launch into a diatribe about them, pointing a finger in their face and telling them what they did, where they'd come from and where they were going wrong. Then somehow he'd turn the whole thing back on himself, as if to redeem the person he'd been attacking. He was absolutely extraordinary, and I loved him to bits.

One day I happened to mention to Litvinoff that my favourite play was *The Caretaker*, and that I'd seen the film hundreds of times. When he heard this, he hinted that he knew the man that Pinter had based the character of the tramp, Davies, on. The next thing I knew, he turned up with this guy, whose name was John Ivor Golding. He was a full-blown tramp, wearing pinstriped trousers and a sort of worn-out frock coat over layers and layers of clothing. He was very eloquent, but quite mad, and, just like Davies did in the play, he moved in and took over, manipulating us with his charm. Then, of course, we couldn't get rid of him, and as far as I remember, he was still there after I moved out.

The Pheasantry was a fantastic place to live in 1967. Being right in the middle of the King's Road, there was always a lot of street activity, and it was within strolling distance of all the places where I used to hang out. I was dressing in a mixture of antique and second-hand clothes, and also new stuff, bought from places like the Chelsea Antique Market, Hung On You and Granny Takes A Trip. Often accompanied by Litvinoff, I would work my way down to the World's End from the Picasso, look in at Granny's, and then wander back up to the Pheasantry, where we'd have a cup of tea and a joint. I won't name-drop, but it was astonishing the amount of different faces that would drop in throughout the course of the afternoon, and our 'tea parties' invariably evolved into whole evenings listening to music. Whether it might be the first pirated disc of Dylan's *Basement Tapes*, which I remember Litvinoff once producing, or an acetate of a new Beatles song, or just me sitting in the corner playing guitar, there was always something going on.

When Cream played the seventh Windsor Jazz Festival at the beginning of the third week of August, just over a year to the day after our debut, it did not escape our attention how little we had really progressed. In terms of record sales we were still way behind the Beatles and the Stones, and even below Hendrix. Our touring round the same old circuit had been patchy, and we felt disappointed that Stigwood had not allowed us to play the Monterey Pop Festival, especially having seen the incredible success that Hendrix and the Who had had there. Even though we had been champing at the bit to go there, Stigwood, in his wisdom, had decided that if we were going to conquer America, then we should do it by going in the back door, not by performing at a huge outdoor event at which we would be lost amongst the hundreds of other performers. We bowed to what we assumed was his experience. Now at least our spirits were raised by the fact that, with the release of *Disraeli Gears* set for November, we were leaving for California within a week.

I was actually pretty contemptuous of the West Coast rock 'n' roll scene, as exemplified by the new bands like Jefferson Airplane, Big Brother and the Holding Company and the Grateful Dead. At the time I just didn't understand what they were doing, and thought they sounded pretty second rate. I liked the Byrds and Buffalo Springfield, and I had heard a great album by a San Francisco band called Moby Grape, but I had never seen them play live, and I thought that most of the so-called psychedelic stuff that people were talking about was pretty dull.

Bill Graham, who was inviting us to play in San Francisco, was an entrepreneur and visionary, and had opened the Fillmore Auditorium as a rock venue at the beginning of 1966. Formerly the Majestic Academy of Dancing, it stood on the corner of Fillmore and Geary Streets and had already become one of San Francisco's institutions. Bill loved the idea of free expression and fostering new talent, and his vision had been to start a venue where people could come and, under minimum supervision, do what they wanted. San Francisco was, in those days, the home of the drug culture, and I think he pretty well turned a blind eye to drug using, so, as long as no one was endangering anyone else, they were free to trip out or smoke pot. In many ways he was like a father figure to all the bands and a lot of the other creative people who inhabited the city, like the artists who designed the posters, and he was very well respected and loved by all the people who worked with him. There were those people who intimated that he was involved with some shady characters, and was connected to the Mafia, but I loved him and never saw any evidence of that.

We were told by Bill that we could play anything we liked for as long as we liked, even if this meant us playing till dawn, and this is where we started openly exploring stuff. Anywhere else, we would probably have been a lot more concerned about presentation, but playing in the Fillmore, we soon realised that no one could see us because they were projecting light shows on to the band, so that we were actually in the light show. It was very liberating. We could just play our hearts out, without inhibition, knowing the audience were all really into whatever was being projected on to the screen behind us. I'm sure a good deal of them were out of their heads, half of them maybe, but it didn't matter. They were *listening*, and that encouraged us to go places we'd never been before. We started doing extended solos, and were soon playing fewer and fewer songs but for much longer. We'd go off in our own directions, but sometimes we would hit these coincidental points in the music when we would all arrive at the same conclusion, be it a riff or a chord or just an idea, and we would jam on it for a little while and then go back into our own thing. I had never experienced anything like it. It was nothing to do with lyrics or ideas; it was much deeper, something purely musical. We were at our peak during that period.

It was an incredible time for me, and I met some amazing people, like Terry the Tramp, head of the San Francisco chapter of the Hell's Angels, Addison Smith, who lived on a houseboat in Sausalito and lived the pure hippie life that most people could only pretend to, and Owsley, the chemist who made most of the acid that we were all taking. We were staying in a great little hotel called the Sausalito Inn, which at one time had been a bordello, and hanging out with musicians like Mike Bloomfield and David Crosby, smoking pot and dropping a lot of acid. Some of the time I was actually playing on acid. I don't really know how I got through it, because sometimes I didn't know if my hands were working, what the guitar was that I was playing, or even what it was made of. On one trip it was in my head that I could turn the audience into angels or devils according to which note I played.

Our first American tour lasted seven weeks, culminating in a return to New York to play twelve nights at the Café Au Go Go, and a couple at the Village Theater, where we shared the bill with one of Martin Sharp's favourite artists, Tiny Tim. One night I had a call from Ahmet asking me to drop by Atlantic Studios next day as there was someone he would like me to meet. So I went up there, and Aretha Franklin was in the control room with all her family, her sisters and her father. There was a powerful feeling in the room. Nesuhi Ertegun was there, Ahmet and Tommy Dowd, and there were at least five guitar players on the floor, including, I think, Joe South, Jimmy Johnson and Bobby Womack, with Spooner Oldham, David Hood and Roger Hawkins as the rhythm section. All these incredible musicians had come up from Muscle Shoals and Memphis to play on the album Aretha was making called *Lady Soul*. Ahmet said to me, 'I want you to go in there and play on this song,' and he pulled all these guitarists out of the room, and put me in there on my own. I felt so nervous, because I couldn't read music, and they were playing from music sheets on stands. Aretha came in and sang a song called 'Be As Good To Me As I Am To You', and I played lead guitar. I have to say that playing on that album for Ahmet and Aretha, with all of those incredible musicians, is still one of the highlights of my life.

It was touring America that made Cream as famous as we became. They really couldn't get enough of us, and I think once Stigwood saw this, he saw dollar signs, not just for him, but for us too. Before we knew where we were, we were back on the road in the States, this time for a massive five months. Part of me loved these whistle-stop tours where you'd jump into the car after one gig to drive to the next. Musically we were flying high. The other great part for me was arriving in some faraway town and going off with my nose to the ground, to see what was happening. I was really interested in American underground literature at the time. Two friends in London, Charlie and Diane Radcliffe, had turned me on to Kenneth Patchen and his book *The Journal of Albion Moonlight*. It had been my bible for a little while, and even though I had no idea what it was about, it just felt great to read, like listening to avant-garde music. So I would search out kindred spirits who looked like they'd be into the same kind of thing, and just go up and introduce myself, and then hang out with them and see where it led. Would I do it now? I'm not sure, but in this way I made a lot of friends all over America, and I met some incredibly interesting people. I remember, for instance, playing somewhere on the East Coast, and as I was walking through the audience between sets, I smelled this very powerful smell of what turned out to be patchouli oil. The guy who was wearing it told me that his name was David, and that he lived in a tepee, and would I like to come and visit him the following day. He was interested in Native American culture, and had decided to try to live like them, in the old way. We became good friends and we still communicate occasionally, to this very day. I met people like him all over the country. Wherever I went I was always on a quest to find like-minded souls, eccentrics, musicians, or people I could maybe learn something from.

In LA, hanging out with the guitarist and songwriter Stephen Stills, my career with Cream nearly came to an abrupt end. Stephen had asked me to come down to his ranch in Topanga Canyon to watch his band, Buffalo Springfield, rehearse. I went down there with a girl called Mary Hughes, who was the It girl of the day in LA, and we made ourselves comfortable while the band warmed up. It was a loud session, and a neighbour must have called the cops, who came knocking on the door. It didn't take them long to cotton on to the fact that we were all smoking dope, as the smell was quite overpowering, and the next thing we knew was we were all being hauled off, first to the Malibu sheriff's office and from there to the LA County Gaol. It was Friday night and I was thrown into a cell with a group of black guys who I immediately concluded must be Black Panthers. I was wearing pink boots from Mr Gohill in Chelsea, and had hair down to my waist, and I thought, 'I'm in trouble here.' Luckily for me, word of my predicament had somehow reached Ahmet, and he bailed me out. I then had to go to court and swear on the Bible that I had no idea what marijuana was. I was English after all, and we didn't do things like that in England. I walked out of there without a blemish on my character, but it really shook me up. It was a scary enough experience being locked up in LA County Gaol for the weekend, but a drug conviction would have put an instant end to Cream's American career, and the future of mine too.

The five months we spent touring were a time of deep political unrest in America, with anti-war demonstrations taking place on campuses across the country, and racial tension simmering in the cities. I had never been interested in politics, so was deliberately oblivious to it all, taking no interest in what was happening. From time to time I would run into people on the underground circuit who were politically very active, and I would go out of my way to avoid them if at all possible. The closest we came to trouble was in Boston on 4 April, the night Martin Luther King was assassinated. James Brown was playing in the theatre opposite us, and we had to be smuggled out of our venue through the back door because the people who were coming out of the James Brown show were trashing everything they could get their hands on. That night, anybody white was in danger, and over the next few weeks, playing in places like Detroit and Philadelphia, you could really feel the tension.

I had never really understood or been directly affected by racial conflict; I suppose being a musician helped me to tran-scend the physical side of that issue. When I listened to music I was fairly disinterested in where the players came from, or what colour their skin was. Interesting, then, that ten years later I would be labelled a racist for making drunken remarks about Enoch Powell on stage in Birmingham. Since then I have learned to keep my opinions to myself, even though that was never meant to be a racial statement. It was more of an attack on that government's policies on cheap labour, and the cultural confusion and overcrowding that resulted from what was clearly a greed-based policy. I had been in Jamaica just before, and had seen countless commercials on TV advertising a 'new life' in Great Britain, and then at Heathrow had witnessed whole families of West Indians being harassed and humiliated by the immigration people, who had no intention of letting them in. It was appalling. Of course it might have also had something to do with the fact that Pattie had just been leered at by a member of the Saudi royal family – a combination of the two perhaps.

Whistle-stop touring America was the beginning of the end for Cream, because once we started constantly working in such an intense way, it became impossible to keep the music afloat and we began to drown. Everybody always believes that the demise of Cream was predominantly to do with the clash of our personalities. True though it may have been that Jack and Ginger were often at each other's throats, this was only a tiny part of the picture. When you are playing night after night of a punishing schedule, often not because you want to but because you are contractually obliged to, it is only too easy to forget the ideals which once brought you together. There were times too when, playing to audiences who were only too happy to worship us, complacency set in. I began to be quite ashamed of being in Cream, because I thought it was a con. It wasn't really developing from where we were. As we made our voyage across America, we were being exposed to extremely strong and powerful influences, with jazz and rock 'n' roll music that was growing up around us, and it seemed that we weren't learning from it.

What brought me up short more than anything else was being introduced to the music of the Band by a friend of mine called Alan Pariser, an entrepreneur from LA, who knew just about everybody in the music business and who could connect you with anyone you wanted to meet. He had tapes of their first album called *Music From Big Pink*, and it was fantastic. It stopped me in my tracks, and it also highlighted all of the problems that I thought we had. Here was a band that was really doing it right, incorporating influences from country music, blues, jazz and rock, and writing great songs. I couldn't help but compare them to us, which was stupid and futile, but I was frantically looking for a yardstick, and here it was. Listening to that album, as great as it was, just made me feel that we were stuck, and I wanted out. Stigwood began to get regular calls from me after gigs telling him, 'I've gotta go home, I can't do this, you gotta get me out of here.' To which he would reply, 'Just do one more week.'

CHAPTER FIVE
BLIND FAITH

When we returned to England in the early summer of 1968, commercially speaking we were in very good shape. We could have sold out concert halls wherever we were twice over. *Disraeli Gears* was a best-selling album in the States, and we had a hit single there with 'Sunshine Of Your Love'. As far as I was concerned, all this counted for nothing because we had lost our direction. Musically I was fed up with the virtuoso thing. Our gigs had become nothing more than an excuse for us to show off as individuals, and any sense of unity that we might have had when we started out seemed to have gone out of the window. We also suffered from an inability to get on. We would just run away from one another. We never socialised together, we never really shared ideas any more. We just got together on stage and played and then went our separate ways. In the end this was the undoing of the music. I think if we had been able to listen to each other, and care for one another more, then Cream might have had a chance of further life, but at that point it was beyond our grasp as individuals. We were immature, and incapable of putting aside our differences. Maybe too, a little rest now and then might have helped.

Our decision to go our separate ways may have upset Stigwood, but it was certainly no surprise to him. He'd been the recipient of too many increasingly desperate phone calls from America for that. He had told us from the very beginning that he had all our interests at heart, but as time went by, I came to believe that it was me that he was starting to pin his hopes on. In the meantime, we struck a deal agreeing to two more albums, one of which we had partially recorded before leaving the States, a farewell tour of America in the autumn, and two last shows in London on our return.

It was great to be back at the Pheasantry, where Litvinoff was in an excitable mood, having been employed as dialogue coach and technical advisor on a film, *Performance*, which was being shot in Chelsea by Donald Cammell and Nick Roeg. The particular expertise for which he had been hired was his knowledge of the underworld, as the movie, which was basically a star vehicle for Mick Jagger playing a faded rock idol, was set in the world of London gangsters. He was full of ideas about how he felt the story should develop, and every day he would come and see me to tell me about all the goings-on on set and to fill me in on whatever was going to be happening next day. One night he brought round the director, Donald Cammell, who managed to stage a power cut in the flat, and then tried to grope my girlfriend Charlotte in the dark. A peculiar chap.

Life soon settled into the old routine, with people dropping in for tea and musical soirées. A regular visitor was George Harrison, who I had known since we met when I was in the Yardbirds. Not being the kind of guy, in those days, to instigate a friendship, I had just considered him a fellow musician. He used to drop by on the way home from his office in Savile Row to his bungalow in Esher, often bringing with him acetates of records the Beatles were working on.

Sometimes I would go down to George's house in Esher, and

we'd play together and take acid, and bit by bit a friendship began to form. One day, early in September, George drove me over to Abbey Road Studios where he was recording. When I arrived there, he told me that they were going to record one of his songs and asked me to play guitar on it. I was quite taken aback by this, considering it a funny thing to ask, since he was the Beatles guitar player, and had always done great work on their records up until then. I was also quite flattered, thinking that not many people get asked to play on a Beatles record. I hadn't even brought my guitar with me, so I had to borrow his.

My reading of the situation was that Paul and John were known to have been quite disparaging about both George's and Ringo's contributions to the group. He would put songs forward on every project only to find them pushed into the background. I think that George felt our friendship would give him some support, and that having me there to play might stabilise the situation, and maybe even draw some respect. I was a little nervous because John and Paul were pretty fast on their feet, and I was an outsider, but it went well. The song was called 'While My Guitar Gently Weeps'. We did just one take, and I thought it sounded fantastic; John and Paul were fairly non-committal, but I knew George was happy because he listened to it over and over in the control room, and after adding some effects and doing a rough mix, the other guys played some of the other songs they had already recorded. It felt like I had been brought into their inner sanctum.

A couple of weeks later, George dropped by the Pheasantry and left me acetates of the double album on which the song was going to appear. This was the *White Album*, and was the long-awaited successor to *Sgt Pepper*. When I left the following month to go to America on Cream's farewell tour, I took these with me. While I was in LA, I had been playing some of the songs on the album to various friends, when I got a phone call from George.

Word had got back to him that I had been playing the album around town and he was furious and gave me a huge bollocking. I remember being incredibly hurt because I thought I'd been doing a grand job of promoting their music to really discriminating people. It brought me down to earth with a bang, and it was a good lesson to learn about boundaries, and not making assumptions, but it hurt like hell. For a while I steered clear of him, but in time we became friends again, although after that, I was always a little wary of letting my guard down around him.

On 26 November, 1968, Cream played their final two shows at the Royal Albert Hall in London. Before the gig started, I just wanted to get it over with, but once I was up on stage, I became quite excited. I thought it was great that we could do this and keep our heads high, and walk away from the whole thing with a fair amount of good grace. It also meant a lot to me knowing that out there in the audience there were not just fans, but musician friends, and people on the scene who had all come to say their goodbyes. My overwhelming emotion, however, was that we had done the right thing. I think we all knew that. At the end of the second show, there was no party, no speeches. We just went our separate ways.

For a while I was quite happy just to be a sideman. I would play with anybody and I loved it. One of the first gigs like this I played, only two weeks after the Albert Hall shows, was with the Rolling Stones. It was a bizarre occasion. I had a call from Mick asking me to come up to a studio in Wembley where the Stones were recording a TV special called *The Rolling Stones' Rock 'n' Roll Circus*. I was intrigued because he told me that another of the contributing artists was Taj Mahal, an American blues musician who I really wanted to see. It was certainly an amazing line-up, and included, as well as Taj, John Lennon and Yoko Ono, Jethro Tull, Marianne Faithfull and the Who.

It was an interesting gig. Mick played the part of the

ringmaster, complete with top hat and tails, and introduced the different acts. Jesse Ed Davis, who played guitar with Taj Mahal, was brilliant, and there was a curious duet between Yoko Ono and Ivry Gitlis, a classical violinist. I played guitar with John Lennon on 'Yer Blues', in a band put together for the night, which also featured Keith Richards on bass, Mitch Mitchell on drums and Ivry Gitlis on violin, and which went by the name of Winston Legthigh and the Dirty Macs. Yoko Ono added vocals. Unfortunately the whole project was unhinged by the fact that the Stones were in pretty poor shape at the time. Brian, who had been as good as sacked from the band, was clearly under a lot of pressure, and you could tell that they were all a bit depressed. The result was that they didn't sound very good. They gave a performance that was lacklustre and out of tune, and apparently when Mick saw the finished tapes, he made the decision not to release the show.

Not long afterwards, I was sitting around at the Pheasantry when I had a visit from Ginger. He told me that I had to get out of town, the reason being that I was on 'Pilcher's List'. Detective Sergeant Norman Pilcher was a notorious London copper, a kind of police groupie, who had made a name for himself in the drugs squad by busting a number of famous rock stars including Donovan, John Lennon, George Harrison, Keith Richards and Mick Jagger. According to Ginger, he had had a tip-off from someone he knew in the police force to the effect that I was next on the list. I immediately called Stigwood, who had a pile in North London, the Old Barn, Stanford, to ask him what I should do, and he told me to come and stay with him for a few days. That first night that I spent at Stigwood's, the Pheasantry was raided by Pilcher. Pilcher got his comeuppance when sometime later he was convicted of conspiring to pervert the court of justice. I felt terrible, because they busted Martin and Philippe, and I had not warned them, thinking that Pilcher would only be interested in me; I will never forgive myself for that.

The bust at the Pheasantry seemed to have been some kind of warning, because a few days later Ginger told me he had heard on the grapevine that Pilcher wanted to do some kind of deal with me, which was that if I got out of town, and right away from his patch – his territory – he wouldn't bother me. In fact, I felt quite ready to move, and as for the first time in my life I now had some money, I realised that I could use it to buy a house. Up until that point I hadn't really thought much about earnings. Rather than pass through our hands, it went straight to management, and we were paid a weekly salary. Things like rent were paid directly from the office. On a day-to-day basis, I really didn't spend that much, and most of what I had went on clothes at Granny Takes A Trip. So I didn't pay much attention to what was going on with our money until I made the decision to move out of town.

The panic to get out of Chelsea was a catalyst to go and buy some property magazines. I knew that if I was going to live in the country, then I wanted to be somewhere near Ripley, and I went to look at a few houses near Box Hill, and places like that, which were in nice countryside and had views of the Surrey Hills. One day I was looking through *Country Life* and I stopped at a photograph of what looked like an Italian villa, complete with tiled terrace and a balcony. I rang the agent and arranged to meet him there. When I drove there for the first time, my initial impression as I approached the house down the drive was how perfectly situated it was, perched on the side of a hill, surrounded by beautiful woodland and with a great view looking out towards the South Coast. I remember going in the front door and it still had a few furnishings and the odd curtain from the previous owner. It was all rotting and musty, but I just fell in love with it. As soon as I walked in, I had the most incredible feeling of coming home.

The house was called Hurtwood Edge, and was rumoured to have been designed by the great Victorian architect, Sir Edwin

Lutyens, designer of the imperial capital of New Delhi. This turned out to be false, the real architect having been a man called Robert Bolton. The front door had a little porch attached to it, to stop draughts coming in, and you could look straight into the living room, which had windows on three sides, one looking out over a terrace, and the others with views across the hills. When I walked round the garden, I was amazed to find five or six fully grown redwoods planted there, which I imagined must be hundreds of years old and had been there long before the house was built. There was a palm tree too, and poplars, which gave the whole place a Mediterranean feel. It was also falsely rumoured that the garden had been designed by the celebrated horticulturist Gertrude Jekyll. I wanted to buy it there and then, and move in right away. When I returned a second time to check to see if my initial impression had been sound, I surprised the agent and his girlfriend sunbathing naked on the terrace. It turned out they were using the house, which had been empty for two years, no one before me having shown any interest in it. I think it gave them a bit of a shock to realise that they would have to stop doing so.

The price that was being asked for Hurtwood was £30,000, which at that time was by far the biggest amount of money I had ever heard of. I knew nothing about how to do business, let alone doing something like buying a house, so I went to see Stigwood for help. He clearly didn't think that thirty grand was that much, and he said I should buy it. Next thing I knew, the deal was done and the house was mine. It was an extraordinary feeling. I'd never owned my own home. All my life, I'd been bumming around, from the first day I left Ripley, spending the night on stations or sleeping in the park, or staying on the couch at friends' houses, and then going back to Ripley. The most I'd had was a lease at the Pheasantry, and now I had Hurtwood, and the satisfaction of having a place in which I could do anything I pleased.

What I liked about Hurtwood was the solitariness and the peace. I also loved the road that led to it, which went from Shere to Ewhurst and at some point became a single-track road that looked like a riverbed, dug down between sheer high rock walls. It looked as though it was thousands of years old, and there were all kinds of myths about it having been a smugglers' route. In the winter, when there was snow on the overhanging trees, it was like being in a white tunnel. When I drove down there, I felt like I was entering Hobbit land. I decided very quickly that this was going to be the place where I would live for the rest of my life. I was absolutely sure of that.

I moved in very quickly, with my guitars, a couple of armchairs in the living room and a bed upstairs. I also had a 1912 Douglas motorbike, which I had bought in a shop in Ripley. It didn't actually work. I just pushed it around, and eventually I had it standing in the middle of the living room like a sculpture. There was one other expensive present I gave myself, a pair of huge six-feet high cinema loudspeakers, made by Altec Lansing, and called 'The Voice of the Theatre'. Made of wood, each one had a metal trumpet on top of it, and they gave a great sound to my music system.

After a few months of living at Hurtwood in a very spartan way, I decided it was time for a change. At around this time in London, there was a group of people on the scene who were what could be best described as aristocratic hippies, members of the upper classes who had dropped out and were living a kind of gipsy life. The leaders of this set were Sir Mark Palmer, who ran a model agency called English Boys, Christopher Gibbs, an antique dealer who had designed the sets for *Performance*, and Jane, Julian and Victoria Ormsby-Gore, the older children of David Harlech, who had been British Ambassador to Washington during the Kennedy era. Stylish in dress and leaders of fashion, they were surrounded by artistic and interesting people and used to hang out in a lot of the places I frequented, like Granny's, the Chelsea Antique Market and the Picasso. We had a mutual friend in a guy called Ian Dallas, who I had met at the Pheasantry and who was very interested in Sufism. One night he took me down to the Baghdad House, an Arabic restaurant in the Fulham Road, the basement of which was decked out like an oriental bazaar and was an ultra-cool hangout, often frequented by various Stones and Beatles. There I was introduced to an up-and-coming young interior designer called David Mlinaric. His nickname was 'Monster'.

At my request, Monster, who had done a lot of work for Mick Jagger, came down to take a look at Hurtwood, which I had been trying to furnish. I wanted it to have a Spanish or Italian feel and had been buying furniture from antique shops in Chelsea and Fulham, eighteenth- and nineteenth-century pieces, but without good advice I was being ripped off right, left and centre. The house had central heating, so the furniture would warp and crack and began to fall to bits. I also had some Arabic furniture, some Indian carved chairs and a big old refectory table in the hall, so there was a funny mixture of bits and pieces. Monster called in Christopher Gibbs to help and, bit by bit, they turned it into something nice. They put some woven carpet in the front room, which made it more comfortable, and a lovely old four-poster in the bedroom, and lots of Persian and Moroccan hangings, and gradually it started to take shape.

I was so pleased with the way Hurtwood was coming together that I wanted to create something like that for my grandparents. I found a beautiful cottage in Shamley Green, and took Rose and Jack to look at it. They were delighted, at least Rose was, I'm not so sure about Jack. We had become a little distant from one another, and maybe he was a bit jealous. Rose was always so excited about the way my life was unfolding, and I don't think he really understood what was so special about it all. He was a proud man, and although I would try to think of things to say when I saw him, when the time came, the moment would slip by without either one of us being able to express anything. It was such a shame. Nevertheless, Rose and Jack had many happy years together in that cottage, and for a pretty long time, things were good.

I was seeing more and more of George Harrison during this period, especially since we were now virtually neighbours. George and his wife Pattie lived on a residential estate in Esher, about half an hour's drive away, in a sprawling bungalow called Kinfauns. It had round windows, and a huge fireplace decorated by the Fool, who had also painted murals everywhere. We started to hang out a lot together. Sometimes he and Pattie would come over to Hurtwood to show me a new car, or to have dinner and listen to music. It was in the early days at Hurtwood that George wrote one of his most beautiful songs, 'Here Comes The Sun'. It was a beautiful spring morning and we were sitting at the top of a big paddock at the bottom of the garden. We had our guitars and were just strumming away when he started singing, 'De da de de, it's been a long cold lonely winter,' and bit by bit fleshed it out, until the first verse was finished and it was time for lunch. Other times I used to go over to them, to play guitar with George, or just hang out. I remember them also indulging in a bit of match-making, trying to get me off with different pretty ladies. I wasn't really interested, however, because something else quite unexpected was happening. I was falling in love with Pattie.

I think initially, I was motivated by a mixture of lust and envy, but it all changed once I got to know her. I had first set eyes on Pattie backstage at the Savile Theatre in London, after a Cream concert, and had thought then that she was unusually beautiful. This impression grew stronger the more I observed her. I remember thinking that her beauty was also an internal thing. It wasn't just the way she looked, although she was definitely the most beautiful woman I had ever seen. It was deeper. It came from within her too. It was her entire being, and the way she carried herself, that captivated me. I had never met a woman who was so complete, and I was overwhelmed. I realised that I would have to stop seeing her and George, or give in to my emotions and tell her how I felt. The overflow from all these feelings finally put paid to my relationship with Charlotte. We had been together for over two years, and I loved her as much as I was capable of really loving anyone, but she was in the way of someone else, who, even though I couldn't have her, was commanding my every thought. She went back to Paris for a while, and eventually began a long-lasting affair with Jimmy Page. I didn't see her again for a long time.

I also coveted Pattie because she belonged to a powerful man who seemed to have everything I wanted – amazing cars, an incredible career and a beautiful wife. This was not an emotion that was new to me. I remember that when my mum came home with her new family, I wanted my half-brother's toys because they seemed more expensive and better than mine. It was a feeling that had never gone away, and it was definitely part of the way I felt toward Pattie, but for the time being I kept all these emotions strictly under lock and key, and buried myself in trying to sort out what I was going to do next musically.

When Cream broke up, it wasn't like the Yardbirds, when I had another band to go to. I didn't really have anything else set up, and for a while I was in a vacuum, just playing here and there. Sitting alone at Hurtwood, I had been thinking a lot about Steve Winwood, who I had heard had left Traffic. It was a logical conclusion to go and see Steve, because in the days when I was having my first doubts about Cream, it used to cross my mind that he was the only person I knew with the musicianship and the power to keep the band together. If the others had shared my interest in making it a quartet and let him in, then Cream could have evolved into another unit, a quartet, with Steve as the frontman, a role for which I lacked not the capability but the confidence.

Steve had a cottage in the country, at Aston Tirrold, in a remote part of the Berkshire Downs, where Traffic had written a lot of the *Mr Fantasy* album, so I called him up and started to go over there. We'd drink and smoke, and talk a lot, and play our guitars. I played him a song I had written about finding Hurtwood, called 'Presence Of The Lord', the second verse of which has the line 'I have finally found a place to live just like I never could before.' For most of the time, it was just the two of us hanging out, and we walked round the idea of a band, without actually getting into a discussion about it. We were deliberately killing time, just having fun and getting to know one another.

One night Steve and I were at the cottage, smoking joints and jamming, when there was a knock at the door. It was Ginger. Somehow he had got wind of what we were doing, and had tracked us down, in spite of the fact that Steve's cottage was way off the beaten track, surrounded by furrowed fields. I saw Steve's face light up when he saw Ginger, while my heart sank, because up till that moment, we were only having fun. There was no agenda. I had been very cautious about not springing anything on Steve, just intending to let the thing evolve and see where we would go. Ginger's appearance frightened me because I felt that before we knew where we were we'd be a band, and with that would come the whole Stigwood machine and all the hype that had surrounded Cream. I thought to myself, 'Oh no. Whatever's going to happen now, I know it's all going to go wrong.'

All these feelings I kept to myself, because I still hadn't really found my voice. When things were going well it was easy to go with the flow, but when things became difficult or disagreeable, I would feel a certain amount of resentment about what the flow was, rather than try to do something about it, and then when I'd had enough I would just pull out or disappear without actually speaking up. Despite my concerns about Ginger, I was so keen to work with Steve that I compromised my intuition, thinking every-thing would turn out all right because he would see it through. I invested in his vision and, rather than stick my heels in, made the decision to go along with things and see where they went.

As we began to give birth to a new band, an extraordinary girl came into my life. She was brought down to Hurtwood by Monster, and her name was Alice Ormsby-Gore. The youngest daughter of David Harlech, she was barely sixteen, and hauntingly beautiful, with thick curly brown hair and huge eyes. She had an enigmatic smile and a wonderfully infectious giggle. I thought she was astonishing, but though I was very taken with her it never occurred to me then that anything could come from it. The age gap seemed enormous, and she seemed very fragile and slightly other-worldly. She asked me to go to a party in London with her, which kind of surprised me. I went and she completely ignored me all evening, even though, apart from Monster and Ian Dallas, I didn't know a soul there. For some reason in spite of myself, for we didn't seem remotely compatible, I found her completely compelling. With her wistful quality and the Arabic clothes she used to dress in, she seemed to have stepped straight out of a fairy story. This was a fantasy that was encouraged by Ian Dallas, who told me the story of Layla and Majnun, a romantic Persian love story in which a young man, Majnun, falls passionately in love with the beautiful Layla, but is forbidden by her father to marry her and goes crazy with love. Ian was forever saying that Alice was the perfect Layla, and while he thought Steve should be her Majnun, I had other ideas. I have no idea what she saw in me, maybe it was because I was an outsider to her group, and she saw me as a means to spite them, who knows, but after a few days of clumsy courting, she moved in with me, and the madness began.

From the beginning it was a very stiff, uncomfortable situation. I wasn't in love with Alice, my heart, and a good deal of everything else, being with Pattie. I also felt very ill at ease about the age difference, especially since she had told me she was still a virgin. In fact sex played very little part in our lives. We were more like brother and sister, although I was hoping that eventually it would blossom into a normal relationship. Her father was a serious jazz enthusiast, and she had inherited a love of music from him, so we listened to a lot of records, and we smoked a lot of dope. There was also another extraordinary thing that struck me later on. When I was a kid in the playground, aged seven or eight, my friend Guy and me had a game in which we would fall about laughing over the most ridiculous names we could think of, and the silliest name we came up with was Ormsby-Gore. When things had begun to go badly wrong between me and Alice, I had a terrible fear that getting attached to an upper-class girl like her was part of a childhood resentment, connected to my feelings about my mother, to bring down women, and that deep inside I was thinking, 'Here's an Ormsby-Gore, and I'm going to make her suffer.'

Steve came over to Hurtwood in the first few weeks after Alice arrived, and we spent hours playing together. I had set up the front room as a music-cum-living room, with a table and chairs and a large couch, as well as a drum set, keyboards and amps for the guitars. There was equipment everywhere, with tape recorders and microphones for recording, and cables running down the hall. It was a semi-studio, really, and we would jam and jam and record and record, all the time testing the air. During those first days we worked with a little drum machine, until Steve said that he wanted to ask Ginger to join us. So Ginger came to stay too, and once we had a drummer, we started to look around for a bass player. I was still very reluctant to go through my Cream experience with Ginger again, but I felt that if Steve was happy with him, then I should at least try to make a go of it. As for a bass player, I knew Rick Grech, who played with the group Family, from the Speakeasy. We were good mates, and he was a great guy, so he just kind of fell in with us.

All the early rehearsals of the new band took place at Hurtwood. We would start work at about midday, and jam late into the night. We had a lot of fun, but it soon got out of hand, in that we were just wandering around musically without ever getting anywhere. Once we got in the studio, however, it started to take shape. I had already written 'Presence Of The Lord', and I also came up with the idea of doing a cover of the Buddy Holly song 'Well . . . All Right', but it was Steve that provided the real songs, like 'Sea Of Joy', 'Can't Find My Way Home' and 'Had To Cry Today'. Outside of that, we were basically still a jam band and didn't really care what we were doing. Eventually, someone came up with the bright idea of bringing in Jimmy Miller to try to give the music some focus, and gather up the album. Jimmy had worked with Steve on the Traffic albums, and it seemed the most logical way forward. Soon, however, word leaked out in the music press that I was playing again with Ginger, and that Steve, who was a big star himself, was involved. The dreaded word 'Supergroup' reared its head again. That's when I saw the red light, but I decided to go through with all of this to see where it led, mainly because Steve was involved, and also because there was simply nothing else to do. Subliminally, my ambition perhaps, was to re-create the Band in England, an idea I knew was a huge gamble, which is probably why I named the new band Blind Faith.

We started our professional career on 7 June, 1969, with a free concert in Hyde Park. This was the first ever rock show in the park, and an audience of over 100,000 people turned up to watch. We all met at Stigwood's office before the show, and as soon as I saw Ginger, my heart sank. Over the years, on and off, Ginger had

had sporadic clashes with heroin. He would go through periods when he was using, and then he would be clean for a while. His using often seemed to be triggered by stressful situations, first nights, unfamiliar social situations etc., but we had been jamming and rehearsing for a good long while, and he had seemed pretty happy, I took one look at his eyes and I was sure he was back on it. It made me so angry, and I had the same feeling that I had had on the night he knocked on Steve's door. I felt that once again I was stepping back into the nightmare that had been part of Cream.

We played in front of this vast crowd on a beautiful sunny summer's afternoon, and I wasn't really there. I had zoned out. Maybe I was wrong, and that Ginger had not picked up, but I felt that whatever we had achieved up till that point in terms of bonding, rehearsing and playing seemed to have been a complete waste of time, and I remember thinking, 'If this is the first gig, where the hell do we go from here?' The audience may have loved it, and the atmosphere was great, but I really didn't want to be there. It wasn't helped by the fact that we were completely underpowered. We didn't really have enough amplification for playing outdoors in the park, and we sounded small and tinny. I came off the stage shaking like a leaf and feeling that I'd let people down. My blaming mechanism laid the fault at Ginger's feet, setting up a resentment within me that just grew and grew.

Stigwood didn't give us time to think. We went straight out on the road for a tour of Scandinavia to settle the band in, and actually it was a tactic that worked. Ginger came back from the edge, and we began, for the first time, to sound very good. We got some of our power back, playing smaller venues, and the band started to forge ahead. On our return home, we went into the studio to finish the album with Jimmy. One day I got a call from Bob Seidemann, who I had met in San Francisco. Bob, a brilliant photographer, was/is an eccentric and funny man. We spent a lot of great times together in the days of the Pheasantry. He looked like something out of a drawing by Robert Crumb, who was also a friend of his. He was very tall, with long frizzy hair which stood out behind him, a great big face and nose, and long thin legs.

Bob told me that he had an idea for an album cover for us. He wouldn't say what it was, just that he was going to put it together and then show us. When he finally presented it, I remember thinking that it was rather sweet. It was a photograph of a young, barely pubescent girl, with curly red hair, photographed from the waist up, naked, and holding in her hands a silver, very modernistic aeroplane, designed by my friend the jeweller, Micko Milligan. Behind her was a landscape of a green hill, like the Berkshire Downs, and a blue sky, with white clouds scudding across it. I immediately loved it because I thought it captured the definition of the name of our band really well – the juxtaposition of innocence, in the shape of the girl, and experience, science, the future, represented by the aeroplane. I told Bob that we should not spoil the image by putting the name of the band on the front cover, so he came up with the idea of writing it on the wrapper instead. When the wrapper came off, it left a virgin photograph. The cover caused a huge outcry. People said the representation of the young girl was pornographic, and in the States record dealers threatened to boycott it. Since we were about to embark on a major tour, we had no alternative but to replace it over there with a shot of us standing in the front room at Hurtwood.

It was quite clear from the opening night at Madison Square Garden in New York on 12 July, 1969, that Blind Faith were not going to have to work hard to pull in the crowds. There were too many Cream and Traffic fans around for that, and the truth is we didn't really know or care which we were. Looking back, I realise that from the start I knew that this was not what I really wanted to do, but I was lazy. Instead of putting more time and effort into making the band into what I thought it ought to be, I opted instead for the laid-back approach, which was just to look for something else that already had an identity. I completely ducked the responsibility of being a group member, and settled for the role of just being the guitar player. This frustrated many people who felt that I should play a more dominant role, not least of all Steve, who became more and more frustrated at the fact that I would not step forward and do more vocal work. The Blind Faith tour made us all very rich, pushing the album straight to the top of the American charts, but it ended with the disintegration of the band. This was probably my fault and was down to one thing. As I became more and more disenchanted with what we were doing, I was falling increasingly under the spell of our support group, Delaney and Bonnie.

Sometime early in the summer, my friend Alan Pariser had sent me an acetate of a band he was managing, consisting of a husband and wife, Delaney and Bonnie Bramlett, who both came from the South, and sang under the name Delaney and Bonnie. They had the distinction of being the first white group ever to be signed by Stax, the Tennessee-based record company founded by Jim Stewart and Estelle Axton, which had pioneered the sound of Memphis and Southern soul music. I immediately loved the record, *The Original Delaney and Bonnie – Accept No Substitute*, which was hardcore R&B, and was very soulful, with great guitar playing and a fantastic horn section. When I told Alan how I felt about them, he asked if he could put them on the bill with us when we toured America.

For me, going on after Delaney and Bonnie was really, really tough, because I thought they were miles better than us. Their band was made up of all these great Southern musicians, who had such a strong sound and performed with absolute confidence. There was the rhythm section consisting of Carl Radle on bass, Bobby Whitlock on keyboards and Jim Gordon on drums, a horn

Me aged four.

Me with my grandfather, Jack Clapp.

My grandparents, Rose and Jack Clapp.

Me aged 16 and (right) 17.

The Yardbirds.
Left to right: Keith Relf, Chris Dreja, Paul Samwell-Smith, Jim McCarty and me.

John Mayall and the Bluesbreakers.
Left to right: John Mayall, me, John McVie and Hughie Flint.

The infamous 'Clapton is God' graffiti.

The *Disraeli Gears* cover.

Me listening to Albert King.

Cream rowing in Central Park. Left to right: me, Ginger Baker and Jack Bruce.

Jack Bruce, me and Ginger Baker in Crystal Palace Park for a Cream photo shoot.

Cream performing
for Top of the Pops.

Me with Cream.

Blind Faith in Hyde Park.

The *Blind Faith* album cover shot by Bob Seidemann.

Hurtwood Edge.

Me on the terrace at Hurtwood.

Me and Alice Ormsby-Gore.

Alice Ormsby-Gore.

Alice and I at Hurtwood.

On the tour bus with Delaney and Bonnie.

Derek and the Dominos.
Left to right: Jim Gordon, Carl Radle, Bobby Whitlock and me

In the gardens
at Hurtwood.

section with Bobby Keys on sax and Jim Price on trumpet, and Rita Coolidge joined Bonnie on vocals. They turned out to be big fans of me and Steve, and started to court us; needless to say it wasn't long before I dropped all my responsibilities as being part of Blind Faith and started to hang out with them. There was something infectious about their approach to music. They would have their guitars on the bus and would play songs all day as we travelled, while we were much more insular and would tend to keep to ourselves. I took to travelling with them and playing with them, which I think quite upset Steve who must have thought I'd become a bit of a traitor. The truth, which I found hard to tell him, was that I had lost faith in our band. I was the man in the hallway, who has come out of one door, only to find it has closed behind him, while another one is opening. Through that door were Delaney and Bonnie, and I was irresistibly drawn towards it, even though I knew it would destroy the band that we had put so much blind faith into.

CHAPTER SIX

CHAPTER SIX

DEREK AND THE DOMINOS

If Delaney and Bonnie had never played on the same bill as us, it is possible that Blind Faith might have survived and regrouped at the end of the tour, and tried to figure out what was wrong and move forward. Maybe. But the temptation Delaney put my way was irresistible. He confronted me with the same issue that Steve had, which was that I had to develop, and not just as a guitarist. Steve had said, when I wanted him to sing my song 'Presence Of The Lord', 'Well, you wrote it, so you ought to sing it.' I had insisted that it should be him, and while we were recording it I kept interrupting him and suggesting that he sing it in such and such a way, until he finally said, 'Eric, if you want it sung that way, sing it yourself!' He was quite definite about it, and I decided to just let him get on with it. Looking back I know he was right. I had written that song upon moving into Hurtwood Edge, and it was a very personal statement, not necessarily a religious one, but more of a statement of fact, 'I have finally found a place to live just like I never could before.' I should have at least had a go at singing it, but I don't think I could have ever enjoyed my version as much as I do his.

123

Delaney shared Steve's opinion, but took a slightly different tack. Raised in Mississippi, he was a very charismatic character, with long hair and a beard, and he had successfully cultivated the persona of a Southern baptist preacher, delivering a fire and brimstone message. It could have been off-putting, if it wasn't for the fact that when he sang, he was totally right, and absolutely inspiring. I completely believed in him. We went out one night to see Sha Na Na, and when we got back to my hotel, we dropped some acid and started to play our guitars. At some point, Delaney looked deep into my eyes and said, 'You know, you really have to start singing, and you ought to be leading your own band. God has given you this gift, and if you don't use it he will take it away.' I was stunned by the certainty of his statement, and it really struck home with me. The acid probably gave it a bit of depth too. I thought to myself, 'He may have a point here. I'd better start doing something about this.' Other than my early fantasies of what Cream could have been, this was the first time I ever really considered the idea of a solo career.

The last Blind Faith concert took place in Honolulu on 24 August, and I then returned to England and Hurtwood. I had barely settled in, however, when one Saturday morning, 13 September, the phone rang. It was John Lennon. 'What are you doing tonight?' he asked me.

'Nothing,' I replied.

'Well, do you want to do a gig with the Plastic Ono Band in Toronto?' he asked.

'Yeah, sure,' I answered, because part of the thing in those days was doing stuff like that, hopping on a plane on the spur of the moment, without giving it a second thought.

'Great!' he said. 'Meet me as soon as you can get there, in the BOAC First Class Lounge at London Airport. I'll explain everything then.'

I drove to the airport, where I found John and Yoko with Klaus

Voorman, the bass player of the band, and the drummer, Alan White. John was going through his white-suit phase, and had long hair and a beard. He told us that we were going to play at something called the Toronto Rock 'n' Roll Revival Festival, and that we could rehearse on the plane. We carried our semi-acoustic electric guitars onboard, and settled into the First Class cabin, which we were sharing with a number of other passengers, including the man who owned the Schick razor company. He happened to be sitting in the same row of seats as us, and tried to humour us by telling us we could all make good use of his razors to shave our beards and moustaches. He didn't get very far since, as soon as we were airborne, we were concentrating on running through the numbers for the show, songs like 'Be Bop A Lula', 'Yer Blues', 'Dizzy Miss Lizzy' and 'Blue Suede Shoes'. We just played sitting in our seats. No one complained which, looking back on it, was not surprising, since John was one of the biggest stars in the world, and the other passengers were probably just astonished to be in the same space as him. Curiously enough, I don't recall Yoko getting involved at all. She just sat quietly in the background.

When we arrived in Toronto it was raining, and we were standing around waiting for the luggage when a huge limo rolled up, and John and Yoko jumped into it and drove away, leaving the rest of us standing in the rain without a clue as to what to do next. 'Well, that's nice,' I thought. In the end we got in the van with the luggage, which I felt was a bit sad, as I thought we deserved a little more respect than that. When we arrived we found that we were all staying together in this very grand house belonging to a guy called Cyrus Eaton, who was one of the richest men in Canada, and that a press conference had been called. Loads of journalists had turned up, but John and Yoko steadfastly refused to come out to talk to them. So I spoke to them instead, and they were very complimentary, saying how eloquent I was for a musician. I bathed in that glory for a while, and then we went to the show. We found out that we were going on between Chuck Berry and Little Richard, and John was terrified, overwhelmed I think by the fact that he was going on stage with all his heroes. Backstage, John and I did so much blow that he threw up, and I had to lie down on the ground for a while. Luckily we had Terry Doran with us, who was John's personal assistant, and he made sure that John was fit to go on stage.

The Plastic Ono Band went on at midnight, and played a tough hardcore set of standard rock 'n' roll numbers. Considering that we had never played together before we rehearsed on the plane, I thought we sounded good. At the end John told us to take off our guitars, turn them up, and lean them against the amplifiers. He did the same thing, and the amps and the guitars just started howling in feedback, while we either stood to one side or got off the stage. Yoko started to sing along with this, a song she had written called 'Oh John'. It sounded pretty strange to me, more like howling than singing, but that was her thing. John thought it was all pretty funny, and that's what closed our set. Then we all piled into four cars which had been organised by Cyrus Eaton's son, and drove back to spend what was left of the night at his sprawling estate. The following afternoon, we flew back to England. My payment for the gig consisted of a few of John's drawings which, over time, I have unfortunately lost.

However much I was enjoying guesting with my friends, I couldn't wait to get back together with Delaney, who had asked me to tour with him and Bonnie under the name Delaney and Bonnie and Friends. I set up a rehearsal room on the top floor at Hurtwood and the band came to live there for a few weeks prior to touring, first in Germany, and then England and Scandinavia, for both legs of which we were joined by George Harrison, who was keen to record Delaney and Bonnie for the Beatles' Apple label. It was an incredibly happy experience for me to play with a group of musicians who were out there for the sheer joy of playing, rather than to make money, which they were hard-pressed to do anyway because there were so many of them. There was a great feeling of love on the stage when we played. Unfortunately there were the occasional ugly scenes triggered by the fact some audiences expected more from me. They had seen the tour posters announcing 'Delaney and Bonnie and Friends, featuring Eric Clapton' and wanted to hear more than the couple of songs I would sing during the show. When I refused to respond to their demands, they would start heckling, which could be quite nasty.

None of this happened on the American leg of the tour, where the Bramletts had a strong following. When we'd finished, I went to stay with them at their home in Sherman Oaks, California, which they shared with Delaney's mother. It was a tiny house, so small they almost had to sleep in the same bed. All around there lived a community of great musicians, all from the South, and Delaney and Bonnie were right there at the centre of it. It was unbelievable to me that from being in a fairly small, though creative, framework back in England with Blind Faith, I was suddenly living in LA and hanging out with these incredible musicians. Delaney turned me on to so many things. He played me the music of J. J. Cale, which was to become an enormous influence. I met and played with King Curtis on his single 'Teasin'', an experience I wanted to go on for ever. I hung out with the Crickets, Stephen Stills and Leon Russell, who had his own recording studio in North Hollywood.

Delaney persuaded me to cut a solo album, with him as producer, and we started worked on it at Amigo Studios. I had only written one song, 'Let It Rain', but Delaney had a few, or we would be on the way to the studio in the morning and Delaney would say 'What about a song about a bottle of red wine?' and he would start singing 'Get up and get your man a bottle of red wine . . .' It would just flow out of him, and by the time we got to the studio, the song would be finished. I remember thinking to myself, 'How does he do it? He just opens his mouth and out comes a song.' We'd then go straight into the studio and record it live. Then I would put a couple of vocal tracks down, with Delaney coaching me, and then it would be time for the girls and the horns. Rita and Bonnie would be given their part and they'd sing it, Jim and Bobby would put some riffs on, and that was the whole thing wrapped up. It was fantastic and I was in my element, recording my own album with the best band in the land. Delaney had brought out something in me that I didn't know I had.

My solo career really began there, I knew I had it in me really, but I had stuffed it down to the point where I had stopped believing in myself. I'll never be able to repay Delaney for his belief in me, he saw something I had stopped looking for. Making that record was one of the most important steps I would ever take, and it was a truly memorable experience. I remember going in one day when we didn't have a song planned, and Leon came up to me and said, 'I've got a line for you' and thinking aloud he said, 'You're a blues musician, but people don't know that you can also rock 'n' roll, so we can say, "I bet you didn't think I knew how to rock 'n' roll/Lord I got the boogie-woogie right down in my very soul/There ain't no need for me to be a wallflower/'Cos now I'm living on blues power."' Just like that, no effort, and that was the birth of the song 'Blues Power' which was one of my favourite songs on the album.

However much I may have been enjoying living in LA and hanging out with all these great musicians, I was also suffering from occasional bouts of homesickness. Alice used to come out to see me and although she got on really well with Delaney, she wasn't that comfortable hanging out with the band, and it was quite clear that she wanted me to go home. I think she was threatened by the gipsy in me, which she saw emerging as I was hanging out with Delaney. I had a restlessness in me, which I still have, that however much I loved my roots of Ripley and Hurtwood, the road always beckoned, and the idea of travelling and making music with a band of musicians in different places never stopped motivating me. At that moment, however, with the album completed, I was ready to go home.

My relationship with Alice, which was always something of an on/off affair, was at that time headed for the rocks, mostly because of my continuing obsession with Pattie. However hard I tried, I just could not get her out of my mind. Even though I didn't consider that I really had any chance of ever being with her, I still thought of all other affairs with women as being merely temporary. I was totally distracted by the idea that I could never love another woman as much as I loved Pattie. In fact, in order to get closer to her, I had even taken up with her sister. The circumstances which had led to this were curious, and had happened a few months before, when Delaney and Bonnie played the Liverpool Empire, with George playing guitar. Pattie had showed up, accompanied by her younger sister, Paula. After the show, when we were all back at the hotel, George, who was motivated just as much by the flesh as he was by the spirit, had taken me aside and suggested that I should spend the night with Pattie so that he could sleep with Paula. The suggestion didn't shock me, because the prevailing morality of the time was that you just went for whatever you could get, but at the last moment, he lost his nerve and nothing happened. The end result was not the one George wanted, as I ended up spending the night with Paula instead of him.

When I got back to Hurtwood, in the spring of 1970, Alice and I had a bust-up and she went off to Glin, her Welsh family home, a manor house outside Harlech. This side of her life, the aristocratic social part, was something that I never wanted to get involved in. I didn't get it and I didn't enjoy it. You'd go up to stay at the house, and the whole place would be full of people who just seemed to sit around all day smoking dope. I had a very strong work ethic at the time, and I didn't particularly enjoy spending time with what appeared to be a bunch of freeloaders. In Alice's absence, Paula, a surrogate Pattie, moved into Hurtwood, where I was almost immediately involved in setting up another band. It was a stopgap relationship, and I think we both knew that, but she reminded me a lot of Pattie, and for the moment I had no qualms about that.

I'd had a call from Carl Radle telling me that Delaney and Bonnie and Friends had disbanded, and asking me whether I might be interested in doing something with him, Bobby Whitlock and Jim Gordon. Having nothing else on, I'd said yes, and they had flown over to England and had come to live at Hurtwood. It was the beginning of one of the most extraordinary periods of my life, the memory of which is dominated by one thing – incredible music. It began with me just talking to these guys about music and getting to know them, and then we just played and played and played. I was in absolute awe of these people, and yet they made me feel on the same level as them. We were kindred spirits, made in the same mould. To this day, I would say that Carl Radle, the bass player, and the drummer, Jimmy Gordon, are the most powerful rhythm section I have ever played with. They were absolutely brilliant. When people say that Jimmy Gordon is the greatest rock 'n' roll drummer that ever lived, I think it's true, beyond anybody.

All we did was jam and jam and jam and night would become day and day would become night, and it just felt good to me to stay that way. I had never felt so musically free before. We kept ourselves going with fry-ups and a cocktail of drink and drugs, mostly cocaine and Mandrax. 'Mandies' were quite strong sleeping pills, but instead of letting them put us to sleep, we would ride the effect, staying awake by snorting some coke, or drinking some brandy or vodka, and this would create a unique kind of high. This became the chemistry of our life, mixing all these things together. God knows how our bodies stood it.

There was no game plan at this time. We were just enjoying playing, getting stoned and writing songs. George Harrison was a frequent caller. He had recently moved from Kinfauns, his bungalow in Esher, to a sprawling mansion in Henley called Friar Park, and his visits gave me plenty of opportunity to flirt with Pattie behind Paula's back. One night I called her up and told her that the truth about me was that it was not Paula I was interested in, or any other girl she might see me with, but that it was her who I really wanted. In spite of her protests that she was married to George, and that what I was suggesting was impossible, she agreed to me coming over to talk to her. I drove over there, and we talked about it over a bottle of red wine, and ended up kissing, and I sensed for the first time that there was some kind of hope for me. I knew then what I had suspected for some time, that all was not well in her marriage.

I was so buoyed up by what had happened with Pattie, as well as being a bit drunk, that on the way home, driving a little Ferrari Dino that I'd just bought, I took a corner in Clandon much too fast, hit a fence, and the car flipped over on to its roof. I didn't pass out, but I found myself just hanging there upside down. Somehow I undid the seat belt and got out, and, realising that I didn't even have a driving licence, made the decision to run home and make out that someone had stolen the car. So I set off running, but soon realised that I was heading in the wrong direction, back towards London. I then thought that I would hide somewhere, so I opened a gate in the hedge, walked into what turned out to be a graveyard, and sat down on a grave. After a while, I decided to go back and face the music. I walked back to where the car was, and there were all these people wearing dressing gowns, wandering around with torches looking for the driver. I owned up that it was me. Someone had already called an ambulance, and it arrived straight away and took me to Guildford Hospital for a check-up. Then Bobby Whitlock came and took me home. Miraculously for me, I was unhurt and luckily the police never got involved.

I began to get into the habit of dropping into Friar Park, in the hope that George might be away and I might catch a few moments alone with Pattie. One evening I went over there and found the two of them together with John Hurt. I was slightly taken aback, but George took over the situation and gave me a guitar and we started playing, which by now was a common occurrence with us. There was quite an atmosphere in the house that night. There was a roaring fire going, candles burning, and as the intensity of our playing increased, John sat there with a rapturous look on his face as if he was privy to some fantastic meeting of the giants, or a battle of the sorcerers, and with his actor's imagination, I could see him creating this scenario that we were somehow engaged in a musical duel for the hand of Pattie, who wafted in from time to time bringing us tea and cakes. The truth is we were just jamming, although the mythical rumour of that night may have passed around a few dining-room tables.

George was working on his first solo album, *All Things Must Pass*, and one day he asked if the Tulsa guys and me would play on it. I knew he had Phil Spector producing for him, so we made a deal whereby he would get Spector to produce a couple of tracks for us, in return for having the use of our band for his album. After my dalliance with Ronnie Ronette, who had told me how much I reminded her of her husband, I was curious to meet Phil Spector, and noticed that we actually did have the same kind of facial profile. We recorded two songs with him, 'Roll It Over' and 'Tell The Truth', at Abbey Road Studios, before turning ourselves over to George as his session musicians.

Working with Spector was quite an experience. I thought he was a really sweet guy, maybe just a bit eccentric, but the rumour was that he carried a gun, so I was a little bit wary. Most of the time, though, he was hilariously funny, and him and George certainly seemed to hit it off. His method of working was to get a lot of players in the room, and have them all playing at the same time, creating the famous Wall of Sound. Other than George and us, there seemed to be hundreds of musicians in the studio, percussionists, guitarists, George's group Badfinger, Gary Wright and Spooky Tooth, all hammering away like mad. To my ears it sounded great and big. There were also a lot of drugs around, and I think this was when heroin first came into my life. There was a particular dealer coming round whose deal was that you could buy as much coke as you wanted, on condition that you took a certain amount of smack at the same time. I would snort the coke, and store all the smack in the drawer of an antique desk at Hurtwood.

On a Sunday night in June, we tried the band out in front of an audience at a charity concert at the Lyceum in the Strand, in aid of Dr Spock's Civil Liberties Legal Defense Fund. In the excitement of just forming the group, one thing had slipped our minds and that was that right up to the last minute before we were due to go on stage, we had no name for ourselves. Ashton, Gardner and Dyke were the opening act, and Tony Ashton always used to call me Del, and suggested that we should be Del and the Dominos. When he did finally announce us, without any mention of our real names, it was as Derek and the Dominos, and the name just stuck. Our set consisted of songs from our Delaney days, like 'Blues Power' and 'Bottle Of Red Wine', a couple of blues numbers, 'Crossroads' and 'Spoonful', and, because Dave Mason had joined us for this one show, a Traffic song, 'Feelin' Alright'.

The thing I remember best about that whole evening was not

the show, but a weird meeting I had afterwards with Dr John, who had been in the audience. I had come across the legendary 'Night Tripper' before, in NY on the very night that Delaney had told me that my gift would be taken away from me if I didn't sing. On the way home from seeing Sha Na Na, we had dropped by his hotel, where he had sung a great song for us called 'You're Giving Me The Push I Need'. It was the first time I had met him, and I was totally mesmerised. Soon after that we went to see him play live, and I just fell in love with him. He's a wonderful man and an incredible musician. Whether or not he really was a practising voodoo doctor, I don't know, but for my own purposes, at that time, I chose to believe he was.

When I ran into him at the Lyceum, I told him that I wanted to consult him as a doctor. He asked me what my problem was and I told him that I needed a remedy. 'What kind of remedy?' he asked, and I told him . . . 'A love potion.' In a way, I was just calling his bluff, but he then asked me to tell him some more about the situation. So I told him I was deeply in love with the wife of another man, and that she was no longer happy with him, but wouldn't leave him. He gave me a little box made out of woven straw, and told me to keep it in my pocket, and gave me various long-forgotten instructions as to what to do with it. I do remember that I did exactly as I was told.

A few weeks later, purely by chance, or so it seemed, I ran into Pattie, and we just kind of collided, to the point where there was no turning back. A little while later, I saw George at a party at Stigwood's house, and blurted the whole thing out to him, 'I'm in love with your wife.' The ensuing conversation bordered on the absurd. Although I think he was deeply hurt, I could see that in his eyes, he preferred to make light of it, turning it into a Monty Python situation. In a way though, I think he was relieved, because I'm sure he knew what had been going on all the time, and now I was finally owning up to it.

This was the beginning of a semi-clandestine affair between us, and the end of my relationship with Paula, who moved on to Bobby Whitlock. But however much I tried to persuade her, it was quite clear that Pattie had no intention of leaving George, even though I was convinced that the writing was on the wall for them. Tormented by my feelings for her, I threw myself into my music, starting with a UK tour of the Dominos. The idea was that wherever we went, we should play incognito, and in this way get back to our roots. To begin with it worked. We toured round the country, playing small clubs and halls in towns like Scarborough, Dunstable, Torquay and Redcar, and no one knew who we were, and I loved it. I loved the fact that we were this little quartet, playing in obscure places, sometimes to audiences of no more than fifty or sixty people.

This was an incredibly creative time for me. Driven by my obsession with Pattie, I was writing a lot, and all the songs I wrote for the Dominos' first album are really about her and our relationship. 'Layla' was the key song, and was a conscious attempt to speak to her about the fact that she was holding off, and wouldn't come and move in with me. 'What'll you do when you get lonely?' The *Layla* album was recorded at Criteria Studios in Miami, where we headed in late August. Its beginnings were inauspicious, because we soon found that, apart from 'Layla', which was still no more than a framework, we actually had very little material. Before I left, Pattie had asked me to get her some pairs of these jeans we used to wear called Landlubbers, which were hipsters with two little slip pockets at the front. She had asked for flared rather than straight bottoms, so I had written 'Bell Bottom Blues' for her. Then I had another love song about her called 'I Looked Away', and there were one or two blues covers I was keen to record, but it was all taking a lot of time and for the first couple of weeks, we really weren't getting anywhere.

What we were doing was having a lot of fun. During the day

we would go swimming and have saunas, and then we would go to the studio and jam, sometimes with chemical assistance. We were staying in a funky little hotel on Miami Beach, where you could score hard drugs in the gift shop by the front reception desk. You just placed your order with the girl who worked there, and you'd come back the next day and she'd hand it over to you in a brown paper bag. By this time we were doing quite a lot of different stuff: smack and coke, as well as all kinds of mad stuff like PCP. One night our producer, Tommy Dowd, told me that the Allman Brothers Band were playing the Coconut Grove and suggested that we all go down to see them. With their long, long hair and beards, the band looked amazing, and were great musicians. I loved them, but what really blew me away was Duane Allman's guitar playing. I was mesmerised by him. He was very tall and thin with an air of complete conviction, and although he didn't sing, I felt sure he was the leader of the band, just by his body language. Tom introduced us to the band after the show, and we invited them back to the studio for a jam, which resulted in me asking Duane to play on the sessions while they were in town.

Duane and me became inseparable during the time we were in Florida, and between the two of us we injected the substance into the *Layla* sessions that had seemed to have been missing so far. He was like the musical brother that I never had, but wished I did. More so than Jimi, who was essentially a loner, while Duane was a family man, a brother. Unfortunately for me he already had a family, but I loved it while it lasted. These kind of experiences don't happen every day, and I knew enough by then to cherish it while I could.

Having another guitarist had made our band come alive, and when Duane had to go back to playing with the Allman Brothers, we were never really the same again. We returned to England and carried on touring, but when we put out the album it died a death, because even though word was beginning to seep out that 'Derek is Eric', I wasn't prepared to do any press or help it in any way. I was still a real idealist in those days, and my hope was that the album would sell on its merit. It didn't, of course, because lack of promotion meant that nobody knew it was out there. In the end pressure from the record company on the one hand and Stigwood on the other compelled me to agree first to 'Derek is Eric' badges being released to the press, and secondly to our promoting the album both at home and in the States.

By the time I got back to America, my heart was no longer in the Dominos. We scored masses of coke and smack before we left Florida and took it on tour with us. With the amount of drugs we were taking every day, I really don't know how we got through that tour alive, and by the time we came back to England, everyone was on the same path to becoming full-blown addicts. Tommy Dowd was so worried about me that he asked Ahmet Ertegun to come and see me. Ahmet took me aside and talked to me in a very fatherly way about how concerned he was about my drug taking. He told me all about his experiences with Ray Charles, and how painful it had been for him watching Ray getting more and more caught up in the world of hard drugs. At one point he became very emotional and started to cry. You would think that the fact that I can recall this with such clarity means that it had some effect on me, but the fact is that it didn't make the slightest bit of difference. I was hell-bent on doing what I was going to do, and I really couldn't see that it was that bad.

What I didn't realise then was, after his experiences not just with Ray, but with people in the jazz world who had gone down the drugs road and ended up dead, how scared Ahmet was of what might happen to me. He was just doing his best to dissuade me from carrying on. Drugs were the beginning of the end for the band. We couldn't do anything. We couldn't work. We couldn't agree. We were paralysed, and this led to hostility growing among us. We attempted to make another album, but it just fell to pieces. The final straw came when Jim Gordon and I had a huge row, and I stormed out of the studio in a rage. The band never played together again. Disillusioned, I retired to Hurtwood.

This was the beginning of a period of serious decline in my life, triggered, I think, by several events. The first of these was the death of Jimi Hendrix, on 18 September, 1970. Over the years, when time allowed it, Jimi and I had become good friends, spending time together in London, but particularly in New York, where we used to play a lot together in the clubs. What I found refreshing about him was his intensely self-critical attitude towards his music. He had this enormous gift and a fantastic technique, like that of someone who spent all day playing and practising, yet he didn't seem that aware of it. There was something of the playboy in him. He loved to spend all night hanging out, getting drunk or stoned, and when he did pick up the guitar, it was very throwaway to him, as if he didn't take himself too seriously.

Though Jimi was left-handed, he always played right-handed guitars upside down, a tradition in which he was not unique. Albert King and Stevie Ray Vaughan both played like this, as does Doyle Bramhall II, who plays with my current band. One afternoon I was browsing through some instrument shops in the West End when I saw this white, left-handed Stratocaster and I bought it on impulse to give to Jimi. The scene was so small then that I knew I would be seeing him that night as I was going to a Sly and the Family Stone concert at the Lyceum, and Jimi was bound to be there. I took the guitar with me to the show so that I could give it to him afterwards, but he never turned up. Then the next day I heard that he had died. He had passed out, stoned on a mixture of booze and drugs, and choked on his own vomit. It was the first time that the death of another musician had really affected me. We all felt obliterated when Buddy Holly died, but this was much more personal. I felt incredibly upset and very angry, and was filled with a feeling of terrible loneliness.

Six weeks later, while I was touring the States with the Dominos, I had a call from Stigwood telling me that my grandfather had been taken into hospital in Guildford with suspected cancer. I flew home to see him. He was a sad figure in his hospital bed, diminished both by his illness and by a stroke he had suffered the previous year, which had left him paralysed down one side. I felt stricken with guilt. In my arrogance, I believed that I had somehow contributed to his decline by having bought him a house and given him enough money to take early retirement. I felt that I had offended his pride by depriving him of his way of life. Of course, in reality, I was just doing what any grateful child would do, trying to pay him back for the love and support I had always received from him. But nevertheless, I couldn't help feeling that I was to blame for it all. It never occurred to me that perhaps I wasn't responsible for everything that happened in the world.

Finally there was my unrequited love for Pattie. I had convinced myself that when she heard the completed *Layla* album, with all its references to our situation, she would be so overcome by my cry of love that she would finally leave George and come away with me for good. So I called her up one afternoon and asked her if she'd like to come over for tea, and listen to the new record. Of course it was blatant emotional blackmail and doomed to failure. By this time, I'd already applied quite a lot of pressure, and this was just more of the same. Having said that, the quality of the music was pure, and I really did need to share that with someone, and who better than her? Anyhow, she came over, and listened, and I think she was deeply touched by the fact that I had written these songs about her, but at the same time, the intensity of it all probably scared the living daylights out of her. Needless to say it didn't work, and I was back to square one.

Over the next few months, I blindly kept on trying to persuade Pattie to leave George and come and live with me, but I was getting nowhere. Until one day, after another session of fruitless pleading, I told her that if she didn't leave him, I would start taking heroin full-time. In truth, of course, I had been taking it almost full-time for quite a while. She smiled sadly at me, and I knew the game was over. That was the last time I saw her for any length of time.

CHAPTER SEVEN
LOST YEARS

Threatening Pattie was futile and childish, but it was all bluff, and had nothing to do with me actually becoming a heroin addict. It just doesn't work that way. I have known and met many people who took just as many drugs, and drank just as much booze as I did, but who never became addicted to anything. It's a mysterious phenomenon. Besides that, I would never have deliberately set about going down this road, because since my days with Cream, I had had a healthy regard for the perils of smack. Ginger often lectured me like an older brother, threatening that if he ever found out I was using heroin, he would have my balls, and I believed him. I just assumed I was in some way immune to it, and that I wouldn't get hooked. But addiction doesn't negotiate, and it gradually crept up on me, like a fog. For a year or so I thoroughly enjoyed it, taking it pretty infrequently, while indulging in lots of coke and other drugs, as well as drinking. Then suddenly, from taking it every two weeks, it was once, then twice or three times a week, then once a day. It was so insidious, it took over my life without my really noticing.

All the time I was taking heroin, I thought I knew exactly what I was doing. In no way was I the helpless victim. I did it mostly because I loved the high, but on reflection, also partly to forget, both the pain of my unrequited love for Pattie and the death of my grandfather. I also thought I was endorsing the rock 'n' roll lifestyle. In spite of Ahmet's warnings, I enjoyed the mythology surrounding the lives of the great jazz musicians like Charlie Parker and Ray Charles, and bluesmen like Robert Johnson, and I had a romantic notion of living the kind of life that led them to create their music. I also wanted to prove that I could do it and come out the other side alive. I was very determined and wanted no help from anybody. I remember George coming to see me one night, and he had Leon with him, who got very angry when he saw the state I was in, and demanded to know what the hell I was up to. I told him that I was on a journey into the darkness and that I had to see it through, to find out what was on the other side. I can't begin to imagine how they must have felt hearing that. These were people I knew well and who loved me. But my addiction had cut me off from the feelings of other people. The concerns of others meant nothing to me, because I was feeling great, and would continue to feel great, as long as I had the powder.

The stuff I was using was pretty strong. It came from Gerard Street in Soho, and was raw and pure. The first time I realised I was completely hooked was an occasion when I had promised Alice that I would drive up to see her in Wales. It suddenly occurred to me that driving stoned 200 miles in a Ferrari would be impossible. I told her I would come in about three days, because I knew enough to know that was the amount of time it would take to come off the drug. I remember the first twenty-four hours of cold turkey as being absolute hell. It was as if I had been poisoned. Every nerve and muscle in my body went into cramp spasms, I curled up in the foetal position and howled with agony. I had never known pain like it. Even when I was a kid and had scarlet fever, there was no comparison. It took all of three days, and I had not a wink of sleep in that time. And the worst thing was, being drug-free and clean felt terrible. My skin felt raw, and my nerves were stood on end, I couldn't wait to take some more, to slip back into comfort. But I had promised Alice, and I was still this side of gone, where I could hold on to the rational world, and make some decisions that I could commit to.

On that occasion, I managed to come off, and move back into life, but from then on, and as my frequency of using began to increase again, I didn't come off very often. It was just too difficult and painful. Alice came back to live with me, and once she became part of the picture, she started using too and took the role as the runner, going to score for us. It never crossed my mind that it was wrong to bring her into my nightmare; my logic determined that if you wanted in, you were in, simple as that. We soon worked out that the trick was to always overlap our supply so that we never got to the point where we'd run out. This was never a problem when we were at home, but anytime I had to travel, I ran into difficulties.

In the summer of 1971, over a year into my self-imposed exile, George called me one day to ask if I'd fly to New York to play in a show he was putting on at the beginning of August at Madison Square Garden, to raise money for the victims of the Bangladesh famine. He was only too aware of my drug problems, and may have seen this as some kind of rescue mission. Whatever the reason, I told him that I could only go if he could guarantee that they could keep me supplied. Since the initial schedule was about a week's rehearsal followed by the show, he was pretty certain he could take care of it. The consensus was that finding stuff in New York would not be a problem, and if there were any difficulties, there were apparently people who knew people who would be able to sort me out.

The journey got off to a very bad start. When Alice and I got to the airport, Pattie was there to see me off. I can't remember how this came about, but it was wonderful and disastrous all at the same time. Alice was furious, and came to the conclusion that I was secretly still seeing Pattie, which wasn't true, but who could blame her for thinking that? I was in such a haze most of the time that situations like this were commonplace. I could make an arrangement to meet someone somewhere, and then forget about it two minutes later. The result was that fantasy and reality shared the same space in my head, which had become a labyrinth of half-formed plans and ideas, none of which I could seriously commit to. Emotionally and spiritually, though, I was bankrupt, and therefore unconcerned, so this sort of situation did not worry me too much. As long as I had enough stuff to get me through whatever was going on, I was happy.

By the time we got to the hotel in New York, the drugs were starting to wear off. As promised, however, there was a good supply of stuff waiting in my room. I tried some, but nothing happened. It turned out that what they had scored for me was street-cut, with a very low amount of actual heroin in it, and cut with something nasty, like strychnine, so that it was about a tenth as strong as what I was used to. The result was that I went into cold turkey for the first two or three days and missed all the rehearsals. I just lay on the bed in our hotel room, shaking and mumbling like a madman, apologising to anybody that came to check on me, while Alice ran around town tirelessly trying to find me the real thing.

Luckily for me, Allen Klein, the Beatles' manager at the time, who was helping George produce the show at the Garden, heard that I was in trouble and offered me some medication that he was taking for his ulcers. I took some and amazingly, at the eleventh hour, it made me feel OK. At the last minute I got to the soundcheck and quickly ran through some of the things I was supposed to do, and although I have a vague memory of this, and then of playing the show, the truth is I wasn't really there. I've only ever seen the concert once on film, and I felt ashamed. No matter how I've tried to rationalise it to myself over the years, I let a lot of people down that night, most of all myself. But if I ever want a reminder of what I might be missing from the 'good old days', then this would be the film to watch.

When we returned home, we retreated to Hurtwood, and closed the door. For a long time I didn't go out at all, leaving Alice to do all the shopping and cooking, and more importantly the scoring. She developed a relationship with a guy called Alex, who lived in Notting Hill. As well as being a dealer, he was a writer who was also a registered drug addict, which meant that every day he would get a prescription for his stuff. It came in pill form, and we would buy it from him if he was unable to score the street stuff. This is what we preferred, because it was raw and much more powerful, whereas the pharmaceutical stuff tended to be pretty tame.

The best heroin looked like brown sugar. It was in little nuggets, which had the colour and consistency of rock candy, and it came in clear plastic bags, with a red paper label that had Chinese writing and a little white elephant on it. We'd get a pestle and mortar and grind it up, and we'd then be left with about an ounce of the stuff, which ought to have lasted us about a week. But we were wasteful junkies, and chose to snort it like you snort cocaine, rather than inject it, mainly because I was terrified of needles, a fear that went back to when I was at primary school. One day, without warning, we were all herded up from the classroom and taken to the village hall in Ripley for our diphtheria jabs. It was a horrible experience, frightening and painful, and I can still remember the smell of the chemicals they were cooking the needles in. But as a result, I have never injected drugs, and for that I am very, very grateful. But that meant we got through copious quantities, about five or ten times what a person injecting it would use. Not only that, but within minutes of taking our initial snort, I would think, 'I need some more,' and top up, even though the effect of what I had originally snorted would have lasted at least another five or six hours. It was a very expensive way of getting stoned.

During those lost years, I scarcely saw my family. I was no support to Rose, who of course was deep in mourning for my grandfather, and who certainly must have known that something was going on, even if she wasn't aware that it was drugs. I later learned that she had decided to stand back, hoping and praying that whatever was wrong would eventually run its course, and everything come out all right in the end. I also avoided even my oldest friends. The front gates of Hurtwood were always left open, so from time to time people would come and visit me, knock on the door and then leave when there was no reply. When Ben Palmer drove down to see me one day, all the way from Wales, I hid upstairs and watched him from the top window sitting in his car, waiting for him to go away. Ginger even came once with a plan to kidnap me and take me off to the Sahara Desert in his Land Rover, reasoning that that was one place where I really wouldn't be able to score. The phone went unanswered. Inside, I would sleep most of the day and get up in the late afternoon. I played the guitar for hours, recording songs on to cassettes, most of which were pretty dreadful. I never labelled the cassettes, so a great deal of time was passed playing through them to find whichever song I was last working on. I also drew a lot, making Escher-like drawings with a Rapidograph. My only other pastime was building model aeroplanes and cars.

One of the few people I did see at this time was Pete Townshend who, during a rare period of my wanting to work, I had asked over to help me finish off some tracks I had recorded with Derek and the Dominos. By the time he arrived, however, I had lost interest in the project and in an effort to explain my total inertia, I confessed to him that I had a problem. I was horrified when he told me that he had known for some time. It turned out that, though I had not seen him personally, he had been to the house several times to talk to Alice. I felt embarrassed when he told me that he was keen to help me, because I'd begun to hate myself for dragging Alice down with me. It may have been a bit late to start developing a moral conscience, but nevertheless it was there, and I felt confused and ashamed by people being concerned about me.

One day, Pete told me that he and Alice's father had devised a plan to help me get back on my feet. It was to be a comeback concert, with all my friends playing. Alice's father, David Harlech, was an extraordinary figure. Tall, with a prominent nose and a rather languid voice. From the moment I met him, we got on very well, and my relationship with him was loving and respectful. He was very understanding and became a kind of stepfather to me. I think one of the reasons we got on so well was that we shared a love of music. He told me that during his time in London as a young man, and later in Washington, he had got to know and befriended a number of well-known jazz musicians, and we used to talk together a lot about them. He also seemed to like what I did musically, and because of that, and because I respected him, it served to heighten my sense of shame about what was going on between me and his daughter. But we were prisoners by then and could not break the spell. It really was time for someone like him to step in.

The plan was for me to join a band put together by Pete to play at a concert at the Rainbow Theatre in London, as part of 'Fanfare for Europe', celebrating Britain's entry into the Common Market. David saw a return to the public arena as a way of giving me the incentive to break my habit. Though this was something that I would never have managed to do on my own, because it was Pete, I went along with it, and I had a good time doing it. All the while I had shut myself away, I had been listening to music and playing the guitar, but to fully develop your craft you need to interact with other people, and what was missing was the fact that, since the concert for Bangladesh, I hadn't actually played with any other musicians. When we got into rehearsals, which took place at Ronnie Wood's house, I made a real attempt to practise, play and compose, if on a limited level. Thank God that Steve Winwood was there to give me confidence, since it must have been quite clear to the other players that there was something seriously lacking in my playing. Fortunately I knew in my head what I wanted to do, as well as what was required of me, it was just the problem of communicating that to my fingers.

On the night of the show, 13 January, 1973, Alice and I, stoned out of our heads, turned up late to find Pete and Stigwood tearing their hair out. The reason for our lateness was that Alice had to let out the waist of the trousers of my white suit because I had taken to eating so much chocolate of late that I couldn't get them on any more. Ahmet was in the audience, along with George and Ringo, Jimmy Page, Elton John and Joe Cocker among others, while on the stage the band, which we called the Palpitations, included Pete, Steve, Jim Karstein, Jim Capaldi and Rick Grech. We opened with 'Layla', and included songs like 'Badge', 'Bottle Of Red Wine', 'Bell Bottom Blues' and 'Presence Of The Lord', and having such a great band pushed me to the limits of my playing in the state that I was in. Though it wasn't bad, listening to the tapes later made me realise that my playing and singing were miles off course. It sounded just like the charity benefit that it really was. I had a great time doing it, however, and the incredible welcome I was given by the audience was very moving. After the Rainbow concert, I went back into hiding, and even though I understood that Pete cared for me and wanted to help by getting me back into the music scene, I just wasn't ready. In the days that immediately followed I sank to new lows, with Alice following close behind. I was soon taking vast quantities of

LOST YEARS

heroin every day, and my cravings had become so powerful that Alice was giving me virtually everything that she was able to score, compensating for the heroin which she was missing by drinking large quantities of neat vodka, up to two bottles a day. She too had now become a recluse, unwilling to connect with anyone who was going to obstruct us in what we were up to. The doors remained closed. The post went unopened, and we existed on a diet that consisted for the most part of chocolate and junk food, so I soon became not only overweight, but spotty and generally unfit. Heroin also completely took away my libido, so there was no sexual activity of any kind, and I became chronically constipated.

The cost of our lifestyle was not just high in human terms, it was beginning to cripple me financially. Each week I was spending about £1,000 on heroin, the equivalent of £8,000 today. For a period of time I had managed to hide from Stigwood the true amount, but eventually he had cottoned on to what was going on, and I had received a message from the office to say that funds were running low and I would soon have to start selling things to pay for my habit. If that gave me something to think about, then so did a letter I received from David in which he told me in no uncertain terms that he was quite happy to turn us both over to the police, if I wasn't prepared to stop what I was doing to myself and, more importantly, to his daughter. His letter was quite ruthless, but compassionate at the same time. 'I love you both so much,' he wrote, 'that I cannot bear to see what you are doing to yourselves. For all that you can do and all you can have in your lives, please let me help you.' He finished off by saying, 'I will probably never know how much courage it will take, dear Eric, but for your own sake, please do it.'

It was fairly clear that he meant business, and I knew deep down that I was inflicting serious damage on an unsuspecting innocent, somebody that I had no right to meddle with. I realised that I had to put the brakes on, if not for my sake, then for hers.

151

Finally the light went on, and I called him up and said, 'You're right. We need help, but what can we do?' He then told me he had come across an extraordinary woman called Dr Meg Patterson, a Scottish neurosurgeon who had worked for years in Hong Kong, where she had developed a method of treating opiate-withdrawal symptoms using a form of electrical acupuncture she called Neuroelectric Therapy. She had recently returned to Britain and had set up a clinic in Harley Street with her husband, George. They had already had a meeting with him, and had put together a programme for me and Alice.

I knew I had to go through with this. I had total faith in David's reasoning, and I realised that this was not a step he had taken lightly. We agreed to go for an interview with them at their home in Harley Street, and, as usual, arrived stoned. I took to Meg straight away. She was a very charismatic woman, petite and attractive with auburn hair and a pretty face, and she had a motherly kind of personality, very loving and concerned. She struck me as a good person. Her stories of living and working in Hong Kong and China among the street addicts were fascinating and she seemed confident that she could help me. George, her husband, was interesting too and had spent a lot of time in Tibet, getting to know the guerrillas who were fighting back against the Chinese. Their cure was a form of acupuncture, using an electrical stimulator made in China, which Meg had bought in Hong Kong. This took the form of a small black box with wires radiating out of it, attached to small clips holding tiny needles which were applied to various points within the contour of the ear. The treatment involved three hour-long sessions a day and would necessitate the Pattersons coming to live with us at Hurtwood for at least the first week. Cautiously, we agreed.

To begin with, things were very difficult. George was a committed Christian and came on quite strong about God and Christianity and Jesus, and I found this a little overwhelming because I felt so vulnerable. To a certain extent I felt he was taking advantage of my situation to lay this on me, so I was a bit guarded around both of them. Though I had certainly looked at religion, I have always been resistant to doctrine, and any spirituality I had experienced thus far in my life had been fairly abstract and not aligned with any recognised religion. For me, the most trustworthy vehicle for spirituality had always proven to be music. It cannot be manipulated, or politicised, and when it is, that becomes immediately obvious. But of course, I could not explain that to them back then, although I'm sure I tried, so I thought the best thing to do was to follow their programme, and see what would happen.

The first thing that Meg explained to us was that we were not allowed to touch any heroin from day one. This really did come as a shock as I had somehow thought we would be weaned slowly off it. She set up her apparatus in the room we used as a den, next to our sitting room. The method was that the clip with the needles was attached to various pressure points in your ear lobes, like a clip-on earring, and when the machine was switched on it would pass a very mild electric current through the needles. You could control the strength of this with a knob, which you could turn to the point where it started to get tingly, and then you would turn it down till you could only just feel it. It eventually produced in you a state of euphoria, and you could actually end up going into a kind of half-sleep. They talk about heroin as 'the nod', because it does send you into a stupor, and the black box was supposed to have the same effect. So the treatment was really comprised of trying to wean you off heroin both psychologically and emotionally, while the box physically reduced the withdrawal symptoms. Theoretically, as you progressed the treatment, the amount of time you spent plugged into the box decreased.

After about five days, Meg told me that she and George had decided that the treatment was not going to work unless Alice and

I were treated separately. It was the nights that were the problem, because neither of us could sleep, and this was wearing us all down. I was also having serious misgivings; at first I had felt like we were being given a demonstration of what this thing could do, but now it was dawning on me that this was really it, this was all we were going to get, and I was panicking. They decided that, to make things more manageable, I should go and live with them in Harley Street, while Alice was to go to a clinic elsewhere. Her problems were compounded by the fact that she was also drinking heavily. I didn't like the fact that they were splitting us up at all, and wondered why, if one of us had to be shipped off to some strange nursing home, it should be Alice and not me. I still feel quite puzzled about them in this respect. Could it have been that they saw me as a golden opportunity, a high-profile person with whom they might have success? This would undoubtedly give a boost to their clinic, which I think had been quite slow in getting off the ground.

It was unnerving going to live on my own with a strange, completely straight family, but I knew I had to accept everything that was being offered. Looking back on it, I suppose the idea was that the 'cure' was a purely physical technique coupled with lots of tender loving care and dietary supervision, with George's Christian ethic added to the whole thing. They also had what appeared to be a very strong family unit on display, two sons and a daughter who were shining examples of how good kids could be. It was as if they were saying, 'Look how it can be when everyone's in harmony.' But this just made it all the more difficult.

I remember one time they let me out on my own, and I went to see some friends and got my hands on some Viseptone, which is a methadone syrup used to wean people off heroin. I smuggled it back to Meg's house, and hid it in some clothes. What I didn't realise was that she used to go through my things. The next day at lunch, in front of the children, she produced the bottle and told me that I had betrayed her and that my behaviour was disgusting. She then poured it down the sink. I have never seen eye to eye with shaming people, no matter what the justification is, and I couldn't understand how it could be part of their programme. It didn't work, and it was humiliating. It was at this point that I inwardly decided to have nothing more to do with them, and quietly shut down.

I did make a kind of recovery while I was there, and they did help, a great deal in fact, by encouraging me to listen to and play music again. It was by doing this that I got in touch with my feelings again, and they came back in a flood. Looking back, I honestly believe that Meg and George did the best they could with what they had. But it wasn't enough. Because for all the good they may have done in getting me off heroin, to then let me loose without any real aftercare was uninformed and dangerous. They seemed to have had no knowledge of, or interest in, any of the twelve-step programmes like AA or NA which have been active and flourishing in London and throughout England since the mid-forties. Their idea of rehabilitation, planned with the help of David, was to send me to live on a farm outside Oswestry, run by his youngest son Frank Ormsby-Gore. The idea was that I should get physically well and sort myself out. The reality was, the minute I got up to the farm, I simply traded one substance for another.

CHAPTER EIGHT

461 OCEAN BOULEVARD

Frank Gore was nine years younger than me, aged twenty, when I went to work on the family farm in Shropshire early in 1974. Though I had known him since he was fourteen, it was only as Alice's little brother, and now we hit it off right away. I drove myself up from Hurtwood in a car which I had been given by George Harrison, a Mini Cooper Radford, a deluxe custom-built Mini, that he had had painted with tantric Indian symbols by a coach-painter. I took with me an acoustic guitar and some of my record collection, and since Frank turned out to be a huge music fan, that immediately gave us something in common. He was a great person to listen to music with and bounce ideas off, and he became my sounding board as to how I was going to get back into playing. We were living in a tiny cottage with a couple of bed-rooms, a kitchen and a living room. It was pretty funky, but Frank was a good cook and we lived mostly in the kitchen.

Since I was so unfit, after three years of doing little more than lying in a nod on a couch in front of the TV, the agreement was that to begin with I would work according to my condition. There was a lot of work to be done. Frank was running a farm that barely broke even, and was doing it virtually single-handed. A friend of his, Mike Crunchie, and another man called Dai were the only farmhands I met, and it was Crunchie who showed me the ropes. I was soon up at dawn, working like a maniac, baling hay, chopping logs, sawing trees and mucking out the cows. It was the kind of manual labour I hadn't done since working with my grandfather on a building site, and I really loved it. I was soon becoming very fit and, even though it was winter, I was getting brown too from windburn. In the meantime, Frank was swanning around doing stuff with trucks and mechanical devices. He fancied himself as a trader, and loved to talk about the massive deals he was doing with people for lorries and tractors and things.

Around five or six o'clock, he would pick us up and we'd go down to the local town, Oswestry, and hit the pubs, where we'd listen to the jukebox and drink until we could hardly stand up. Sometimes we'd make complete arses of ourselves, but we were doing it in public, in an outward manner, and after the reclusive way I'd been living, that seemed very healthy. Then we'd go back to the cottage and Frank would fix us some dinner, and we'd drink some more. I was having the best time I'd had for a long time. Frank did something very important for me. He helped me to feel good about myself again. When I was around the Pattersons, I always felt slightly ashamed of myself, as if I was a rehabilitating criminal, but when I was with him, although a good deal of it was fuelled by alcohol, I felt confident and funny, as if I was finally coming out of my shell. He was very loving and very kind to me, and best of all he seemed to have no agenda. I think he truly liked my company and just accepted me for who I was.

All the time I stayed with Frank, I began to collect songs and ideas for a new album. I was listening to all kinds of different stuff, and even trying to write the odd line or two. Needless to say the blues featured high in my priorities, and I was starting to get quite excited about making a start on something soon. Going from a very isolated existence to a very gregarious one had a lot to do with me wanting to make music again, and for this I am truly indebted to David Harlech and the Pattersons, for this was the one area on which they were absolutely right to focus my energies. Apart from the material I had in mind, there was a possible band too, waiting in the wings. Carl Radle had sent me some tapes he had made of a combo he was playing with in the clubs in Tulsa, along with a little note saying 'You should listen to this. I think you'd like working with these guys.' It was Carl on bass, Dick Sims on keyboards and Jamie Oldaker on drums. It sounded great, and I could tell they were really gifted players.

Carl himself was a fascinating character. A Tulsa musician of German descent, he was quite European-looking. He always wore pebble-shaped glasses and had hair that was balding at the front and long and straggly at the back. Though he was only three years older than me, he had an age to him and a great deal of experience and wisdom. He was a natural philosopher, as well as being a musicologist with a wide taste in music from all over the world. We could talk for hours about anything from movies to hunting dogs, he was a real soulmate for me. But of course, more than anything, he was a brilliant bass player, with a minimal and melodic style which really swung. During the Dominos period I had become very close with Carl, and he had held on to the idea that he would like to work with me again. He could see through all my nonsense, and knew what I was capable of. As much as I had been moved by David's intervention to help me, I was much more motivated by this approach of Carl's, because as a musician who really had aspirations to be in America, to be holed up in the middle of nowhere in England was hell for me. All my heroes were in the States and Carl's message that 'We're waiting for you' was a real incentive to resurface. The memory of this little outfit stayed with me, and when I started piecing together the ingredients for this new album, up at Frank's, this was the band that I pictured playing with.

When I am trying to write songs, I like to leave things as unfinished as I can, so that whoever I am going to play the song with has a chance to influence, by the way they play, the way the song will end up. What I was doing in my mind, in this case, was preparing small groups of ideas that I could take to Carl, Jamie and Dick, and say, 'Let's work on this.' Then, hopefully, when we actually came to play it, the song would almost finish itself. One of the songs I had started was coming on quite well, and I was very proud of my inventiveness in the verse. This was 'Let It Grow', and it was several years before I realised that I had totally ripped off 'Stairway To Heaven', the famous Zeppelin anthem, a cruel justice seeing as how I'd always been such a severe critic of theirs.

One day while I was at the farm, I had a call from Pete Townshend asking me if I would like to make a cameo appearance in the movie version of *Tommy*, which was being filmed at Pinewood Studios. He wanted me to play an old Sonny Boy Williamson song, 'Eyesight To The Blind', and I was to do this in the character of a preacher in a church that worshipped Marilyn Monroe. Even though I thought the whole idea sounded like a load of bollocks, I couldn't resist the thought of trying to do it, of getting back into the work of playing and singing a song and recording a track. They sent a car to pick me up from the farm and drove me down to the studios for the day. It was a surreal experience. I spent the whole time getting smashed with Keith Moon, and seeing him in full flight made me feel like I didn't have a problem at all. Compared to him, I viewed myself as a lightweight.

Halfway through my time at Frank's, Alice came up to join me, having been released from the clinic she was attending. It was a tense, edgy visit, as we were under strict instructions from Meg not to share a room or get involved in any way, the theory being that it might take us back to where we'd been. This actually suited me quite well because as my senses had begun to come back to life, so had thoughts of Pattie, which had been dormant for the past three years. They were rekindled when George and Pattie turned up in Wales, quite out of the blue, to see how I was getting on. Touched though I was by their friendship, I remember thinking that I would rather Pattie had come on her own. We all went to a pub for a drink and though they seemed like they were still a couple, I got the distinct impression that she was looking at me with more than just friendly concern. All the old feelings came flooding back.

When I left Frank's, I was fit, clean and buzzing with excitement at all the possibilities that lay ahead of me. In a moment of gratitude to Meg, I sent her my 24-carat gold coke spoon, along with a handwritten note which read 'Thanks Meg. I won't be needing this any more.' I was feeling good, because life was starting to look good again. I was conscious of the fact that I had never stopped listening to music and playing, and even when I was at my lowest ebb, I had managed to maintain some kind of craft, and had something to go back to. I also made the painful decision to split with Alice for good, something that Meg had always recommended, for fear that we would end up destroying each other. There was nothing left in that relationship but dependence, and now my thoughts were only of Pattie.

Throughout the course of my addiction, Stigwood had always had faith that I would come through. Even though it was an enormous gamble for him, he stuck by me, and one of the first things I did on my return was to arrange a meeting with him.

'What do you want to do?' he asked, 'Because I know what I want you to do.'

I said, 'Well, I've got all these ideas, and I think I want to make a record.'

'Well that's great,' he said, 'because that's exactly what I had in mind. I want you to go straight out to Miami, the studio's already booked, with Tom Dowd to produce it and engineer it, if you want him.'

And that was it. It had all been prearranged, and they were just waiting for me. I remember thinking how great it was that he had shown such foresight in putting together something that I could just step into. He'd also rented a house, 461 Ocean Boulevard, a luxury home right on the seafront in Miami Beach, and I flew straight out there.

When I arrived in Miami, I was greeted by Carl, who then drove me to the airport to meet Jamie and Dick. They were very feisty young guys, bright and confident and not in the least impressed by me. They made me feel old, and I was only twenty-nine! The idea was that we should play as a quartet, augmented in the studio by other artists, and I instinctively understood that the success of the record depended entirely on the kind of chemistry that developed. The first and most important thing for me was to find a way to restore my playing capabilities in the company of proper musicians. What we ended up doing was finding a compromise solution in which they played minimally to my capabilities. This gave a certain charm to the music, in that it was very basic.

One of the extra musicians who Stigwood had brought in to join us was Yvonne Elliman, a brilliant young singer who had played the part of Mary Magdalene both on Broadway and in the movie of *Jesus Christ Superstar*. Of Irish and Hawaiian descent, she was incredibly pretty and exotic-looking, with long dark hair, and Stiggy was very keen that we should collaborate. Since I had had virtually no sex life in the last few years, it is not hard to imagine what happened in the heady atmosphere of recording in Miami. Yvonne and I fell in lust with each other, and were soon flirting and mucking around and enjoying a passionate affair. She was a great lady, who liked to have fun and drink and do dope and generally hang out with the guys, and we became good friends. She also had a terrific voice, and it wasn't long before I asked her to join the band.

The guitar I chose to use for my return to recording was one that I had built myself, a black Fender Stratocaster which I had nicknamed 'Blackie'. In the early days, in spite of my admiration for both Buddy Holly and Buddy Guy, both Strat players, I had predominantly played a Gibson Les Paul, but one day, while I was on tour with the Dominos, I saw Steve Winwood with a white Strat, and, inspired by him, I went into Sho-Bud in Nashville, which had a stack of Strats in the back of the shop. They were completely out of fashion at the time and I bought six or seven of them for a song, no more than about $100 each. These were vintage instruments, which today would be worth about a hundred times that. When I got home I gave one to Steve, one to Pete Townshend, another to George Harrison, and kept the rest. I then took three of them and made one guitar out of the three, using the best components of each.

Having come from the Dominos, who were hard-playing musicians, very full on, who played loud and strong, it was a very different experience playing with such a laid-back attitude, and I enjoyed it. We jammed and played for hours, and listening to these guys play, I realised that I was miles behind, and needed to catch up with everybody. I wanted to know what everyone was listening to and what was going on in the world of music. I had been hibernating for years, and was completely out of touch, but I knew I could still play from the heart. No matter how primitive or sloppy it sounded, it would be real, and that was my strength. Also I was tired of the guitar-hero thing, I wanted to just blend into the band and play more rhythm.

I was starting to follow the example of J. J. Cale, who Delaney had turned me on to in the late sixties, and these guys actually knew him, Carl had played on some of his records. It all seemed to fit that I should be playing with minimalist players, since that's exactly where I wanted to go.

Apart from 'Let It Grow', which I had finished on my own, most of the material for this album was cover versions of songs like 'Willie And The Hand Jive', 'Steady Rollin' Man' and 'I Can't Hold Out', which had been rolling around my head for a long time, waiting for the opportunity to pop out. 'Get Ready' was written for what was happening, and the way I felt about Yvonne, and 'Mainline Florida' was written by George Terry, a local musician, who had mysteriously joined our happy throng. He was a friend of Alby Galutin, another local player who I had met and hung out with during the recording of *Layla*. 'Give Me Strength' was a song I had first heard in London during the early sixties, while I was living in the Fulham Road with Charlie and Diana Radcliffe. It seemed to perfectly fit the occasion, and also gave me the unforgettable opportunity of playing with Al Jackson, the drummer of the MG's, a legend among players.

One day, George Terry came in with an album called *Burnin'* by Bob Marley and the Wailers, a band I'd never heard of. When he played it to me I was mesmerised. He especially liked the track 'I Shot The Sheriff', and kept saying to me, 'You ought to cut this, you ought to cut this. We could make it sound great,' but it was hardcore reggae, and I wasn't sure we could do it justice. We did a version of it anyway, but I wasn't that enamoured with the way it turned out. Ska, bluebeat and reggae were familiar mediums to me, I had grown up hearing them in the clubs and on the radio because of our growing communities of West Indians, but it was quite new to the Americans, and they weren't as finicky as I was about the way it should be played. Not that I knew myself how to play it, I just knew we weren't doing it right. When we got to the end of the sessions and started to collate the songs that we had, I told them that I didn't think 'Sheriff' should be included, as it didn't do the Wailers' version justice. But everyone said, 'No, no.

Honestly this is a hit,' and sure enough, when the album was eventually released, and the record company chose it as a single, to my utter astonishment, it went straight to number one. Though I didn't meet Bob Marley till much later, he did call me up when the single came out and seemed pretty happy with what we had done. I tried to ask him what the song was all about, but couldn't understand much of his reply. I was just relieved that he liked it.

The album *461 Ocean Boulevard* was recorded in a month, after which I returned to England, where I decided to make another move towards Pattie. I knew through go-betweens that things were bad between her and George and that they were living in virtual open warfare at Friar Park, with him flying the 'OM' flag at one end of the house and her flying a Jolly Roger at the other, but the general advice from my friends was 'Bide your time and she'll leave him.' One night I had gone into the studio with Pete Townshend to complete the recording work I had done on *Tommy*, and when we had finished I suddenly had this urge to go and see Pattie. I managed to persuade Pete to drive me down to Henley under the pretext that George was very keen to meet him and that we didn't have to stay too long. In fact we were just marauders. When we got there, George took Pete into his studio to show it off and play him some of the stuff he'd been working on, while I spent the time canoodling with Pattie and trying to talk her into finally leaving George. I eventually left without her having made a decision, but it turned out to have been a seminal moment in our relationship.

I went to see Stigwood who at that time was as heavily involved with other projects as he was with me. On stage he had *Hair, Jesus Christ Superstar* and *Oh! Calcutta!*, he was producing the film of *Tommy* and he was managing the Bee Gees, so he told me he was going to appoint someone full-time to give me the time and attention he felt I deserved. The guy he chose was Roger Forrester, a sharp, humorous Northerner, who had been working at his company, RSO, for some time as a booking agent. I knew Roger, as he'd organised some of my tours, and with his big, tinted TV-shaped glasses, his natty suits, kipper ties, and his combover haircut, I'd always regarded him as a bit of a character. Jack and Ginger were always trying to make his life a misery – Ginger, for example, loved to take his dogs into his office and encourage them to chew the place up – but they rarely got the better of Roger who could always see them off with his sharp patter and witty one-liners. He was no novice in the world of show business, having started his career promoting wrestling matches in working men's clubs, before going on to work with pop groups like the Honeycombs and Pickety Witch. It is extraordinary that he ended up with me, as we were such different people, poles apart really. I was into fairly esoteric things, art, cinema and street fashion, while he liked to portray himself as a sort of Andy Capp working-class lad, living on a diet of bangers and mash. Somehow we met in the middle and got on very well.

With the huge success of 'I Shot the Sheriff' and the subsequent release of the album *461 Ocean Boulevard* in July 1974, it was time to go out on the road again, and Stigwood had planned a massive six-week, 28-city tour of North American stadiums, a decision that the newly appointed Roger apparently profoundly disagreed with. He felt that I should be brought back slowly and gently, with a shorter tour playing in smaller venues. For whatever reason, the Stigwood plan held, and we were off again, big time.

During his pre-Stigwood career, Roger had made some interesting connections in the East End, including Laurie O'Leary who had managed Esmeralda's Barn for the Krays before taking over the Speakeasy. He brought in Laurie's brother, Alphi, to work for me as my personal assistant and bodyguard. Alphi was an unforgettable character, a huge, powerfully built man, with permed hair, who stood at least six feet four. He had a strange kind of neck movement, as if he'd broken it at some time, and because he could hardly move his head, when he turned to look at you he had to move the whole of the top half of his torso, which gave him rather a sinister air. Menacing though he may have looked, it was all a front, because he was in fact an extremely deep and gentle man. But as my minder, he often had to do things that would be morally difficult for anyone, like forcibly ejecting people from situations where they were not wanted. This would make him suffer dreadful remorse for days, but he would swallow it, and continue to put on a fierce front. In truth, he was the definitive gentle giant.

Roger may have had misgivings about my going on tour, but I didn't. I had buried myself away for quite long enough. Anyway I was too drunk most of the time to have noticed whether or not the tour was doing me any harm. Drink turned me into the worst kind of prankster. For example, Stigwood decided that rehearsals for the tour should take place in Barbados and rented us a large villa on the beach. I remember arriving there to find that the staff had prepared a delicious dinner of spaghetti bolognese in our honour. We had scarcely sat down before I picked up my plate and threw it over somebody. Soon food was flying round the room, leaving the walls and furniture dripping with pasta and meat sauce.

Some of the best times I ever had in my drinking years were in the company of Stigwood and Co. We loved high-stakes pranking, with virtually no limit, and it could get quite rough, until there would eventually have to be some kind of truce in order to prevent someone getting hurt. Stiggy liked to play the role of the indignant victim who, pushed too far, would suddenly lash out in furious self-defence, and he always gave as good as he got. It sounds pretty childish, and it was, but we had great fun. Apart from me, two of Stiggy's most vicious tormentors were Ahmet and Earl McGrath, who ran the Rolling Stones record company. I once heard that they stripped him to his underpants in the middle of an airport and emptied the contents of his briefcase all over the floor. One Christmas I had a full-size stuffed camel delivered to his house, and in return three dairy cows were delivered to Hurtwood, and so it would go on. Once in Barbados, Ahmet, Earl and me went to visit him in his rented villa, where we set about totally trashing the whole place, while he sat in a hammock outside, crying and whimpering, 'How dare you? I've never been so humiliated in my whole life.' We were like kids, and if one of us switched sides and went to Stiggy's aid, then there would be an immediate change of power, and the victim would become the aggressor. On reflection, it required a lot of love and trust to play games like this on a large scale, and that was definitely there for all of us, drunk or sober.

The 461 Ocean Boulevard tour opened on 28 June, 1974, at the Yale Bowl in Newhaven, Connecticut, playing to a capacity crowd of 70,000. The band remained the same as played on the album – Carl Radle, Jamie Oldaker, Dick Sims, George Terry and Yvonne Elliman, but the set also included songs such as 'Badge' and 'Crossroads' from my Cream days, 'Presence Of The Lord' from *Blind Faith* and 'Layla' and 'Have You Ever Loved A Woman?' from the Dominos repertoire. This was, after all, supposed to be my comeback tour. It was a flamboyant show and we went out with Legs Larry Smith as our opening act. He was the drummer with the Bonzo Dog Doo-Dah Band, who would often wear a tutu and come out from behind the drums to do a tap dance. His performance on our tour consisted of him coming on dressed as a Roman centurion and miming to the Who song 'My Generation' with a ukelele. We would all stand at the side of the stage and throw things at him, fruit, bread rolls, or whatever came to hand. Sometimes we used to fill up his ukelele with soup just before he went on. We made his life a misery. It was quite an extraordinary act. The audience had no idea how to take it, and he would invariably be booed off, which was also part of the act, feigning terrible grief and humiliation.

Legs and I became good friends and drinking buddies. He liked to wear very warm clothes in hot climates. For instance, in New Orleans in the middle of July, I remember him wearing a three-piece, Harris tweed suit, with an overcoat folded over his arm. He also had a beautifully tailored suit made from Holiday Inn towels. He was extremely stylish, and his taste in clothes began to rub off on me. My standard outfit became a pair of worn-out Lee bib-overalls that I'd bought in a second-hand store, with a plastic see-through mac over the top, adorned with hundreds of badges.

I wasn't too concerned about what people thought, I was drunk most of the time and having fun, fooling around and playing with the guys. Brandy was my drink of choice, but I couldn't drink it neat. Like most alcoholics I have met since, I didn't like the taste of alcohol, so I would mix it with something sweet, like ginger ale or 7-Up. I drank round the clock, and it didn't matter to me whether or not there was a show that night, because I was always convinced that I could handle it. There were many times, of course, when I couldn't, in which case I'd just wander off the stage and somebody, usually Roger, would have to try to persuade me to go back on.

There seemed to be a post-psychedelia drunkenness which swept over everybody in the entertainment business during the early seventies. To be on stage, you were almost expected to be drunk. I remember doing one entire show lying down on the stage with the microphone stand lying beside me, and nobody batted an eyelid. Not too many complaints came back either, probably because the audience was as drunk as I was. Of course there were shining lights working on the road at that time, artists with high ethical and professional standards, people like Stevie Wonder, Ray Charles and B. B. King. And if I had had the courage or the clarity of mind to have understood the example they were setting, maybe I would have been able to start doing something about my steady decline. But this is alcoholism we're talking about, and I was already in deep denial about the direction my life was taking.

Private concern over my condition was building, but without proper information. The only thing that the people in my immediate circle knew how to do was preserve the status quo, and Roger became part of that. Apparently his brief from Stiggy had been to keep everything working and functioning, and so he became my enabler, making sure I had everything that I wanted, encouraging me just enough, playing the party animal with me and making me laugh. We became incredibly close, and I began to look upon him as a father figure. He travelled everywhere with me, and all the time he kept an eye on me, asking everybody, 'Where's Eric? What's he up to? Is he all right? Give me a report.' I, in the meantime, was in a happy alcoholic haze, failing to notice that everybody who worked for me now worked for Roger, and the balance of power had shifted.

Roger's real coup, and the thing that really cemented our relationship, was to produce Pattie. It was the first time he waved his magic wand, and the fact that it made a long-held wish come true left me totally under his spell. Roger had heard through the grapevine that Pattie had actually left George and gone to stay in LA with her sister, Jenny, who was married to Mick Fleetwood. He suggested that I call her up and get her to come and join me on the tour. This all came quite out of the blue, but I summoned up the courage to ring and she said yes. It was a lot to take in considering how little I'd seen of her during the previous three years. She joined us in Buffalo on 6 July, where we were playing to a crowd of 45,000 at the War Memorial Stadium. It was not an auspicious start. I was almost blind from a severe bout of conjunctivitis, caught from Yvonne Elliman, with whom I was still carrying on, and so drunk from nerves that I managed to crash into a huge potted plant on the stage. But that night, when I played 'Have You Ever Loved a Woman?' the words had a very special meaning.

CHAPTER NINE
EL AND NELL

My relationship with Pattie, now that we could actually be together, was not the incredibly romantic affair that it has been portrayed as being. Rather than being a mature, grounded relationship, it was built on drunken forays into the unknown. With what I know now about my condition, I don't know if we ever really had a chance for anything better, even if we had got together earlier, because there was always going to be my addiction in the way. Having said that, we were having a lot of fun, and we were really in love with each other, but we were on the road, and although it was great to finally be together without having to hide, reality would have to be faced sooner or later.

Part of my denial about what was going on in my life encompassed the way I needed to identify Pattie. Calling her Pattie really meant acknowledging that she was still George's wife, so as a kind of subconscious sidestep I nicknamed her 'Nell', or 'Nelly', sometimes 'Nello'. She didn't seem to mind, even though it meant becoming known in this persona by everyone involved in her new life. I suppose I may have been paying homage to my favourite great-aunt, or just trying to relegate her to a sort of barmaid status, so that I wasn't so much in awe of her.

Difficult to say. Back then, my thoughts and actions were never easy to interpret, even for me. But it suited her, and it stuck.

The Ocean Boulevard tour continued throughout most of 1974. We played forty-nine sold-out shows in the US, Japan and Europe, almost all of them in huge stadiums, and much of the time is a blackout. Looking back on this time, however, I think that Roger was probably right to have been worried about sending me out to play in these vast arenas. After having been out in the cold for so long, I was nervous and rusty on stage, and so tended to avoid playing the solos that people had paid to come and hear. My live guitar playing didn't really pick up until we started playing smaller venues in the US the following year. Nell stayed till the end of the first leg of the American tour and then went home. The minute she left, I was off having one-night stands and behaving outrageously with any woman who happened to come my way, so my moral health was in appalling condition and only likely to get worse, while my drinking was steadily increasing. It seemed like I was already trying to sabotage my relationship with Pattie, as if now that I had her, I didn't want her any more. There were only a couple of other people who were inclined to keep up with me, Legs Larry and, to a certain extent, Carl, but a lot of the others would try to avoid us. Occasionally Roger would tell me to slow up, and I might think about it for a while, before pouring myself another drink to drown it, or I would get angry and tell him to mind his own business.

When the tour was over, because of the success of 'I Shot The Sheriff', Tom and Roger thought it would be good to head down to the Caribbean to follow up the reggae thing, and they arranged a trip to record in Jamaica, where they felt we might dig around and get some roots influence. Tom was a great believer in tapping the source, and I was happy to go along with this since it would mean that Pattie and me would also be able to have a kind of honeymoon. Kingston was a great place to work. Wherever we went, there was music in the air. Everyone was singing all the time, even the maids in the hotel, and it really got into my blood, but recording with the Jamaicans was something else. I really couldn't keep up with their intake of ganja, which was massive. If I had tried to do what they were doing, I would either have passed out or started having hallucinations. We were working at Dynamic Sound Studios in Kingston, and there were people coming in and out all the time, smoking these huge 'trumpet' joints and making so much smoke in the room that you couldn't see who was there and who wasn't. We were doing a couple of songs with Peter Tosh, who looked like he was unconscious a lot of the time, just slumped in a chair. Then he would play brilliantly while we were cutting the track, playing his wah-wah reggae chop, but as soon as we stopped, he would just go back into a kind of trance.

I was seriously interested in reggae, but having already got acquainted with Bob Marley and the Wailers, I wasn't sure where to go next. On reflection, Toots and the Maytals would have been ideal, they are now one of my all-time favourite bands, but back then we hadn't made that connection. The problem was, in my drunkenness, I was being led around quite a lot by Tom, and sometimes even Roger, with them making assumptive artistic choices on my behalf, sometimes disastrously so. Just going to Jamaica was not going to be enough, and trying to make a bridge between reggae and rock music, without having some kind of plan, was not going to be an easy thing to do. It had happened, in a very naive way, with 'I Shot The Sheriff', but we had done that without really thinking about it, and when we did start to think about it, it was already too late. We found ourselves either playing full reggae or rock 'n' roll. We did one song on the album called 'Don't Blame Me', written by George Terry, which was a sort of sequel to 'I Shot The Sheriff', but it didn't sit well. It felt like we were milking a formula, which in effect was what we were doing, and that almost always backfires. Though there was a lot of stuff in the can, the album we ended up with, which I called *There's One in Every Crowd*, was really just another rock 'n' roll record, which owed little to Jamaican music or reggae.

The fact is, I was trying to find my way. I was also beginning to discover during this period that the more I heard great musicians and singers, the more I wanted to step back. For example we brought in Marcy Levy, a beautiful singer from Detroit, who sang with Delaney and Bonnie and Leon Russell, to work on this album, and in order to give her more opportunity to sing I began to minimise my output. I found I liked playing the role of sideman, and I was happy to push the others to the front. It was my band, after all, so there was no doubt as to who was leader. I ended up asking her to join the band full-time, apparently much to the dismay of Leon, who had already accused me of 'stealing' two other young musicians he had been playing with, Jamie Oldaker and Dick Sims. So far as they were concerned, however, it was probably a much more attractive proposition to come and work with me, and tour the world.

The 'honeymoon' that Nell and I had planned was short-lived. She flew out to join me in Ocho Rios where, after a few days, I broke my toe trying to kick down the door of the bathroom, in which she had locked herself after a playful fight, and had to be taken to Kingston Hospital to have it strapped up. This was followed by the news that my half-brother, Brian, had been killed in a motorcycle accident in Canada. Though I hadn't seen much of him since we were teenagers and we were hardly close, the news still saddened me because I had liked him a lot. I asked Nell to accompany me to the funeral, but I don't remember much about the journey there. It was a grand excuse for me to get blitzed. But it was a tough event for her. She had never met my family, and I had seen very little of my mother over the years. I recall that the funeral service was a Catholic one and that I had no idea what was going on, never having attended a Catholic ceremony before. The other thing I remember was being unable to feel my own grief, maybe because my mother's was so strong. She was seriously devastated by Brian's sudden death, and I was too numb to be able to properly console her.

For the first year of our life together, Nell and I were constantly on the move. I had made so much money from the Ocean Boulevard tour that Roger insisted that we moved to the Bahamas for a year to save us from what would have been punitive income tax. This was to be our real honeymoon. We rented an estate on Paradise Island, a beautiful, tiny island at the north-east end of Nassau, which is connected to the main island by a bridge. Richard Harris had a house at one end, while at the other was a large hotel complex. Smack in the middle, going right across the island, was an estate that belonged to a man called, coincidentally, Sam Clapp, a partner of the international financier Bernie Cornfeld, and it consisted of a big Miami-style house and another Polynesian-style one. It was all beautifully done and quite modern, and one of the things I liked best about it was the fact that it had a music system which extended to every room. I'd never seen anything like this. It seemed quite revolutionary.

To begin with, life on Paradise Island was idyllic. We soaked up the sun, the sea and the sand, and basked in the pleasure of being alone and together. My drinking ceased to be abusive or solitary and became restricted to enjoying a few beers throughout the day. It was a way of life that didn't last long, however, because as I got used to Paradise, and I was brown and healthy, my tendency became more and more to live indoors in the air con-ditioning. I couldn't take the outside any more. I just withdrew and started to drink, mostly brandy and vodka. Because drink was dirt cheap over there, hard drinking was a way of life for the residents. Virtually overnight my drinking escalated, and within the space of that year, I became a 100 per cent, full-blown alcoholic.

From Paradise Island I embarked with the band on a tour of Australia, where my drunkenness seemed to fit in, as if one was encouraged to behave like that. I remember that one of the forms it took was an obsession I developed with arm-wrestling. I'd pick on people in bars and challenge them. They could always beat me on my right arm, but no one, even huge people, could defeat me on my left arm, which is very strong. This was pretty harmless, but every now and then I would go over the top and do things in public in front of Nell that were totally inappropriate. I remember getting into trouble one night at a big dinner, when I loudly asked the wife of the host if she'd like to take a bath with me. This seemed funny to me at the time, but it wasn't for Nell or any of the other people who were directly affected. There was always this madman inside of me trying to get out, and drink gave him permission. A diary entry of mine from the mid-seventies, written while on holiday on a yacht in Greece, reads: 'I am sitting here drinking vodka and lemonade . . . having a party of my own. I am very sad and pissed . . . I've been dreaming about what I would do to the first customs man who questions me about my guitar, or who, worse still, just touches it.' It was my normal thing when I was pissed, to always contest authority, so a customs official, or a policeman, or a concierge or anyone else with a uniform, would get the sharp end of my tongue, and then it would be left up to someone like Roger or Alphi to clean up the mess, or bail me out, make apologies, pay the bill or whatever it might take to redress the situation. Sometimes I'd invent mock situations in order to pick a fight. I'd say 'You've insulted my wife,' and use that as a launch pad for an indignant shouting match against some innocent person I'd taken a dislike to.

A notorious incident of this kind took place during the time we were living on Paradise Island, when I was invited to go to

Tulsa, Oklahoma, to perform in a jam to celebrate the anniversary of Cain's Ballroom, a very famous dance hall that had been open since the days of vaudeville, and which was a popular venue for bands. Because of my connection with all the Tulsa musicians, I decided I was going to go. I flew to Miami and from there to Tulsa, but by the time I got there I was so drunk I was warlike. I had got in some kind of altercation on the plane and they had called ahead to the Tulsa police who were waiting for me when the plane landed, and I was arrested. When we got to the County Gaol, one of the cops involved used my middle name when charging me, saying 'Are you Eric Patrick Clapton?' I replied to this, 'Nobody calls me Patrick. You don't have the right to call me that,' and then launched into a tirade against him. As a result of this I was thrown in the Drunk Tank. I kept trying to tell them who I was, but they refused to believe me, so I told them to go and find a guitar and I would prove who I was by playing to them. They did this, and then they let me out. The following morning there was a large photograph of me staring out from behind the bars of the Tank on the front page of the local newspaper, the *Tulsa Tribune*.

Flying off to jam with other artists was a good excuse to get away from Paradise Island. I played twice with the Stones, in New York and LA, as part of their Tour of the Americas, and in August I flew to New York for a session with Dylan, who was working on the album that was to become *Desire*. I remember feeling very elated that I had been asked to play, but when I arrived it turned out to be a very odd situation. There were already two or three bands waiting to go into the studio with him, including an English band called Kokomo, and every now and then you'd get a bunch of people who had come out, and everyone would ask 'Well, what was it like?' It was not unlike being in a doctor's waiting room. I was one of five guitarists present, and when I went in he wasn't particularly communicative. It was one of those awkward times when I didn't really know what was expected of me. There was no question of a rehearsal. He played the song once or twice and then moved on to the next one.

There were something like twenty-four musicians in the studio that night, all playing these incredibly incongruous instruments, like accordion and violin, and it sounded great, but I had no idea what was going on. I felt like Mr Jones again, and remembered the first time we had met in London. I played along as best I could, but it was very hard to keep up with him, he was racing from song to song. Then it was suddenly over and he left. I couldn't wait to get out for some fresh air. Later he told me that he had recut all the songs again with just a drummer and a bass, and that those were the tracks he was going to use.

I did eventually cut a track with Bob, on our next studio album, *No Reason To Cry*, which was recorded during the winter of 1975 at the Band's Shangri-La Studios in Malibu, California. This was a drunk and disorderly kind of album and we didn't really know where we were going. We had no producer to begin with, other than our engineer, Ralph Moss, and we just lost direction. Part of the problem was that the setting of the studios and the situation were so idyllic that I for one couldn't get myself together sufficiently to write any songs. After a couple of days, I was ready to leave, so I called in the Band's own producer, Rob Fraboni, to help us. Richard Manuel then came up with a song called 'Beautiful Thing', which was the first number we recorded and got us off to a start.

At the time, Bob was living in a tent in the garden of the studios, and every now and then he would appear and have a drink and then disappear again just as quickly. I asked him if he would contribute something for the album, write, sing, play, anything. One day he came in and offered me a song called 'Sign Language', which he had played me in New York. He told me that he had written the whole song in one sitting, without any understanding of what it was about. I said I didn't care what it was about, I just loved the words and the melody, and the chord sequence was great. Since Bob doesn't restrict himself to any one way of doing a song, we recorded it three different ways, with me dueting with him. It also gave me the opportunity to overdub Robbie Robertson, doing his wang-bar thing that I love so much; all in all it's my favourite track on the album.

One of the more bizarre guest appearances I made during this period was in the south of Ireland in September, when I was approached by Kevin McClory, the Irish producer of the James Bond movie *Thunderball*. He was mounting a charity extravaganza at Straffan House, his home in Kildare, in the form of a celebrity circus, which he called Circasia, in which he wanted me to perform alongside stars like Sean Connery, John Huston, Burgess Meredith and Shirley MacLaine. Roger thought it would be a good idea, and as Burgess Meredith, star of *Day of the Locusts*, was one of my heroes, I agreed to turn up. It turned out to be an unforgettable event, and led to another interesting fork in the road.

On the first night I met John Huston and sat in a circle of people around him, all of us spellbound, listening to his reminiscences. The following day, myself, Burgess and Shirley were gathered up and given our skit to rehearse. I had always had a crush on Shirley, since seeing her in *Irma la Douce* wearing a tiny little teddy. What legs! I was keen to meet her, as she was known to be a very feisty lady. Our routine was loosely based on a piece of Chaplinesque slapstick. Burgess and I were dressed as clowns, with wigs, big funny noses and great big shoes, and she was playing the Chaplin tramp. The idea was that she would wander around the ring and we would follow, each carrying a custard pie behind our backs. We would sneak up behind her, with the intention of hitting her on each side of her face with the pies, but just as we were about to hit her, she would bend down to do up her shoelaces, and we would end up hitting each other in the face, across her bent back. There were two shows, the first was a free performance for handicapped kids, where the routine went without a hitch, with me and Burgess smothering one another with whipped cream, which the audience thought was hilarious. The evening show was the earner with tickets going for £5,000 a head, and of course by this time, bearing in mind that we were in Ireland, the entire cast, with the exception of Shirley, had got blind drunk. Poor Mr Connery lost control and went round the ring hanging underneath the horse he was supposed to be riding, which was five times more entertaining than what he was supposed to do, and Burgess and I took our cue from that. When Shirley bent down to do her laces, instead of hitting each other, we waited for her to straighten up again and then hit her full in the face, one on each side. She was furious, and chased us out of the ring, screaming blue murder. Roger told me that after that, she would occasionally call the office to remark on whatever media trouble I had got myself into, still smouldering. Gorgeous woman.

The place where we were put to stay was a charming little hotel in the village of Straffan, called Barberstown Castle, part of which dates back to the thirteenth century. I immediately fell in love with it, possibly because the first night we were there, I got blind drunk without parting with a penny. I literally stood at the bar and drank all night and I never saw any money change hands. I thought to myself, 'This is heaven,' and I rang Roger the next day and told him, 'You've got to come and see this. You won't believe it.' A few weeks later, we came out together and stayed the night and had the best time, getting pissed with the locals, all of whom, through our rose-tinted spectacles, seemed to be incredible characters and great singers. It had the same effect on Roger as it had on me, and we made the decision between the two of us to buy it.

Over the next few years, we got some good use out of it, and a lot of very funny and sometimes strange stuff would go on there, usually in the bar. The restaurant was the actual earning part of the business, and the bar was where the locals and myself would get completely legless every night. At the end of a good night, it would look like a hurricane had swept through the room, broken glass and furniture everywhere, bodies half hidden under carpets, and me unconscious behind the bar. In the morning the cleaning girls would come in and within ten minutes the place would look as good as new, ready for a lunchtime session. When, eventually, I became sober, it was decided that we should sell it. By then I hardly went there, and in fact it would have been a reasonably dangerous place to go. But I have extremely fond memories of my times there, in the company of wonderful characters, like Breda, our manageress, and her erstwhile boyfriend Joe Kilduff, my drinking buddy. They were great days.

In the spring of 1976, after a year of living in the Bahamas and touring Australia, America and Japan, I eventually returned to England where, for a while, Nell and I enjoyed a period of real domestic bliss. Hurtwood was in a terrible state back then. It hadn't had a lick of paint or much care of any kind, because Alice and me had ignored and neglected it from the day that Monster had started to restore it. It was borderline squalid. When we had a couple of dogs living there, Jeep, a Weimaraner, who was my first dog since childhood, and Sunshine, a Golden Retriever, we would let them crap in the house because we were too stoned to clear it up. The curtains and upholstery were beginning to rot. Nell immediately threw herself into trying to make the house nice again, starting with putting an Aga in the kitchen. She was a very social lady, and wanted to make the place ready to receive visitors.

Like me, Nell enjoyed a drink, though it may not have been to the same extent, and so drinking became an accepted part of our life, and our activities branched off from that. The heroin culture, which I had been immersed in with Alice, had consisted mostly of watching TV or movies, when we were not actually pursuing the drug itself. What now followed on from that was a much more pub-orientated lifestyle, starting with the Windmill, the pub at the top of the drive, and going over to Ripley to watch cricket matches and drink in a convivial manner with friends at the cricket club.

Nell met Guy and Gordon, my old school friends, and once again they became part of my network. We were an outgoing couple, and we started to collect other couples. Local married couples became part of our social circle; some were drinkers, others just liked to come round and have dinner. My life suddenly changed from being very introverted to becoming part of this golden duo, holding dinner parties and going out to premieres and things like that. It was much the same for Nell who had been holed up for years in the gothic gloom of Friar Park with George. It was a fantastic time for me, getting to know all my Ripley friends again. We started something called the Ripley Spoons Orchestra. We'd all go to the cricket club, where Chris Stainton would play the piano and there'd be ten or fifteen people, all playing spoons and having a great sing-song. For a while, Nell and I really felt part of the community.

Sometime during this period, Nell asked if I would meet a man who had begun dating her youngest sister Paula. The idea was that as the acting head of the family, I was supposed to give this guy the once-over, to ascertain whether he was worthy or not. This suited my grandiose view of myself, and I went up to town to have lunch with him. His name was Nigel Carroll and I liked him instantly. We had a lot of things in common and became good friends, and of course he got the thumbs up from me. He was pretty much in love with Paula, and I could tell that he was a capable and honest man, but unfortunately for him she wasn't ready to settle. It was tragic, because Paula had a little boy called

William, who Nigel had become very attached to, and when the affair ended, he was broken-hearted. I asked him if he would like to come on the road with me to take his mind off things, and for the next several years he was my personal assistant.

I still saw George, who never lost the habit of coming round to play with me if he'd written something. One Christmas Eve he came over and when I answered the door, he squirted a water pistol in my mouth, and it was full of brandy. There would be this edgy relationship going on between us, and he'd often make sarcastic little remarks referring to what had taken place. He wouldn't hide it under the carpet. Sometimes we'd laugh, and sometimes it would be uncomfortable, but it was the only way we could go on. One night we were sitting in the hall at Hurtwood when he said, 'Well, I suppose I'd better divorce her,' to which I replied, 'Well, if you divorce her, then that means I've got to marry her!' like something out of a Woody Allen script. Over the years our relationship developed into a sort of cagey brotherliness, with him, of course, being the elder brother. There was no doubt that we loved one another, but when we actually got together it could get quite competitive and edgy, and I very rarely got the last word.

Towards the end of the year, an invitation came in to attend a big party celebrating the demise of the Band. It came as a bit of a shock. I had no idea that they were intending to stop working, but I remember Robbie grizzling about 'the road', back at Shangri-La Studios. It was a tremendous honour to be asked to play. A lot of very respectable players were scheduled to perform, including Van Morrison and Muddy Waters, not to mention Bob himself. The new hotshot director of *Taxi Driver*, Martin Scorsese, was filming it for posterity, and the Band were going to play their final set, with a host of guests getting up. The show was being staged at Winterland, a big dance hall in San Francisco that had flourished through the sixties alongside the Fillmore. Pattie and I flew over a couple of days before, and started some hardcore partying. It was great to meet up with Robbie and Richard again. Needless to say, me and Richard got along famously. We were cut out of the same cloth, and I loved all the other guys. They were like family to me. The gig was great, except at the beginning of 'Further Up The Road' my guitar strap came undone, and I just about caught my guitar before it fell to the floor. Van and Muddy stole the show, although 'The Night They Drove Old Dixie Down' stands as one of my favourite filmed live performances of all time.

One day, an old beaten-up bus rolled up the drive at Hurtwood, and out of it stepped Ronnie Lane, whom I had known since I first met the Small Faces in a guitar shop in the West End. We had got talking and they had invited me down to the studio where they were practising. I remember watching them playing and thinking how great they were. The one I was attracted to most, in terms of personality, was Ronnie. He was sharp and well dressed and very funny, as well as being very gifted musically. Then, when we were doing rehearsals at Ronnie Wood's for the Rainbow concert, he would drop by and I remember thinking that I'd like to spend more time with him one day.

Ronnie was about to turn a corner in his life. He had left his first wife, Sue, and had taken up with a woman called Kate Lambert, who was into the world of travellers and carts, and the gipsy lifestyle, so he was going down a road that was already familiar to me from the Ormsby-Gore clan. I was immediately interested, particularly since I'd always known that we had a lot in common and that sooner or later we'd probably get together. They parked their bus outside the house and stayed with us for a while. They told us that they had bought a 100-acre farm on the Welsh borders called Fishbowl, and were living there with a motley group of musicians and friends. It caught me like a bug, and I couldn't wait to go up and visit them.

My fascination with the life that Ronnie described to me went back to something that I had been exposed to a little bit with Steve when he was forming Traffic and I was forming Cream, and we had discussed the philosophy of what we wanted to do. Steve had said for him it was all about unskilled labour, where you just played with your friends, and fitted the music around that. It was the opposite of virtuosity, and it rang a bell with me because I was trying so hard to escape the pseudo-virtuoso image that I had helped create for myself. Ronnie was into the same kind of thing, but it was much more convoluted because he was actually trying to combine his music with the running of a circus. It was called *Ronnie Lane's Passing Show*, and it featured circus acts like jugglers, fire-eaters and dancing girls, as well as the band he had assembled, which he called Slim Chance, featuring, amongst others, Bruce Rowland, Kevin Westlake, and Gallagher and Lyle. They would put up a big tent, and then put up posters in the village, all done with a very casual approach. Whereas a real circus would have to get permission to go on the land a year in advance, they'd just turn up and put it up before anyone knew they were coming, and hope to get away with it. A certain number of the community would turn up and, if they were lucky, they'd probably make enough money to break even. This was a rarity, however, and the whole thing eventually fell to pieces.

Nell and I started to go and visit Ronnie and Kate in Wales. We'd just turn up and blend in, and although there wasn't a lot of room in the cottage, it didn't seem to matter. I loved hanging out with Ronnie, because we were both drinkers, and as we spent more time together, Ronnie's musicality also began to rub off on me. Just like him, I was going through a very different period in my music. I was getting increasingly interested in country music, and making music just for fun. I remember we once chartered a boat and sailed round the Med, and did a few shows off the boat in places like Ibiza and Barcelona. The band consisted of me and Ronnie, Charlie Hart on violin, Bruce Rowland on drums and

Brian Belshaw on bass, and we'd sometimes set up on the quay and play like buskers, while Nell and Katy would dress up in cancan outfits and dance. It was a complete fiasco and we certainly didn't make any money, but it was a lot of fun. On another occasion, on St Valentine's Day 1977, we played a secret gig at the village hall in Cranleigh, a village near Hurtwood, under the name of Eddie Earthquake and the Tremors, playing songs like 'Alberta' and 'Goodnight Irene', and encouraging the audience of locals to dance and join in the singing.

What it was about, for me, was drinking and escaping my responsibilities as a band leader, and the music reflected this. It was very homespun and mostly acoustic. It was in just this spirit that the song 'Wonderful Tonight' was written. I wrote the words for this song one night at Hurtwood, while I was waiting for Nell to get dressed to go out to dinner. We had a busy social life at that time, and Nell was invariably late getting ready. I was downstairs waiting, and was playing the guitar to kill time. Eventually I got fed up, and went upstairs to the bedroom where she was still deciding what to wear. I remember telling her, 'Look, you look wonderful, OK? Please don't change again. We must go, or we'll be late.' It was the classic domestic situation between a couple; I was ready and she wasn't. I went back downstairs to my guitar, and the words of the song just came out very quickly. They were written in about ten minutes, and actually written in anger and frustration. I wasn't that enamoured with it as a song. It was just a ditty as far as I was concerned, that I could just as easily have thrown away. The first time I played it was round the campfire up at Ronnie's, when I was playing it for Nell, and playing it for Ronnie too, and he liked it. I remember thinking, 'I suppose I'd better keep this.'

'Wonderful Tonight' ended up on the album *Slowhand*, which was the first record I cut with Glyn Johns as producer in the spring of 1977. Over the years, the name 'Slowhand' had stuck, and was especially popular with the American band members, maybe because it had a western ring to it. Glyn had a terrific track record. He was best known in England for his work with the Stones, but he had also worked with the Eagles and really understood American musicians. He was a disciplinarian who didn't like people mucking about or wasting time. When we were in the studio he expected to work, and would get frustrated if there was any time-wasting. Even though we were all getting stoned and drunk, we responded to that quite well. He brought out the best in us, and as a result that album has great playing and a great atmosphere.

Me and Nell and Dave Stewart designed the artwork for the album, which is credited to 'El and Nell Ink'. Amongst the various snapshots pasted across the inside cover, including one of me and Nell kissing, was a photograph of a smashed-up Ferrari, a reminder of an incident that very nearly led to my premature demise. I collect Ferraris, an obsession that goes back to my friendship with George. One day in the late sixties he arrived at my house in a dark blue Ferrari 356 GTC. I'd never seen one in the flesh before and my heart melted. At that point, it was like seeing the most beautiful woman on earth, and I decided, there and then, that even though I couldn't drive, I was going to have one too. He gave me the number of the dealers, I called them, and got driven over to the showroom in Egham, where I ordered a new 356 GTC like George's, for the princely sum of four grand. They delivered it to Hurtwood, and asked me if I'd like to test drive it, to which I replied, coolly, 'No, I'm too busy. Just leave it, thank you very much.' So they left it in front of the house.

I had no licence, and had only ever driven an automatic, so I set about teaching myself to drive using a clutch, in that Ferrari on the drive at Hurtwood. I loved that car, and when I was in the Dominos I toured in it, with Carl and me driving me all over England. Then I bought a Daytona and a 275 GTB, followed by a

250 GT Lusso. In those days I only had garage space for two cars, so I would buy and sell and buy and sell. The crash in the picture took place soon after we got back from touring Australia. I had been drinking on the flight all the way home, and it was still in my system. As soon as I got home, I got into the Ferrari and had probably hit about 90 mph in a very short time when a laundry van appeared and I drove straight into it. I turned his van right over. My skid marks were in a straight line and they found me with my head hanging through a side window. They had to cut me out of the car and I was badly concussed and had a pierced eardrum. I didn't know where I was for two weeks afterwards. It was a very close shave.

My drinking was getting worse all the time and I was starting to get into trouble at the Windmill, usually just verbal, but sometimes becoming physical. Then I would get into the car and crash it into the fence between the pub and the house, a distance of about 300 yards. Drink was also affecting my performance. During one London concert in April 1977, I just walked off the stage after about forty-five minutes. It was the end of a British tour, and we'd added on another show at the Rainbow, and my system just couldn't take it. Halfway through the set I started to feel pretty strange, and it got worse and worse and I thought, 'Well, if I don't walk off now, I'm going to fall over,' so I stumbled off. Roger took me outside for some fresh air, telling me, 'You don't have to go back on boy, you don't have to go back on. Don't worry about it, if you're not feeling all right, we'll call it a day.' I sat in the dressing room for a while, then Pete Townshend, who was guesting with the band, came in and said, quite angrily, 'Is this what you call show business?' or something like that. The end result was that I traipsed back on after Pete, and got through the rest of the performance by literally miming to him playing and singing.

There were also times when I endangered my life. Returning

from Japan in the autumn of 1977, we stopped off to do a couple of shows in Honolulu. On one of the nights, I happened to know that my drummer, Jamie Oldaker, had pulled a girl and taken her back to his room, and I decided that I would spoil it, and also give him a fright. I had a ceremonial Samurai sword with me, a tourist souvenir rather than a real one, so I got myself dressed up in a pair of pyjama bottoms, into which I somehow tucked the sword and, naked apart from that, climbed out on to the balcony of my hotel room. Then, edging myself round the ledge which protruded from the wall of the hotel, and which connected the balconies, I climbed from balcony to balcony to the room where I knew Jamie was sleeping. When I finally climbed through his window, he was furious. We were thirty floors up and I was drunk, and the poor girl was freaked out of her mind. I was a bit disappointed and I couldn't see what all the fuss was about. It was supposed to be a brilliant joke.

Worse was to come. There was a knock at the door, and when Jamie opened it, there were two guys with guns outside, pointing them at the door from a crouch position. Someone had spotted me out on the ledge and thought I was some kind of an assassin, and had called the police. When they realised that it was just a drunken idiot making a fool of himself, they begrudgingly let me go, but it took a lot of sweet talk from Roger, who was getting quite good at this sort of thing. Unfortunately such behaviour did little for my reputation, and when in November 1978 Roger had to cancel a show in Frankfurt for technical reasons, the headlines of one of the big national papers screamed 'ERIC CLAPTON – TOO DRUNK TO PLAY'. The tour in question was a little jaunt dreamed up by Roger, both to promote our new album and to be the subject of a candid documentary film about life on the road, to be called *Eric Clapton's Rolling Hotel*. The idea was that the band would tour Europe by rail, aboard not an ordinary train, but three coaches that had once been part of Goering's own private train, which Roger had tracked down somewhere in Europe. They consisted of a drawing room coach, a restaurant coach and a sleeping car, and they would be hooked up to trains which happened to be going in the direction we wanted. Roger thought this would be great fun for one and all. I thought so too, and went along with it. After all, I loved trains, and would be able to drink and lord it up without offending members of the public. Maybe that's why Roger dreamed it up in the first place, to keep me out of harm's way. I remember we had a great promoter on the tour, a Danish guy called Erik Thomsen, who was a friend of Roger's and who was in Stiggy's league when it came to pranks. He would bait me or Roger, hurling pathetic insults at us in a very strong Danish accent until we would finally have to do something about it. Usually it would be something fairly mild, like throwing his shoe out the window of a travelling coach, or running over his precious aluminium briefcase with a lorry. But on this one occasion we went too far and we cut off all his hair, painted his head with blue ink, cut off the legs of his trousers, and threw him off the train in Hamburg in the middle of the night, leaving him in the goods yard with no money, knowing full well that he was supposed to have a business meeting with Sammy Davis Jr the following morning. Sadly, he is no longer with us. He passed away quite recently and I miss him. He was a great character, and an incredible sport, and we will not see his like again.

The film, which was produced by a guy called Rex Pyke, a BBC producer famous for his documentary *Akenfield*, was luckily never released. It showed me in an extremely unflattering light, as I was intoxicated and deranged in most of the footage. It includes a sequence shot in Paris, during a visit to one of the shows by Stigwood, in which, fuelled by drink, I grabbed the camera, aimed it at him and started to aggressively question him on the subject of an old chestnut of mine, namely my suspicion that he had 'creamed off' most of the profits from Cream to finance the Bee

Gees. Robert remained quite unfazed by this, and quietly replied, in his posh English accent, 'This is not the right time to speak about this. We should talk about this another time,' while I shouted maniacally, 'This is my film, and I want it in.'

The album we were promoting on this tour was the follow-up to *Slowhand*, which we had named *Backless*, a title which came about after we had played a gig with Dylan at Blackbushe Airport. It referred to the fact that I thought he had eyes in the back of his head, and knew exactly what was going on around him all the time. It had been a difficult album to cut, drugs and alcohol taking centre stage, which Glyn found hard to cope with, and there was bad blood building up everywhere. The only song on the album that I really rated was 'Golden Ring', which was written about the situation between me, Nell and George. It referred, in part, to her response to the news that George was getting married again. She took it quite hard, and I, in my arrogance, found that hard to understand. So I wrote this song about the peculiarity of our triangle, which finishes with the words 'If I gave to you a golden ring,/Would I make you happy, would I make you sing?'

The fact is that at this time, for whatever reason, me and Nell were not particularly happy. My diary for 6 September, 1978, reads 'Sex life is pretty barren at the moment, we don't seem to be getting on too well, there's nothing in particular to blame, unless it's the stars, we just seem to be heading in different directions.' Nor did my often chauvinistic behaviour improve the situation. For example I noted on 16 October, 'In the evening Nell…was giving advice to Simon's ex-girlfriend in the kitchen for two hours, so my dinner was taken out of the oven and popped back in again, by the time I got it, it was burned and dried up, so I shouted at her good, loud and long, but she didn't seem very repentant, and I got a sore throat.' I was also picking up girls as soon as I got on the road, aided and abetted by Roger. 'Roger started to wind me up,' I wrote in Madrid on 5 November, 'about some incredible-looking bird who he says has turned up at the gig.' Later that day, I continued: 'I have got a £150 bet with Roger that he can't pull a nice clean normal bird for me . . . He had better, cause there was nothing under fifty years old in sight.' Then when on 19 November, Nell finally came to visit me in Brussels for a couple of days, I noted: 'I went to sleep with all my clothes on, I just can't get it on with Nell now that she is here; it's so sad for us, but the road is the road and home is home and never the twix should mix.'

Coming to visit me on tour was a rarity for Nell, as Roger and I had long ago come to a strict agreement that there should be no women on tour. This was a rule that applied to everybody, from the band leader downwards and it was completely transparent; everyone knew what it was really about. Nell, of course, was not too happy about this, and she often told me she felt isolated and lonely. The situation wasn't helped by the fact that whenever I was unfaithful I'd tell her all about it, on the basis that if I was honest with her, and confessed to what I had been doing, then it would somehow make it all OK. She would rail at me occasionally, but I think her main concern was to try to somehow preserve the status quo, in the hope that things would change, but what was her alternative? To leave and start again with someone else?

Everything finally came to a head when I found myself falling in love with one of these girls, or at least thinking I was falling in love. 'No more tequila for me boy,' I wrote in the diary on 28 November, 'woke up with all the clobber on – I am in love again and it hurts.' The woman in question was a young girl called Jenny McLean, and the unforgivable thing I did was to allow Nell, sometime early in the following year, to catch us together at Hurtwood. She left the house in floods of tears, having packed her bags and phoned her sister Jenny to come and collect her. A couple of days later she flew to LA, where she went to stay with Rob Fraboni and his wife Myel. At that point, I did not give up

Jenny, but went on tour to Ireland, where she came out to visit me. On 17 March, which was Nell's birthday, I recorded in my diary that 'the gig was great and sweet Jen flew in to make the day perfect. We talked and talked about our respective wounds.' The entry finishes with the words 'I am a bad man and I think the world better roll on without me for a while anyway. All in love is fair.'

Ironically it was Roger who saved the day for me and Nell. When I got back home from Ireland, he told me over a game of pool at his house that I should be discreet in my meetings with Jenny, or we'd get snapped by a photographer and it would be all over the papers. I said that was rubbish, and ended up drunkenly betting him the ridiculous sum of £10,000 that he couldn't get my picture in the papers. The following morning, to my utter amazement and horror, Nigel Dempster's column in the *Daily Mail* announced 'Rock star Eric Clapton will marry Pattie Boyd'.

Roger had pulled a fast one. I screamed at him that he had no right to make such huge decisions about my personal life. When I'd calmed down a bit, he asked me if it wasn't time to decide whether or not I wanted to stay with Nell, or break with her forever. 'How do I get her back?' I replied. He said that she wouldn't have seen the story yet, and that I should call her and ask her to marry me. When I phoned Rob's house in LA, Nell was out, down at the beach in Malibu. I told him to give her a simple message: 'Please marry me.' When she called back later, I swore to her that I had given up Jenny, and proposed. She burst into tears and accepted.

The ceremony finally took place on 27 March at the Apostolic Assembly of Faith in Christ Church in Tucson, Arizona, the town where, the following day, we were due to play the first date of a major American tour. There was a Mexican preacher, the Revd Daniel Sanchez, and a black organist, who looked a bit like Billy Preston. The band and roadies all wore rented tuxedoes and my outfit consisted of a white tux with black edging round the jacket, a $200 white cowboy hat and cowboy boots, while Nell wore a cream satin dress by Ozzie Clarke. Roger gave her away, and she was attended by two maids of honour, Myel Fraboni and Chris O'Dell. Rob Fraboni acted as my best man. The preacher read from the First Letter of St Paul to the Corinthians, in which he praises love. The service was short and sweet, funky and soulful, which was just what we wanted.

When the ceremony was over, we all returned to our hotel where they'd put aside a room for the reception. The table was dominated by the usual wedding cake about five tiers tall, and there was a photographer who Roger had hired to take pictures. Typically, after the cutting of the cake, when he came over to photograph me and Nell together, I threw a piece of cake at him, covering his beautiful Nikon camera. He obviously felt completely out of his depth, because he didn't dare make a fuss, and then a food fight started. Soon everyone was covered in cake. We didn't eat the cake, we just wore it. The following night we played our first show of a three-month tour at the community centre in Tucson, and when we played 'Wonderful Tonight', I brought Nell up on stage so that I could sing it to her. The reception from the crowd was ecstatic.

WHAT A GOOD LITTLE BOY
AM i (THE NEW e.c.) ugh!

CHAPTER TEN

THE END OF THE ROAD

However much I might have thought I loved Pattie at the time, the truth is that the only thing that I couldn't live without was alcohol. This really made my need or ability to commit to anything, even marriage, pretty inconsequential, and anyway, it was only a matter of time before the 'no women on the road' rule was invoked, and then I'd be off and running again. Pattie came with me to Albuquerque, New Mexico, then to El Paso, and from there to all the gigs till we got to San Antonio, Texas. At each show I would bring her up on stage and sing 'Wonderful Tonight' to her. But after the San Antonio gig, I told her that she must go back to England. It was men-only time again, and I had had enough of domestic bliss. She was not at all happy about this, and of course as soon as she was gone, it was back to business as usual.

One of the first things that Pattie did when she got back to England was set about organising a party for all our English friends to celebrate our wedding. It was set for Saturday, 19 May, when there was a break in my tour schedule, and was to take place in the garden at Hurtwood, where a huge marquee had been erected. Guests were instructed to turn up 'about 3.00 p.m.' and were told that they didn't have to bring presents if they didn't want to. 'If you are free,' we had printed on the invites, 'try and make it, it's bound to be a laugh.' There was no real form to the party. People were just expected to turn up whenever they wanted, wearing whatever they liked, and have a good time.

The first person I remember arriving was Lonnie Donegan, who arrived far too early at about 10.00 a.m., followed closely by Georgie Fame. I didn't have a clue what to do with them, and we ended up going upstairs to a small bedroom where Georgie began rolling joints. I stayed up there for most of the day getting stoned and becoming more and more paranoid as people were arriving. I really had no idea how to be a host, and couldn't cope, so instead of being around to greet everybody and offer them drinks, I hid. Eventually, some time during the evening, I went downstairs to the marquee to find this huge party going on, with hundreds of people, from all my famous musician friends to the grocer and the butcher and all the Ripleyites milling around, chattering, eating and drinking and making out in the bushes, it actually looked like the kind of party I would like to go to.

There was a stage in the marquee, the idea being that the band would consist of anyone who felt like getting up and playing. A succession of great musicians joined in the jam session that took place later in the evening, including Georgie and Lonnie, Jeff Beck, Bill Wyman, Mick Jagger, Jack Bruce and Denny Laine. I remember Denny's wife, Jo Jo, getting up to sing and then we couldn't get her off, so whoever was at the mixing board had to keep switching off whichever mike she was using, and she would just move to another one. George, Paul and Ringo also played, only missing John, who later phoned me to say that he would have been there too if he had known about it. How that came about I'll never know, suffice to say I had little to do with the invitations. Pattie had also made the mistake of giving our bedroom to Mick Jagger and Jerry Hall, so we couldn't go to bed, which I thought was completely ridiculous. So I decided to target a friend of Pattie's called Belinda, who I was convinced was going to make herself available to me at any moment. I hid in a cupboard, with the intention of pouncing on her at some point, but instead I fell asleep, and woke up later that day to find a mess that was to take two weeks to clear up.

Among the guests at this wonderful party was my mother Pat, who had become part of my life again after the death of my half-brother, Brian. Her loss had put a lot of strain on her marriage to Mac, which had gradually started to erode. To get away from it all, she came back to Ripley, where, as she slowly rekindled her child-hood friendships, she eventually decided to stay. At first she lived with Rose, until I bought her a little house on the village high street, right next to a restaurant called the Toby Jug. To begin with I was rather frightened of her. She had a quick temper, and our relationship was inclined to be tempestuous. I'd seen so little of her in my life that most of what I knew about her had come from outside sources, and I couldn't really ever be sure just what the truth about her was.

At that stage in my life, however, I made the decision that this didn't really matter, and that instead of constantly stirring things up, I should just learn to get on with her and have fun. I liked the surface that I saw, because she was very like me, particularly in the things that made us laugh, so I decided that we should use Ripley and its social scene as a way of getting reacquainted. She enjoyed a drink, so what we did was to go out to the pub to drink and socialise and use the company of others to get to know one another again. It may not have been a very direct approach to the relation-ship, because I didn't spend much time alone with her, but on the surface level it worked very well, and the fact is that, as an alco-holic, I wasn't well enough to know how to deal with deeper things.

Soon after her return, Pat had struck up a friendship with her childhood friend Sid Perrin, a charismatic man, handsome, not in the Errol Flynn mould, but rather more like W. C. Fields. Sid was extremely popular and well loved, and a kind of hero in Ripley, through his achievements as a good cricketer and footballer, but most of all as a singer. He had a tenor voice in the style of Mario Lanza, which was a bit melodramatic, almost a caricature of a voice, but he could actually carry a song very well, with a great deal of emotion. He was very gregarious and he loved the spotlight, though only on a small scale, because given the opportunity to step on to a stage, which I gave him from time to time, for instance when we played local gigs, like the Guildford civic hall, he would blanch with fear. In his own environment, however, in the village pub or in the cricket club, he shone, and Pat adored him. This made me happy too, as I had always hero-worshipped him, and I hung out with them a lot.

My developing relationship with my mum was also greatly helped by the fact that Pattie and her got on really well, and had become firm friends. As I did, they also shared an irreverent sense of humour, which could be sarcastic and cruel at times, though without any real malice. This form of humour was a Ripley trait, and a number of my boyhood friends like Guy and Gordon were all fast-witted in this area. Their repartee was quick and cutting, with a lot of teasing involved, and if you could handle yourself in those witty situations, then you were in.

Since I had begun to develop a bit of a home life with Pattie and the Ripleyites, my English humour was in full flow, and unfortunately it was the one area in which I did not gel with my band. They all came from Oklahoma, and their humour was very different. Though it too was very dry, it was parochial, and rather cowboy-orientated, having to do with events and things that were taking place in their neck of the woods, whereas ours was more music-hall stuff and silly humour. There was little cross-fertilisation in the days before Monty Python took off in America. All this struck home at the beginning of 1979 when, owing to prior commitments, George Terry left the band and I hired an English guitarist, Albert Lee.

Albert was a great guitar player who I had known since the John Mayall days, when he played in Chris Farlowe's band, and my take on him then had been that he was a brilliant player, but that he came from a more jazz or rockabilly direction, so I could admire him without thinking of him as a rival. He went on to play with Head, Hands and Feet, and over the years we became good friends and would, if one of us had to drop out of a gig for some reason, occasionally stand in for one another. Then he moved to America where he was in high demand as a session musician. When George left, Roger suggested that I should bring an English guitarist into the band, instead of always playing with Americans, and recommended Albert as a possible replacement. I thought this was a great idea, though knowing Roger, I suspected he'd probably had it all worked out for ages.

When I got together with Albert, we immediately bonded in our humour, sharing a love of Python and Spike Milligan. To a certain extent, music became incidental, because the kind we made, blues and R&B, came from such a strong source that it would never be threatened by the difference in our influences. We formed ourselves into a mock duo called the Duck Brothers, and spent our spare time on the road entertaining ourselves by playing tunes on a couple of rare Acme Bakelite duck whistles which we had found, and which had a great tone. Unfortunately this didn't go down at all well with the Americans, who just didn't get it, and things were not helped by the fact that me and Albert were boozers, while Carl, Jamie and Dick were doing drugs of a more isolationist variety. It was the beginning of a rift which began to form between me and Albert and the rest of the guys.

By the spring and early summer of 1979, when we were

touring the States, promoting our latest album, *Backless*, this division had grown into marked bad feeling. There was a lot of paranoia in the air, reminiscent of the days of the break-up of the Dominos, and we were not spending enough time with one another in a clear-headed way for us to overcome these feelings. It just became accepted that I was going down one road with Albert, having the kind of fun we were having, while the others were doing their own thing. It got to the stage where we were even keeping different timetables. When we were on stage, it was all OK, but everything else was suffering. Unbeknownst to me, Carl Radle had become a serious heroin addict, and my condition was going downhill too. I was drinking at least two bottles a day of anything I could get my hands on. By the time the tour ended in June, things had got to such a bad state that I knew there had to be a change, so, with great trepidation, I instructed Roger to get rid of the band. He fired them all by telegram, while I looked the other way.

Over the next two years, my drinking brought me to rock bottom. It infiltrated everything I did. Even my new band was born in a pub. Gary Brooker was an old friend of mine from the Yardbirds days, when he had been keyboard player for the Paramounts. We had toured together and got on very well, and over the years I would bump into him occasionally, when he was with Procol Harum, and we had developed a friendship and mutual respect. Then in the mid-seventies he became involved in a pub not far from Hurtwood, the Parrot Inn in Forest Green, where he used to play two or three times a week, and when I was at home I would sometimes go over and jam. This had become more frequent since Pattie and I had married, and Joe Cocker's brilliant keyboard player, Chris Stainton, had also become involved. Gradually we began to put together a new outfit, consisting of me and Gary, Chris, Albert, Dave Markee on bass guitar and Henry Spinetti on drums.

After trying ourselves out on a local audience in Cranleigh village hall, we went out on the road, round Europe and the Far East, the concerts in Budokan, Tokyo, being recorded for our first album together, which was released in May, under the title of *Just One Night*. But I missed Carl, and I was riddled with guilt, because he had saved my neck at one point by sending me that tape, and I'd turned my back on him. I never saw him again. In May 1980 the news reached me that he had died of kidney failure, brought on by the effects of alcohol and narcotics, something that deep down I felt partly responsible for.

When I heard about Carl, we had just completed a UK tour, our first for eighteen months, so I was at home for a prolonged period. I became depressed and lost myself in drinking. My normal day became just sitting in front of the TV, and responding very aggressively to anybody who came to the door or who wanted me to do any work. I became very negative about everything. I just wanted to stay at home and get drunk, with Pattie as a slave-cum-partner. I was drinking copious amounts of Special Brew, which I was secretly topping up with vodka, so that it looked like I was only drinking beer. Then I would take coke on top of this, which was the only point at which Pattie would join in with me, as she liked to do cocaine without the booze, so this became our meeting place.

At some point in the day, we would go off to the pub together, either to the Windmill, where we'd hang out with the landlord, or to the Ship to meet the Ripleyites. Nor did Pattie's presence get in the way of my trying to get something going with one of the barmaids, or indeed any woman that walked in the door. Then I would round people up and invite them back home, often complete strangers. My favourite thing was to pick up derelicts, or 'men of the road' as I preferred to call them, my thinking being that these were 'real' people. I'd see them walking along the road, and I'd stop the car and pick them up. They were often barking mad and talking gibberish, and I'd take them home and Pattie would have to cook dinner for them. It wasn't long before she was having to tell people not to offer me drinks if we were out, because she could see I was getting worse.

I couldn't get Carl out of my mind. The band did a short tour of Scandinavia in September and October, during which the coroner's report into his death was published. The next day, I wrote the following entry in my diary: 'I have written (unwittingly) a song for Carl Dean, and as a result I am drinking too much and wallowing in the glory of being the one who had the strings of altrering [sic] his destiny, so they say . . . doesn't it occur to anyone that I was in the front line with him? Dicken knows this . . . I haven't even read the report so why should I be so hurt and angry? I will tell you why – I loved and left the man and there will never be a day go by when he doesn't enter my heart . . . if I am guilty, then God alone will cut me down, and all will be forgiven, even those who calm me and tell me it's all a bad dream . . . We cut the song beautifully and it shall be called "e.c.c.d."'

By the time we set off, at the beginning of 1981, on a major 57-date tour of the USA, my booze intake was supplemented by large quantities of Veganin, a codeine-based sedative. I was suffering from a bad back caused, I thought, by a hefty slap from my Irish pal Joe Kilduff who I'd been drinking with a couple of months previously on one of my visits to Barberstown Castle. To begin with, I was taking around nine at a go, several times a day, but then, as the pain got worse and I couldn't sleep, I began to take more and more till I was swallowing up to fifty tablets a day. The upshot was that on Friday, 13 March, seven dates into the tour, I collapsed in agony as I came off stage in Madison, Wisconsin. We flew to St Paul, Minnesota, where Roger had me rushed into hospital. I was diagnosed with five bleeding ulcers, one of which was the size of a small orange. The doctors told Roger, who wanted to fly me back to England, that I could die at any moment since one of the ulcers was pressing on my pancreas and could burst imminently.

I was immediately admitted into United Hospital, and the following morning Roger spent his time cancelling the remains of the tour, which numbered fifty shows. It was a big enough insurance disaster for the bell to be rung at Lloyd's. They kept me in hospital for about six weeks, treating me with a drug called Tagamet. I remember one of the first questions they asked me was, 'How much are you drinking, because we think that might be your problem?' to which I replied, 'Don't be ridiculous, I'm English. We all drink there, you know. It's part of our lifestyle, and we drink strong ale, not Budweiser.' So they said, 'Well, would you ever consider trying to cut back?' and I replied, 'Of course.' The funny thing is that I don't recall missing alcohol at all while I was in hospital, perhaps because I was on so much medication, and they also allowed me to smoke, out in the corridor or outside. I actually enjoyed feeling well again and being in good health.

When I was finally released from the hospital, I felt like I had a new lease of life because my physical condition was restored. My sanity, however, hadn't been addressed at all. The doctors who treated me had cured my ulcers with drugs and repaired my overall well-being, but my mental state was still the same. I was totally ignorant about the whole subject of alcoholism. I was quite happy to admit to being an alcoholic, but only in a jokey way, I wasn't prepared to admit that it was a problem. I was still at that stage where I would say, 'I don't have a problem. I never spill a drop.'

They did address my situation mildly by telling me that it would be a good thing for me to give up drinking altogether after I left the hospital. So I made deals with them along the lines of, 'Well, if I moderate and cut it down to two or three Scotches a day, would that be all right?' and they would say, 'Fine,' without realising that they were dealing with a chronic alcoholic to whom two or three Scotches was just breakfast. When I did eventually get home, for the satisfaction of Pattie I made a half-hearted attempt to moderate, but it was really no more than me saying 'Let's have a glass of wine at lunch today instead of Special Brew.' After a couple of months, I was back on two bottles of spirits a day, and I didn't give a damn about my health.

One person who eventually shocked some sense into me regarding my drinking was Sid Perrin, whose health had rapidly deteriorated over the past year, much to the distress of my mother. He had first of all had to have a colostomy, which hit him hard. His dignity and self-respect were destroyed by having to wear the bag. Then he developed liver and kidney problems, all of which were drink-related, and he really lost his will to live. On the last occasion I saw him, visiting him in hospital with Pat, he was hallucinating and talking to people who weren't in the room. I had never seen anything like this before.

Sid died early in November, and, to a certain extent, for me Ripley died with him. It was the end of the good times. Uncle Adrian and me got incredibly drunk at his funeral and behaved in the most awful way in front of everybody, our excuse being that it was the way Sid would have liked us to behave. It was unforgivable and my mother was livid. I was very upset by Sid's passing, and in a way it showed me where I was heading. I thought to myself, 'It won't be long before this kind of thing is going to happen to me,' but instead of slowing my drinking down, it spurred me on to drink even more in a desperate attempt to try to blot it out. The fallacy about drinking, however, is that when people say they drink to forget, all it does is magnify the problem. I would have a drink to banish the problem and then, when it didn't go away, I would have another one, so the end of my drinking was really insane, because I was constantly spurred on by the hope that I could somehow get to another place. I was hiding booze everywhere, smuggling it in and out and concealing it in places I thought no one would look. I'd usually, for example, have a half bottle of vodka underneath the mat where the pedals are in the car.

My rock bottom was preceded by a number of warnings, the first of which took place during a weekend away visiting some friends in the country. We had been invited to stay with Bob Pridden, the sound engineer for the Who, who was married to Maria Noel, one of the daughters of the Earl of Gainsborough, and they lived in a house in the grounds of Exton Park, the family home in Rutland. Being full of bravado and therefore having no idea what I was taking on, I promised Pattie that I would not drink during the trip. We set off on the journey, and when we were quite close to the destination, we got lost. I spotted a telephone box and stopped to call Bob to get the final directions. While I was talking to him, I suddenly felt faint and a bit dizzy, and fell against the side of the kiosk. The blood soon came back to my head and I straightened up and finished the conversation, but I was a little perturbed.

When we arrived at the house, we were met by Bob and Maria, who showed us our room and then we had something to eat. I noticed there was no booze to be seen, and then it struck me, because I knew that Bob liked a drink, that they had obviously been told to hide or lock up all the drink. I remember getting up in the middle of the night and prowling round the house, opening every cupboard to try to find some alcohol, without any success. The next day, Bob was going duck shooting and I went with him and helped him carry his stuff, and by the time we returned I was feeling a bit agitated by not having any alcohol and suffering the first signs of withdrawal.

That night, we went out to a local restaurant, the George at Stamford, for dinner. It was a grand occasion with a lot of very posh county people, and I noticed that while we were sitting in the bar before dinner, everyone was drinking water or orange juice, which made me think that these people too had been given the 'EC Brief'. We went into dinner and I'd hardly sat down at the table when I felt the earth revolve. I was sitting upright, but the room went sideways, and the next thing I remember was coming round in the back of an ambulance. Pattie was with me, literally shaking with fear, as she had no idea what had happened to me. It turned out that I had suffered something called a 'grand mal' seizure, a kind of fit brought on by the abrupt cessation of a heavy intake of alcohol or narcotics without medical supervision. I was admitted into the Wellington Hospital in London for tests, where I was soon diagnosed as having a late-arriving form of epilepsy, which they said could have been dormant in my system for years. They then gave me the appropriate medication, which was fine, because it was more stuff to throw into the mix, more chemicals to play with.

Soon after this, at the end of November, we flew to Japan for a short eight-date tour, opening in Niigata. When we arrived at our hotel in Tokyo a few days later, I went up to my room to find I'd been given a bottle of sake, which had flakes of pure gold floating about in it, a very highly regarded gift in Japan. I drank it in one sitting, and within a few hours, I had a serious physical reaction. My body became covered from head to foot with an enormous rash, and my skin started peeling off. Somehow I got through the show, and that night I showed Roger, and he reiterated what he had been saying for months: 'You're an alcoholic.' Of course, I refused to accept it.

That Christmas we had lots of people staying at Hurtwood, close friends and family of all ages. I had asked Santa for some special thermal underwear for fishing, and on Christmas Eve, after everyone was asleep, I decided to open my presents. There I was, blind drunk, in the middle of the night, sitting under the tree opening parcels, the kind of thing I would have done when I was five. I found my precious bright green thermal underwear and put it on and went wandering. When I came to, hours later, I was lying in the cellar in my new thermals, looking like Kermit the Frog, with torches shining in my face. It was Christmas morning and everyone had panicked because I had disappeared and no one knew where I was.

Pattie had been particularly scared, because I was prone to walk out of the house in the middle of the night with no clothes on, and try to get into the car and drive off. She was at her wits' end when they found me in the cellar, and I was laughing and crying at the same time. It was a pretty ghastly experience and I remember seeing the fear in the eyes of the people that were looking at me. Pattie was understandably furious. She took me upstairs, and put me to bed. 'You're staying here till everyone's gone,' she told me. 'We're going to enjoy Christmas without you,' and she left the room, locking the door behind her. She was very clever and very wise, and she kept me in the room, feeding me just enough food and alcohol to keep me sedated. I was so confused about what had taken place, and so ashamed of the damage I had done, that I didn't put up any fight whatsoever. I knew that she was right and that I had to lie low, and just do as I was ordered for a little while.

If that wasn't bad enough, my real rock bottom took place a few days later, after the guests had all left. Early in the morning, wearing my new thermal underwear, I crept out of the house to go fishing. I drove down to the river Wey to try out the water near one of the locks. I had some brand new equipment – two Hardy carp rods and a couple of Garcia reels – and I set up to fish for pike. I'm a country boy, and I've always thought of myself as a reasonably good fisherman, but on the opposite bank were a couple of professional carp fishermen, with a tent and everything beautifully laid out. They had probably been there a day or two, and they were watching me. I was drunk, and I had just about managed to get all my gear set up when I lost my balance and fell over on to one of the rods, breaking it clean off at the handle. The other fishermen witnessed this scene, and I saw them look away in embarrassment.

That was it for me. The last vestige of my self-respect had been ripped away. In my mind being a good fisherman was the one place where I still had some self-esteem. I packed everything up again, put it in the back of the car and drove home. I picked up the phone and called Roger. When he answered, I just said to him, 'You're right. I'm in trouble. I need help,' and right away I remember having this incredible feeling of relief, mixed with terror, because I'd finally admitted to someone what I had been denying to myself for so long.

CHAPTER ELEVEN

HAZELDEN: PICKING UP THE PIECES

The reason I called Roger rather than Pattie on that fateful day was that he had become the most important person in my life. More than anybody, he was the one who had seen me in all my different conditions, and who had also pronounced, with absolute certainty, what no one else had had the nerve to tell me, that I was an alcoholic. He had obviously been researching the subject for some time, because he had already booked me into Hazelden, which was then said to be the best treatment centre for alcoholics in the world. I had no idea where it was and I didn't really care. My only stipulation was that I didn't want to know when I was going until the last moment.

On the day we left, on a cold January morning in 1982, Roger picked me up from Hurtwood and took me to Gatwick Airport. I was a bag of nerves. He flew with me on a Northwest Orient flight to St Paul, Minneapolis, the scene of my ulcer treatment only nine months previously. On the flight over, I drank the plane dry, so terrified was I that I might never be able to drink again. This is the most common fear of alcoholics. In the lowest moments of my life, the only reason that I didn't commit suicide was the fact that I knew I wouldn't be able to drink any more if I was dead. It was the only thing that I thought was worth living for, and the idea that people were about to try to remove me from alcohol was really terrible, so I drank and drank and drank, and they had to practically carry me into the clinic.

Hazelden turned out to be way out in the middle of nowhere, in a place called Centre City, somewhere between St Paul and Minneapolis. The nearest town was a one-horse place called St Croix. The clinic itself was grim and looked something like Fort Knox, with low, concrete buildings that gave it the appearance of a high-security prison. It didn't surprise me to learn that when they tried to get Elvis to go there, he apparently took one look at it and refused to get out of his limo. Most of the people arriving there were either pissed, like I was, or dying for a drink, or possibly comatose with the amount of alcohol in their system and in need of immediate detoxification. They wouldn't even let me bring in my guitar. All I wanted to do when I saw the place was run away.

After checking in, I spent the first week in the hospital part of the clinic, which is where most new inmates go, because they are usually seriously addicted and have to be withdrawn medically. I was given a drug called Librium, which helps you to come off the alcohol and balances you out. It left me feeling very woozy. I didn't really know who I was, or who the other people were, or what I was doing there. It was all just like being stoned again. Four times a day I was given my medicine in a little paper cup, and gradually they weaned me off.

Before you start, you are asked to write down a list of everything you have been taking and, since they often don't have any medical records of new patients, they have to rely on your honesty. Of all the things I had been using, I neglected to include Valium on the list, because I considered that to be a ladies' drug.

The result was that I suffered another 'grand mal' seizure, because they hadn't medicated me for Valium withdrawal; I later learned that this was a very dangerous drug indeed, and highly underestimated.

The clinic, which was founded in 1949, was divided up into a series of units, each one named after a famous person connected with the twelve-step programme. Mine was Silkworth, after William Silkworth, a New York doctor who is quoted in the Big Book of AA. The unit was divided into a living area, a small kitchen and lots of little rooms, shared by two to four people. They had all been through the same as me, the new boy bouncing off the ceiling, and for the first few days they looked after me. I was put into a room with a New York fireman called Tommy who had no idea who I was, and didn't care. He was more concerned with the way I interacted with him on a personal level, and I had no idea how to do that, because I was either above or below everybody. I was either towering above as Clapton the guitar virtuoso, or cringing on the floor, because if you took away my guitar and my musical career, then I was nothing. My fear of loss of identity was phenomenal. This could have been born out of the 'Clapton is God' thing, that had put so much of my self-worth on to my musical career. When the focus shifted towards my well-being as a human being, and that I was an alcoholic and suffering from something that everybody else was, I went into meltdown.

To begin with, I basically withdrew. My counsellor, and most of the other people concerned with me, all reported that I was playing a game in not revealing anything of myself at all, but I think I'd forgotten how, and had little ability to account for myself without my guitar. For over twenty years I had been attached to this thing that gave me my power and my accountability, and without it I didn't have anything to refer to. I didn't know how to begin to relate, so I just sort of shifted around in the background. Then part of my reasoning began to figure out just how much I needed to do in order to get through my 'time' and reach a successful conclusion so that I could leave, just like everybody else. I knew, because they dangled this threat in front of you, that if at the end of the standard period of one month you were not seen to be ready to be released back into society, because you were still in the grip of your addiction, whatever it might be, then they would recommend that you be transferred to another unit called Jelonek. This was a psychiatric unit which involved all kinds of medication and extended care.

Like all the units, Silkworth held twenty-eight people and basically ran itself, though there were a couple of counsellors *in situ* to keep an eye on everybody and make sure that nothing got out of control. Everyone was accountable and you weren't supposed to do anything that was unethical or abusive. We were expected to be honest, supportive, love one another and act with decorum, things I wanted to do without being sure how to go about it. The fact is, it was the first time I'd been in a proper democratic community situation in my entire life, the closest I'd ever come to one having been when I was hanging out with the guys in Long Acre and we would have group sessions getting stoned. In those first few days I really didn't know how to communicate, and I felt quite frightened. I chose to think of myself as shy again and I developed a stutter.

Once it was considered that I could stand on my own two feet, I was given tasks to do, the simplest being to make my own bed, which I'd never done before, and keep myself and my surroundings clean and tidy. Then I was given the job of laying the table for my unit before mealtimes, which was quite hard for someone who lacked any experience of doing anything domestic. Each group had a hierarchy, consisting of a leader and a caretaker, who was known as the 'Pig Master', whose responsibility was to make sure everyone did their duties. There was little chance of skiving off, and if I had done so, the Pig Master would have been after me. The day began with prayers, followed by breakfast, and was then filled with activities, such as group therapy sessions, lectures, psychological tests and exercise, interspersed with mealtimes, and all designed to keep one occupied until you collapsed into bed at the end of the day in a state of mental exhaustion. Sleep came easily, which for me, who had always had to drink to sleep, was great.

At first, the thing that scared me the most was group therapy, where we were encouraged to confront one another about our day-to-day behaviour inside the unit. I had never learned to look honestly at myself. In fact in order to protect my drinking, it was important not to do that. So here I was, feeling raw and vulnerable, wondering how I could even begin to get in touch with the person I had become. But that's what we were there for, and there was no getting round it. The purpose of the group therapy seemed to be for us to see, through direct interaction with one another, the kind of people we had become, and to help one another identify the symptoms of our disease, by honestly recognising the shared defects of the group. Denial seemed to be head of the list, followed by self-centredness, pride and dishonesty. I found it had become almost impossible to be honest, especially with myself. Lying and deflection had become second nature to me. But hanging above all this was the big question – had I truly accepted that I was an alcoholic? – because, until I had done this, progress would be difficult. The struggle of doing this kind of internal work unaided was unthinkable, which is why group therapy was really necessary. We helped each other, sometimes with brutal means, to discover who we really were. After about ten days, I began to enjoy being there. I looked around and saw some amazing people, sometimes real hardliners who had been in Hazelden four or five times and who had much worse stories to tell than me. I started to bond with my inmates, and I remember laughing and laughing for the first time in years. We had a coffee pot on the go all day long, and we'd get 'coffee'd out', sitting up into the night talking about ourselves, our ambitions and the things we had lost. It was a very rich and loving experience.

Most days there were really inspirational lectures, given by people who had been a long time in recovery, who would usually just tell their story. Sometimes they'd highlight certain aspects of recovery like honesty and denial, but they always emphasised how great life was now that they were sober, and you knew it wasn't bullshit. At other times the lectures would take a scientific slant, depicting the nature of the disease in its different phases. It was really good, if not essential, for me to learn, for instance, that alcoholism was regarded, at least in America, as a disease and not a form of moral degeneracy. It was a huge relief to know that I was suffering from a recognised medical condition, no more shameful than diabetes; it made me feel less alone.

These talks riveted me, and I got very excited by some of the personalities who came, people who had been sober for twenty years or more and who had stories to tell that were often hair-raising and sometimes tragic. But some of us were hard to reach, and I heard later that there was quite a lot of drug taking going on in my unit. There was a family visitation day on Sundays, and this is when substances could be smuggled in by friends or family. I didn't do anything myself, only because I didn't know anyone who would bring me anything. My problem was of a different kind. Hazelden was not a single-sex institution, but fraternisation between the sexes was strictly forbidden and patients were expected to report anybody who was seen doing this. But flirtation was a daily practice and attempted liaisons were fairly common. I did manage to have a couple of dalliances with girls without being caught. I achieved this by somehow persuading my counsellor that I was entitled to a room of my own, and once I got this I set about trying to get girls to come and visit me. I succeeded, but only at risk to other people who knew it was happening. If they had been found out for not reporting me, we would all have been thrown out.

Hazelden was one of the first clinics to have a family programme, and towards the end of my stay, Pattie flew out to undergo a five-day course designed to teach spouses and family members what to expect, and how to re-approach their relationships when the patient finally returned home, hopefully sober. It also encouraged them to look at their own role in the family structure, to see whether there would be a possible need for them to get help as well. It has become generally accepted in these matters that no one holds a gun to the head of a person involved with an alcoholic. They are almost invariably there for their own reasons, and in many cases this is because they are addicted themselves, even if it's only in a caretaking fashion. If this is the case, their foundations are often shaken, and their roles threatened when the addict takes steps towards recovery, because they can no longer practise their own addiction with any satisfactory results. The Hazelden family programme, among other things, focused on the need for family members to look really honestly at the nature of their relationships and learn how they could identify and, if necessary, redirect their own needs in order to share their lives successfully with someone who didn't need looking after any more.

For Pattie, these sessions were to prove incredibly helpful, not least because she got to meet other people who were in the same situation as her. I think she felt she had been acting as a surrogate mother most of her life, starting with her siblings, and continuing the role in her relationships. In her life with me, I think she yearned for an independent identity, but was rarely allowed to account for herself, because I was always the prime focus of attention. For years all she would hear was, 'What are we going to do about Eric?' or 'Eric's such an annoyance', 'Eric's done this, Eric's done that. Isn't he wonderful? Isn't he awful?' Until she came to Hazelden, nobody ever asked her, 'Well, who are you, and what's your reason for being with him?'

Of course there were times when I felt I'd never make it through the whole month, and there were those who did give up. One very wealthy guy actually had his wife fly a helicopter into a nearby field, and left in the middle of the night. I got through what was to be the first of two visits to Hazelden by what I later learned was called 'tap-dancing'. I figured out exactly what it was I thought they needed from me, and I gave it to them. I also watched the counsellors very carefully, and tried to mimic them, going to other people in the unit and trying to work out their problems to deflect attention from myself. The result was that I finally got to the end of my stay, having done just enough of the required work to be released.

One of the features about Hazelden was that they had a very good aftercare programme. Before I even left my unit, they had contacted AA in the area where I lived and organised a sponsor to meet me. I was assigned a man who lived in Dorking, named David. It was recommended I stay with my first 'given' sponsor until I had a little time under my belt, and then maybe choose another, based on what my requirements were (it was widely pointed out, by the way, that I would be the last person to know what those requirements were). It was also impressed upon me that it was not a good idea to make any great decisions or embark on any momentous voyages of work for about a year. This was supposedly to allow time for my head to clear, and also gradually be reintroduced to reality. I did the opposite of course.

Before that, however, I had to face the problems of integrating myself with the people at home. One of the initial things I remember was I had a friend who was one of my drinking partners. I didn't know him that well, but every weekend he would come down from Chessington and we would go out boozing round the local pubs. It usually started at the Windmill on Saturday mornings. The first Saturday I got back from America, he turned up as usual. He had no idea where I had been, and I realised that this was going to be one of the first times I was going to have to tell anybody about what had taken place. I was naturally nervous, but I came out of the house and said to him, 'Look, I'm afraid I can't go up the pub. I've stopped drinking.' He looked curiously at me for a minute, and then said, 'Well, fuck you!' got into his car and drove off. I never saw him again. I don't think for a minute there was any malevolence in his reaction. That was normal conversation for us, but in a way it prepared me for the kind of reaction I probably could expect from some quarters, especially old drinking buddies.

Most of the Ripleyites, like Guy Pullen, my oldest and truest friend, were proud of what I'd achieved, but this didn't mean they were going to temper their drinking just to accommodate me. So I had to make some fairly tough choices. Certain people, places and things were dangerous for me, and I needed to carefully identify what was safe and what wasn't safe for my sobriety, from a long list of past associations and haunts. But my judgement was useless, and my value system was completely upside down. What had previously been number one, two and three on my list of life priorities, excitement, danger and risk, now had no place there at all.

For a while I tried to only associate with people who would be good for me, but it was hard, I was angry and disagreeable, and didn't know what to do with all the time that I used to spend drinking. I went to twelve-step meetings, sometimes five or six a week, and would sit there thinking, 'I'm not like these people, I don't really belong here.' What I needed was someone to take an interest in me, but now I was just Eric the alcoholic, and I wasn't too sure that I had totally accepted that.

Amongst the hardest things I had to face on my return from Hazelden was attempting to re-enter my relationship with Pattie.

I came back from treatment with no real idea of how to open the door of intimacy again. It was not something we had covered in treatment and I regret that now. Not that I think it would have made any difference for us, although that is debatable, but because it is a very real issue, and ought to be included in all programmes of this nature. Suffice to say we didn't know what to do. It had been so long since I had done anything without booze, I just didn't know where to start. It was heartbreaking, for both of us. Pattie had been so looking forward to having this clean young man coming home to her, and here I was, partially broken, like a Vietnam vet. I would go to bed with her, and just curl up beside her in the foetal position. I was ashamed and didn't want to talk about it, because for me, the foundations of our relationship had been built on sex, and I'd just assumed that it would all just fall into place the minute I got home.

About this time I started to blame Pattie for everything, after all, hadn't I got sober for her? Where was her gratitude? That was how I was beginning to think. She, meanwhile, was perfectly capable of drinking wine and doing coke in moderation, and to a certain extent, wanted to carry on with our old lifestyle, and who could blame her? But I had to practise abstinence, and for me, sobriety was becoming a drudge. I missed drinking, and was jealous of her for being able to do all that stuff in moderation. I had not really accepted the truth about myself.

The cracks in our relationship caused me to withdraw into myself. I began to spend a lot of time fishing. Though for many years I had been a coarse fisherman, fishing primarily for perch, carp and pike in the waters round Ripley, Gary Brooker had recently taught me to cast a fly. Pike fishing is a cumbersome affair compared to trout fishing. There's an awful lot of gear to cart around, baskets full of stuff, rod stands etc., and green thermal suits to wear, and then when you get out there, you don't really do very much, just sit and wait, and I used to look at Gary with amusement, with his little bag with some flies in it and a rod and reel. I mean he could walk around with this stuff so easily. One day he gave me a lesson in casting on his lawn, and once I'd got the line to go straight out for more than about ten feet, I began to think that there was something in this, and that maybe I could master it.

That first summer of my recovery was one of the most beautiful summers I can remember, perhaps because I was healthy and clean, and I began to rent some trout-fishing days for myself, mostly on stretches of water in the neighbourhood which had been specially stocked for local fishermen. I fished on the Clandon Estate, on the lakes at Willinghurst and at Whitley Farm, near Dunsfold. Fishing is an absorbing pastime and has a Zen quality to it. It's an ideal pursuit for anyone who wants to think a lot and get things in perspective. It was also a perfect way of getting physically fit again, involving, as it does, a great deal of walking. I would go out at the crack of dawn and often stay out till night-time, sometimes proudly returning with a bag of fish that I would present to Pattie to clean and cook. For once I was actually becoming good at something that had nothing to do with guitar playing or music. For the first time in a long time, I was doing something very normal and fairly mundane, and it was really important to me. The fact that it increased Pattie's sense of isolation passed me by.

Believing that work would be one of my greatest therapies, I went on tour with my English band within four months of coming out of Hazelden. It was totally against what the counsellors had recommended, and I imagine they're used to that, but it was a rash decision. The fact is, I wasn't yet ready for work. The first time I stood on stage, at the Paramount Theater in Cedar Rapids, Iowa, I thought to myself, 'This sounds awful,' and I didn't really know why. Like my problem with sex, I hadn't played sober for a long time and had been used to hearing everything through a veil of alcohol and drug distortion, and I just couldn't get used to the sound without it. I went all round America without really knowing what I was doing, but I did go to meetings. At the last show, in Miami, Muddy Waters made a guest appearance and we played 'Blow Wind Blow' together. It was the last time I got to play with him as he died in April of the following year.

On our return from this tour, we went into Compass Point Studios in the Bahamas to cut tracks for a new album. The songs had a pub-rock feel to them, and to me what we were doing was a continuation of what I'd been involved in with Ronnie Lane. To begin with I was happy playing with these guys. We were doing it for fun and companionship and the love of music, all of which seemed to me to be the right reasons. But Roger wasn't too sure, neither was Tom, who was producing again, and to be fair to them, we'd been there for two weeks and hardly completed one track. An atmosphere of apprehension spread over the studio; it started to look like the album wasn't going to get made. Also Gary Brooker and I had become very close, and as a result he was having a lot of input into the way the band worked which, for whatever reason, was not popular with management and production.

After a couple of weeks, Tom Dowd came to me and laid it on the line that nothing was going to happen with this new album unless we had a radical change of musicians. He recommended that I fire the current band, with the exception of Albert Lee, and that we start again from scratch, adding that he could get legendary session musicians Duck Dunn and Roger Hawkins to come and stand in, and even telling me that Ry Cooder was interested in coming down. He said if I wasn't prepared to do the firing myself, then he would do it for me. I was excited by the names he mentioned, people I'd held in high esteem for years, and I decided to take this fork in the road. In my drinking days, I would have got Roger to do my dirty work, but I had learned from my time at Hazelden that I needed to start taking responsibility in these matters. That night I had dinner with the band and told them, 'I'm very sorry, but I've got bad news. This just isn't working and it's been suggested to me that I try something else. So I'm asking you all to go home, and I'll let any of you know if I want you to come back to play on tour.' There was a stunned silence when I told them.

Sacking the band was a huge thing for me to do, and it was very painful. For Henry Spinetti and Gary Brooker, the wounds took a long time to mend, and I've never seen Dave Markee since. As for Chris Stainton, he was the lucky one who got rehired, and has been at my side ever since. Firing them personally had a major effect on me, in that it established my ability to take control over my working life, which was previously totally in the hands of Roger. It also triggered a mini breakdown. The pressure to complete the album, my first since emerging from alcoholism, was enormous, and it had to be good. We had one more song to finish, and at some point I just broke down with Tom, sobbing my heart out in front of him. I think, as much as anything else, I was grieving the loss of my relationship with alcohol, which was a very powerful thing and something that I had not hitherto sufficiently acknowledged. It had been my first relationship and had subsequently played such a significant part in my life. I called the album *Money and Cigarettes*, because that's all that I saw as having left. When we had the playback party, with Tom, Roger, Pattie and a few other people, what would normally be, I suppose, for most artists a joyous celebration, seemed more like a wake. There was definitely something forced about the album, and when we went on the road with it through most of 1983, it was a bit of an anticlimax.

I think subconsciously part of me was rebelling, telling me that all I really wanted to do was play music I loved, with people I loved and cared for. This really struck home when I became involved in the ARMS (Action Research into Multiple Sclerosis) concerts at the end of the year. This was a series of charity concerts, organised by Glyn Johns, to benefit research into MS, a disease that had recently struck down Ronnie Lane. Over the years that I had stayed with Ronnie in Wales, I had noticed that his playing style had become more and more erratic, until he was almost just strumming the air in front of the guitar without actually hitting the strings. I had no idea what that was all about, until now, when it suddenly made sense.

Ronnie had found somebody who could give him hyperbaric treatment, which involved being put into a decompression chamber, and this would alleviate his symptoms and make life bearable for him for quite long periods of time. It was expensive, however, so Glyn had come up with the idea of gathering together a group of his musician friends and holding a concert to raise money for him. Steve Winwood, Jeff Beck, Jimmy Page, Bill Wyman, Charlie Watts, Kenny Jones and Andy Fairweather-Low all rallied to the cause, and after a few days of practice at Glyn's house, we put on a show at the Royal Albert Hall. It was a fantastic success with a terrific atmosphere. We were all playing together for the first time, and because we were doing it for Ronnie, rather than money, we had left our egos at the door and it was great. In fact we enjoyed ourselves so much that it was decided that if everyone would agree, we should take the show on the road to try to make a lot of money for ARMS. The result was a successful tour of America, playing 20,000-seat arenas in Dallas, San Francisco, LA and New York, and thoroughly enjoying ourselves.

CHAPTER TWELVE
RELAPSE

Reflecting on the years after I came out of Hazelden, I now realise that there was no reason why I should have been making records at all. A more intelligent approach to the rebuilding of my life would have been to leave recording for a while to try something else, and to have spent a few years finding out what it was that I really wanted to do rather than just step back into the accepted pattern from the past. But that was not to be. Whether the pressures were contractual or habitual is irrelevant, I was back on the treadmill looking for another formula for a successful album. Roger's suggestion was a collaboration with Phil Collins, who was riding high at the time. Though I wasn't a fan of Genesis, Phil and I had become good friends over the years, a friendship that had been strengthened during the break-up of his marriage to his first wife Andrea, when he used to come over to Hurtwood and pour his heart out to Pattie and me. I had even played guitar on 'If Leaving Me Is Easy', a track on his first album, *Face Value*. Though at first Roger's plan just seemed like a pretty obvious marketing ploy, in the end I decided that it wasn't such a bad idea. It did mean, however, that I had to come up with some new material when I wasn't really ready to.

While considering the best way of going about this, I remembered a trip I had made to Wales many years before, when I had gone there alone with my dog and stayed in the borders for a couple of weeks and had the time of my life. It seemed like that might be a good place to go back to, so I got Nigel Carroll to go down there and find a cottage. He rented a place near Beulah, in the Brecon Beacons, and I went up there with some recording equipment and started writing. Actually, I spent most of my time chopping wood, as all the hot water and the central heating system came from a back boiler that was heated by the fire. The cottage was miles from anywhere and I hardly ever spoke to anyone. I'd go to the pub and have a lemonade and a cheese sandwich, and nobody even looked at me. It was very funny.

Until I started trying to write this new material, I had no idea how difficult it was going to be to shift myself away from writing just for me. I would complete a song and play it back and feel happy with it, and then I'd be out in my car and one of Phil's hits would come on the radio, and I'd think, 'My God, I'm nowhere near this kind of stuff.' It was hard trying to fit into his mould. On my return from Wales, I called Phil and told him I had a few new songs, and we decided to go and work on them in George Martin's Air Studios in Montserrat, in the Caribbean. The idea was to jam a little, try out my songs, see if we could write something together and maybe do some covers. 'Knock On Wood' was one I was keen to try. I had the same band, except that Jamie Oldaker had replaced Roger Hawkins on drums, and Phil had also brought in Peter Robinson to play synthesiser, a different direction for me. We were soon having a great time, and something was working. 'Between now (twelve midnight) and yesterday,' I wrote in my diary on 12 March, 1984, 'we've got five great tracks . . . Phil is so great to work with, you get so much done but it doesn't feel like hard work at all . . . Pete Robinson is a genius and a great bloke too! In fact the whole thing is going so great, I hope it never stops!'

I was amazed by how much we were achieving, and I thought the sound was incredible. 'Good old Phil,' I wrote the following day, 'he's a diamond all right.'

Only one thing jarred, and that was that there seemed to be some kind of conspiracy to keep me from knowing that all the guys were boozing and doing a lot of blow. It was happening in secret, and it was as if they didn't trust me to be able to deal with it. I became very angry. 'Somebody's been holding out on me,' I told them. 'I'm not a kid. I want to know everything that's going on.' But when I voiced my disquiet, they just kind of shouted at me in a jokey way and said, 'But you don't do it any more!'

Before I left home, my attendance at twelve-step meetings had dropped, and I had neglected to find out if there were any meetings where I was going. On my arrival, I had noticed that in the kitchen of the chalet I was staying in there was a courtesy gift of a bottle of local rum on the sideboard, but instead of picking it up and deliberately pouring it all down the drain, I had just put it away in a cupboard, thinking, 'I'm not going to overreact to this by throwing it down the sink, I'll just put it somewhere where I can't see it.' But one night, soon after my row with the band, I went to a club on the far side of the island where I convinced everybody that it would be all right for me to have a couple of drinks. I then went back to my chalet and polished off the bottle of rum in one sitting.

As a celebration, the next day I set about seducing the manageress of the studio, Yvonne Kelly, a beautiful lady from Doncaster, whose father was a Montserratian guitar player. She was very witty and funny, a dark-haired flirtatious beauty who seemed to be interested, and next thing I knew we were embarked on a very passionate and reckless affair, taking no precautions whatsoever. Like the drinking, my rationale was, 'Nobody will know, we're miles away from anywhere.' At the same time, it's as if I wanted to get caught doing something that would rock the domestic boat at home. My disillusionment with my marriage was touched on in some of the songs I had written for the new album, like 'She's Waiting', 'Just Like A Prisoner' and 'Same Old Blues', all very personal numbers about the relationship between me and Pattie.

For some time, I had been finding it increasingly difficult to find a place to exist in my marriage and, at the same time, to have a practising sober life. The two things weren't really jiving very well. I was going to a lot of meetings and also trying to fit in with our social life. But it was difficult going to dinners, because I felt like I was under a microscope, and it was hard too for our friends who were having to moderate their behaviour and act in a way they hadn't had to before. On my return from Montserrat, I chose to hide the fact that I had relapsed by not drinking, and though I managed to do this to begin with, the strain soon became too great.

I was doing a lot of fishing, which helped to keep me calm, and one evening I was driving home from the river when I saw a pub by the side of the road. It was just getting dark and I could see through the windows a throng of people drinking and having fun, and at that moment I had no resistance. My selective memory of what drinking was like told me that standing at the bar in a pub, on a summer's evening with a long, tall glass of lager and lime was heaven, and I chose not to remember the nights on which I had sat with a bottle of vodka, a gram of coke and a shotgun, contemplating suicide.

Suddenly I was at the bar ordering a beer, and it did exactly what I thought it would do. Because I hadn't had a drink in a while, it made me quite tipsy, and I drove back to Hurtwood with some difficulty. When I got there, I decided I would tell Pattie what I had done and make like it was good news, my thinking being that our marriage wasn't working because I was sober, but if I could find a way back into a moderate drinking situation, and become a social drinker again like she was, then all of our problems would be solved and she would be happy. I went to find her and I said, 'I've got something to tell you. I had a drink on the way home, and it felt really good, and I think I can control it.' Her face fell, but even though I saw the anxiety and disappointment in her expression, I'd already made up my mind that that was what I was going to do.

Part of her disappointment was bound up with the fact that a few months previously Pattie and I had visited a fertility clinic, after she had told me she was desperate to have a child. Pattie's problems in getting pregnant stemmed from a blockage in her Fallopian tubes, which had made conceiving a child difficult, if not impossible, during her marriage to George, in the days before IVF. During the first years of our marriage, it was not discussed, as we were too busy racing through life at breakneck speed. Then on 8 February, 1984, I noted in my diary: 'Nell showed me all the bumph she got from the fertility doctor . . . it seems she is suddenly quite keen to have a child . . .' I had realised that having children was the last thing we had to pursue to hold us together, but I was secretly hoping that it wouldn't work, because much as I loved her, I was feeling the need to roam again. I had kind of lost heart.

I now set off on a path of attempting controlled social drinking in the way I saw other people do it. I studied them, and for a while my life consisted of going up to the Windmill for lunch, and having one or two lagers, and then in the evening maybe a glass of wine with dinner or a Scotch after eating. The reality was that as much as I may have been trying to establish some kind of normal day like other people, what it really amounted to was these two drinking sessions with me desperately trying to kill the time in between them, often by sleeping all through the afternoon. This was purely alcoholic in its development and focus, and our life just crumbled as a result.

On our return from Montserrat, with most of the songs recorded and mixed, Roger, who was happy with the material, sent them off to the record company, Warner Brothers, while I set about working on a film score for a new John Hurt movie, *The Hit*. One of the musicians who helped me with this and played on it was Roger Waters, who I had known from my youth, and whose wife, Carolyn, was a close friend of Pattie's. He played me a cassette of a new album he was working on called *The Pros and Cons of Hitchhiking*. It had some great players on it and since I enjoyed his company so much and hanging out with him, I ended up going into the studio with him and working on the album. It was a lot of fun, and at one point I said jokingly, 'You should really take this on the road.' He then asked me if I'd go with him, and since it was the perfect excuse to run away from all the problems at home, I said yes.

Roger Forrester was not happy about this, since he didn't like the idea of me being a sideman to anybody, but he reluctantly agreed to let Roger have me on loan. I was after all his property, and I would have to be given back after the tour. The situation between these two was quite funny in that Roger Waters was very suspicious of Roger Forrester, who in turn thought he had Roger Waters figured out, so there was always a lot of sporting banter bouncing back and forth between them, which I think they quite enjoyed. The tour took place round Europe and America in June and July. Roger works very much to a format, which was multi-media, a combination of visuals and music, which were both meant to emphasise the story he was telling. I had to wear headphones, as a lot of the music had to be in synch with video on the screen, so I needed to follow a click track, which I'd never done before on stage. I thought it was all pretty interesting, although from where I was standing, I never actually saw any of the video stuff. Probably just as well, as from what I gathered there was some very weird stuff going on up there. The first night was in Stockholm, on 16 June. 'The gig was great,' I noted in my diary, 'no bad mistakes and though my own playing could have been better, it wasn't bad at all. Roger was great in front of an audience, quite an eye opener . . . I am back to using Blackie again, it just seems to have that extra bite for stage work, although it's definitely harder to play, perhaps that's what makes it preferable?' The show was like presenting a package, but I became really friendly with the musicians and we all made the most of it, and as usual I got involved in some pretty crazy sexual liaisons, *ménages à trois* and the like, with some scary women, which was all rather sordid.

While we were in Canada playing at the Maple Leaf Gardens in Toronto, I hit a rock bottom, one of a series which was eventually to lead me back to Hazelden. I had been drinking very heavily throughout the tour, and had suffered one or two alcoholic breakdowns, like mini seizures. On this particular occasion, I had bought a couple of six packs of beer, which I drank very quickly, and then I just hit a wall of desperation. It was like a moment of clarity when I saw the absolute squalidness of my life at that moment. I began to write a song called 'Holy Mother', in which I asked for help from a divine source, a female that I couldn't even begin to identify. I still love that song, because I recognise that it came from deep in my heart, as a sincere cry for help.

There were a number of shocks awaiting me on my return to England after the Pros and Cons of Hitchhiking tour. The first was that Warner Brothers had sent back the Montserrat tapes saying that the songs weren't strong enough. There weren't enough potential hit singles amongst them, and we could either re-record the album, removing some of the songs and adding new ones, or we could find another record company. I was incredibly upset, as this was the first time I had ever been rejected. At one point, I even equated it with being sober, because one of the first things that had happened to me when I got back from Hazelden was that I got stopped by the police in my car and was breathalysed, something that had never happened to me while I was drinking. Suddenly, getting a rejection from my record company was just one reflection of all the nastiness one had to face when sober.

After my anger had subsided, I had the presence of mind to sit down quietly and think what might be the proper action to take. I was partly motivated in this by having heard that Warners had recently dropped Van Morrison, and it had occurred to me that if they could drop him, then they could certainly let go of me, and then where would I go? I decided to talk to Roger about it, who had often made sensible decisions in difficult situations, and we both agreed that we should find out what the record company thought hit-single material was. They sent me three songs written by a Texas songwriter they represented called Jerry Lynn Williams – 'Forever Man', 'Something's Happening' and 'See What Love Can Do' – and they were good. I loved the way he sang and I sent back a message to say I would do it, on the condition that they produced the songs and provided the musicians. I think it was, professionally, the first time I'd ever had to back down.

I was pretty scared when I went out to LA, being not quite sure what I was letting myself in for, but as soon as I met him, I got on with Jerry Williams like a house on fire. He was an incredible, larger than life character who looked like Jack Nicholson and sang like Stevie Wonder. The producers were Ted Templeman and Larry Waronker, and they brought in what they called the 'A Team' of Jeff Porcaro on drums, Steve Luthaker on guitar, and Michael Omartin and Greg Phillinganes on synthesisers, all studio musicians who had been used on hit after hit. We recorded these songs, and though I thought the material was pretty good, in the end I believe the original album was better because it was truer to what we had been trying to do. What I really got out of it was the sheer enjoyment of hanging out with Jerry Williams, though he was hardly the best influence I could have had at the time. He was staying up at Shangri-La, where I had recorded *No Reason To Cry*, and I went up and stayed there and played on some of his demos, and before I knew it I was off and running again, with prescription drugs and blow as well as alcohol.

Another piece of shocking news that reached me on my return from the Roger Waters tour was in a letter from Yvonne, who wrote to say that she was pregnant, and that the baby was mine. She emphasised, however, that she wished to keep this news secret and that she didn't have any expectations from me. She was married and she had decided to try to raise the child within her existing marriage. She had told me that things were not good between her and her husband, and I presumed that she was hoping that the baby might save her marriage.

Considering my own behaviour, I suppose I should not have been so shocked at the discovery that during my absence on the road with Roger, Pattie had begun an affair with a society photographer. The irony was that he was the brother of Roger's wife, Carolyn, and I later found out from one of my crew, Peter Jackson, that this had been an open secret on the Pros and Cons tour. They had met socially while I was working on the album. I was devastated, but in many subsequent conversations with her, it became clear that I had been totally blind to the things that had driven her away from me, namely my chauvinistic behaviour and my drinking and depressions. I pleaded with her to come back to me, to no avail, and it was eventually decided that we should have a trial separation. I agreed to rent a flat for her in London, and she moved into an apartment in Devonshire Place. 'I kept on thinking,' I wrote in my diary on 2 October, 'this can't be happening to me.'

I was getting ready for an Australian tour, and I was falling to pieces. I spent the mornings in therapy, which helped me, and the afternoons working, which often knocked me back. 'The problem is that the rehearsals,' I wrote, 'contain all the songs I ever wrote about Pattie, and by the time we're finished, I'm back where I started – jealous and rejected . . .' The evenings back at home were the worst, 'sad, melancholy and negative' I wrote. I could not stop brooding about her and her boyfriend, who I considered to be a complete wimp. One evening, after getting 'further and further down in my pit . . . finally I got in the car and drove . . . with the intention of dragging her back, caveman-style. She wasn't there of course.'

Over the next few weeks, during which I was also rehearsing for the upcoming tour, my state of mind went steadily downhill. 'I feel so lost and desperate,' I wrote on 12 October , '. . . and miss her so much that I can't see the way ahead.' A week later I experienced 'the worst day yet! A complete relapse with all the fears and guilt of the old drinking days, the coke was the worst part of it – never again! The whole day I spent getting more and more suicidal, until finally the phone rang in the evening and it was Roger W who just by being gentle brought me out of it. I stopped drinking, threw the coke away and drank glass after glass of water until finally I came back to a feeling of clarity and ease. I must never let this happen again . . .'

Two things helped me during this dark period. First and foremost was my music, the one thing that was always there for me. 'I want to express all my pain in my music,' I wrote in one entry in my diary; 'I don't want to stifle it, I want it to reach others in pain so that they can know they are not alone.' I also started to see a brilliant therapist who Roger Waters had recommended. 'I saw Gordon today,' I wrote on 16 October, 'and he gave me some good insights on both me and the situation – it seems I must use my head to control my emotions or they will destroy me . . . he is giving me a good foot forward no matter how slow. I wrote and recorded "Behind The Sun" at Phil's house tonight. It's rough, but it says it all . . . I intend giving it to Nell on Thursday.' This song, which consisted of me on guitar and vocals and Phil on synthesiser, expressed all my feelings of sadness at our break-up. I took the title from a line in 'Louisiana Blues', one of my favourite Muddy Waters songs, and it became the title track of the new album, which was released early in 1985.

On 6 November, two days before leaving for Australia, I had one more meeting with Pattie. 'I walked and talked with Nell this afternoon, she is lovelier than ever and I believe she wants to be left alone with her new man and her new life . . . she said that physically there was no attraction for me any more and that she loved being with him, he's a lucky man . . . and I am a fool, but I still believe that she loves me and that I can net her with patience. I can never stop loving her...I have hope and persistence on my side and I will never give in.' Owing to the turmoil I was in, I had avoided further complicating things by involving myself with any other women since my return from America, but the day I flew to Sydney, I went to bed with a girl I had been seeing on and off called Valentina. It released all kinds of feelings. 'Valentina . . . made lunch and we made love. It felt so good to be cared for again, I've been so hungry for so long . . . but it still doesn't stop the deeper yearning which I keep for my wife . . . but maybe that too will fade. I pray that she returns before it does . . . in another hour or so I shall be gone from here and all the ghosts.'

For me, the Australian tour was not a happy one. Not only was I on an emotional roller coaster, but I was not that happy with the sound we were getting on stage. 'The rehearsal was very strange,' I recorded on 12 November, 'the sound was overpowering and I felt like I had dropped acid, my confidence is very low.' The problem was that Albert Lee was not with us this time round, and his place had been taken by Pete Robinson on synthesiser, an instrument I had got used to in the studio, but had some difficulty adjusting to on stage. It seemed to make the show far too loud, which caused problems with my hearing. 'I think the frequency of his synth playing could be what causes my deafness,' I noted on 23 November, adding later, 'the show was OK, for the most part, but towards the end it got too loud again . . . Deb said for her it was too loud from the word go . . . it would be great to do one show that was pleasing to everyone.' (Deb was short for Deborah Russell, a lady I had made friends with in Sydney, and a very fine painter.)

A week into the tour, we were in Sydney when Roger called me to tell me that Nigel Dempster had written up the story of our break-up in his column in the *Daily Mail*. This really hurt, because it hadn't occurred to me up until that point that it was anyone else's business. 'Well it's over,' I wrote, 'I spoke to Nell about divorce and she agrees to it. I have gone back into shock, God help me . . . I called back in remorse and asked her to come with me to somewhere remote for a week just to talk it over.' Two days later I noted 'she has agreed to Florence for a week on the 7th, so I think that will decide it one way or another.'

I returned to England at the beginning of December feeling confused and depressed. 'On mornings like this,' I wrote on my first day back at Hurtwood, 'you really need someone to snuggle up to. It's grey and dark and wet and cold. It's England.' I decided not to press for a divorce, but to leave it to Pattie to ask for one if and when she decided to. I also wrote a letter to her lover in which I unequivocally stated my feelings. I told him that I hoped he was aware of just what he was doing, because Pattie had been the love of my life and he was succeeding in fucking over everyone. That night, out of the blue, Alice called me from Paris, where she was now living, and 'lifted my spirits, in fact snapped me out of it by saying that she always knew that Pattie would end up with a toff'. She suggested that I go to see her in Paris, which did not seem to me like a good idea. Instead I pushed Pattie, who had been having second thoughts, into agreeing to the Florence trip, which turned into a three-day disaster. 'The Florentine experiment proved to be a big let-down,' I wrote. 'The most memorable part was the fact that she has proved, or established that she finds me sexually repulsive.' I was undeterred.

My resolve was soon strengthened by the news that my letter to the boyfriend appeared to have paid off and that he had backed off for a while. So after Christmas, which we spent apart, I decided to press even harder for a reconciliation. Pattie would never have considered this without first consulting 'the Committee', as we called the group of close friends she hung out with. Also known as 'the Blonde Mafia', they were a formidable group of women who used to regularly lunch together and swap gossip. Much to my delight, they gave her the go-ahead, and we flew off together for a holiday in Eilat, Israel. It was just as unsuccessful as the trip to Florence. The problem was that I was convinced that if we could regain the intimate side of our relationship, then everything else would fall into place. So instead of just enjoying her company, I was always trying to push it to the next level. In spite of everything, I persuaded Pattie to give me another chance at making our marriage work, and on our return to England, she came back to live at Hurtwood. Things did not improve. I had placed her on a pedestal, turning her into a person she could never aspire to be and that I would only abuse.

For most of 1985, apart from August and September, I was out on the road promoting *Behind the Sun*. In the early part of that summer I got a phone call from Pete Townshend asking if I would play in a charity event being organised by Bob Geldof to raise money for the victims of famine in Ethiopia. It was to be called Live Aid and was to consist of two concerts which were to be played simultaneously in London and Philadelphia on 13 July, and broadcast live on TV across the world. As it happened, on that date we were to be in the middle of a North American tour. We were booked to play Las Vegas the night before, with shows in Denver, Colorado, on either side, so there were some pretty big leaps involved. I told Roger to cancel the Las Vegas show and called Pete to say we'd do it. Thank God we were in good shape, with the band playing really well, because had we just started our tour, I might have had second thoughts.

Landing in Philadelphia the day before the show, one couldn't help but get swept up in the atmosphere. The place was just buzzing. The moment we landed, you could feel music everywhere. We checked into the Four Seasons Hotel, every room of which was filled with musicians. It was Music City, and like most people I was awake most of the night before the concert. I couldn't sleep with nerves. We were due to go on stage in the evening, and I sat watching the performances of the other acts on the TV during most of the day, which was probably a psychological mistake, as seeing all these great artists giving their best made me a hundred times more psyched up than for a regular gig. How could I ever match the performance of a band like the Four Tops, with their fantastic big Motown orchestra combined with all their energy?

By the time we got out to the stadium, I was in such a state of nerves that I was literally tongue-tied. It was also boiling hot, and the whole band felt faint. In fact Duck Dunn and I later confessed to each other that we'd been close to passing out. The tunnel, which we had to walk through from the dressing rooms to the stage, was crowded with security, which was unnerving in itself, and things weren't helped by the fact that we had been given different guitar amps to those which had been specified by my roadie, who was subsequently screaming blue murder as we reached the stage itself. To say the whole band was jumpy would be an understatement. As I climbed on stage, I luckily saw the reassuring presence of my old mentor, Ahmet Ertegun, standing in the wings, smiling broadly at me and giving me a big thumbs-up sign.

Things got off to a shaky start. When I moved up to the microphone to sing the first line of 'White Room', I got a great big shock off it, further unnerving me, and meaning that I had to sing the rest of the show with my mouth not quite touching the mike, but still close enough to hear myself, since the monitors weren't very good. We played three songs, 'White Room', 'She's Waiting', a song from *Behind the Sun*, and 'Layla', and then we were off and it was all over. Phil Collins came on, followed by Led Zeppelin, then Crosby, Stills, Nash and Young. After that, I remember very little, other than being herded back on stage at the end to join in the finale, singing 'We Are The World'. I think I was just in a state of shock.

The autumn of 1985 found us touring Italy. From my initial visit there, a few years earlier, when I was first exposed to its architecture, fashion, cars and food, I had had a fascination with the country and its lifestyle in general, but I had never dated an Italian woman. I was telling this to the Italian promoter, who told me that he knew a really interesting girl, and that he would introduce us. We were playing a couple of shows in Milan, and after one of them there was a dinner and he brought along a strikingly attractive girl called Lori del Santo. Born in Verona, Lori was the second daughter of a poor Catholic family. When her father had died young, she had been sent to a convent school to be educated, while her mother worked all hours to make ends meet. As soon as she left school, she had made the decision that she would never be poor again. She had gone to Rome with the intention of making a career in modelling and TV, and by the age of twenty had got parts in various films and sitcoms, and had become the girlfriend of the international arms dealer, Adnan Khashoggi. By the time I met her, seven years later, she was famous throughout Italy as the star of a popular weekly TV show called *Drive-In* which was the Italian equivalent of Rowan and Martin's *Laugh-In*. With her long, rich, dark, curly hair, strong bone structure and voluptuous figure, she had a real southern Italian-style beauty, and I was immediately smitten with her.

Lori had a powerful personality, very confident and flirtatious, and I was flattered by her interest in me. Indeed the energy between us was very strong, and had a quality that only exists when you meet someone for the first time. It was also very playful, something that had disappeared from my relationship with Pattie. When the tour ended and I went back home to her, we made a further half-hearted attempt to rekindle our marriage, but it didn't really catch. I realised that my attentions had shifted. I had barely been home more than a few days when I suddenly told Pattie that I was leaving. I had met somebody in Italy and I was going to go and stay with her. I was like a candle in the wind, being blown all over the place, with no concern for other people's feelings or for the consequences of my actions. In my mind I had persuaded myself that, since I had just turned forty, I was going through a midlife crisis, and that was the explanation for everything.

I turned up on Lori's doorstep in Milan, right out of the blue, and told her I'd left Pattie and I was coming to live with her. Funnily enough it was almost as if she was living an existential life herself, because she didn't bat an eyelid. Her attitude was one of 'Come and live here and we'll see where it takes us.' It was an extraordinary moment for me, because having actually got there, I just thought to myself, 'I'm going to start my life again from scratch here in Italy, without any idea at all of where it is going to go.'

To begin with, we lived in Milan for a while, where Lori was starting a new career as a fashion photographer. She had begun to work for the big fashion houses which were going strong then, like Versace and Armani, and it was through her that I became friendly with the Versace family, particularly with Donatella's husband, Paul Beck. I was already a huge fan of Gianni's. I had been buying his things for a while, and thought of him as the best tailor in the world. His ideas were revolutionary, but simple at the same time. I loved both Giorgio Armani and Gianni, but at that moment in time, in my opinion, Gianni was the rock 'n' roll tailor.

For a while I became Lori's model, and spent quite a lot of time doing shoots with her. As our relationship developed, we began to discuss the possibility of having children together. I told her how I had always wanted children, but that Pattie and I had been unable to conceive. I suggested to Lori that the two of us would make the most perfect babies. Looking back on it now, it seems like adolescent nonsense, but at the time it all made perfect sense, she agreed and said that she would stop using birth control.

The façade crumbled when we were in Rome, where Lori had another flat. One day she went out and left me on my own, and I started to poke around, which was not a great idea. I opened a cupboard and found a pile of photograph albums, which I took out and started looking through. They were full of pictures of Lori with famous men – footballers, actors, politicians, musicians, anyone with any kind of notoriety. I noticed that she struck the same pose in every photograph, wearing the sort of smile that wasn't really a smile at all. I felt like someone had punched me in the stomach, I went icy cold, and my hair stood on end. In that moment I knew we were doomed.

However much I might have wanted to walk out at this point, I realised that I had already set in motion something that was out of control, particularly because of the conversation we had had about pregnancy. So I put this experience on file, as a reason why the relationship would never last, and started dissembling the whole thing, mentally and emotionally withdrawing. I stayed in Rome for a while, and then we both flew to London and stayed a couple of nights in the Connaught, before moving into an apartment I had organised for us in Berkeley Square.

Filled with doubts as I was about my life, both the past and the future, it was a hard time for me. After years of living in the country, I also hated the noise and traffic of the city, so to distract myself I filled the apartment with recording equipment to enable myself to make demos for my next album. One of the songs I wrote while living there was called 'Tearing Us Apart', which was about 'the Committee', the group of Pattie's friends who I now blamed for coming between us. 'Your friends are tearing us apart,' I wrote. I could think of little else, so it's not surprising that only two or three weeks after we moved in together, I told Lori that the relationship just wasn't working for me any more, and that I had to go back to my wife. 'That's not good news at all,' she said, 'because I'm pregnant.' At that moment, I couldn't really take this in. I remember getting into my car and driving down to Hurtwood to see Pattie, who had been living there since I had left. Somewhere in my alcoholic mind was the idea that she might be waiting for me. When I arrived, it was night-time, and there were lights on all over the house. I peered in through the kitchen window and saw Pattie and her boyfriend making dinner together. It was like I'd come home to someone else's house. I knocked on the door and said 'I'm back, I'm home!' and Pattie came to the door and said coldly, 'You can't come in here right now. This is not the right time.'

'But this is my home,' I said, to which she replied, 'No, you can't do this . . .' Suddenly my world was absolutely in tatters. I was disenchanted with my now pregnant mistress, and I'd lost my wife. I was in conflict and bewildered, and I felt like I'd opened a vast door into an empty chasm. At some point during this period, I decided that the only answer to my problems was suicide. I happened to have a full bottle of blue 5 mg Valium tablets, and I downed them all, the whole bloody lot. I was convinced they would kill me, but astonishingly enough, I woke up ten hours later, stone-cold sober, and full of the realisation of what a lucky escape I'd had.

As soon as Lori came to understand that she was never going to be able to get me to commit to anything, she went back to Milan, where it was possible for her to make a living. I stayed in England and tried to clear up the mess I'd created by first of all telling Pattie about the pregnancy. Considering how much she had longed for our own child and her deep disappointment at her failure to conceive, it was a dreadful thing to have to tell her. She was utterly devastated, and from then on our life together at Hurtwood was hell. We hacked along for a while, sleeping in different rooms, and living pretty much separate lives until, several months later, on her birthday, 17 March, I had a complete meltdown, and threw her out of the house. It was a cruel and vicious thing to do, and within a few days I was regretting it. I kept replaying our early days over and over in my head, desperately wondering why we couldn't recapture that essence again, but I knew I had crossed a serious barrier this time, and that I would have to leave her alone for a while. Pattie found a very nice apartment in Kensington, and things actually settled down. I visited her once a week, and we were quite civil to one another. I stayed out at Hurtwood, doing bits and pieces, drinking in as controlled a manner as I could, but occasionally going on massive benders. It was like being in limbo again, not quite knowing where things were going, or what the outcome of all of this would be.

CHAPTER THIRTEEN
CONOR

I was sitting at home one day, when I received a mysterious phone call from a lady with a strong European accent. She claimed to know all about my marriage difficulties over the years, and said she knew how to repair them all. I was intrigued, as well as angry. How had this person got my number, and where had she got all the inside information that she appeared to know? Soon after, she began to call quite regularly with bizarre instructions which I followed to the letter, my reasoning being 'What have I got to lose?' Little did I know what I was getting into. To begin with I had to take a bath in an assortment of herbs, which left me looking like the Creature from the Black Lagoon. Gradually the rituals got more convoluted, I read weird incantations at midnight. It got very, very creepy. Then, of course, with great excitement and expectation, I would call Pattie to see if there was any change in her demeanour towards me, which, needless to say, there never was.

The lady on the phone had a very sympathetic manner, and eventually she told me she should meet me. She lived in New York, and I knew I would be there at a particular time, so I agreed to meet her. I knew it was madness, but my rationale was still the same, 'What harm can it do?' She was an extremely strange-looking woman and she told me that I should sleep with a virgin. 'Where do you find a virgin in New York?' I replied, and she said, 'I'm a virgin.' God knows why I didn't just run then. I wish I had, but I was drunk and desperate, and still under the illusion that a reconciliation with Pattie would solve everything, so I went through with it. It was a humiliating experience and I did run, but only after the damage was done.

I escaped to LA to record songs for a new album, which was to be a collaboration between Phil Collins and Tom Dowd. I had asked Tom to co-produce because I didn't feel confident that Phil really knew my musical background well enough to do the job single-handed, and with him involved I felt I could oversee the production. We worked at Sunset Sound Studios in Hollywood, with the basic band consisting of me on guitar, Phil on drums, Greg Phillinganes on keyboards and Nathan East on bass. The horns (Michael Brecker on sax, Randy Brecker and Jon Faddis on trumpet and Dave Bargeron on trombone) were overdubbed in New York, and Tina Turner and myself duetted live on 'Tearing Us Apart'.

For me these were pretty drunken sessions, and looking back, I don't know how I got through them. Nigel, who came with me, had rented us a place on Sunset Plaza, and secretly I would drink and do coke until about six in the morning. Then at about eleven, I would go into the studio and somehow stay sober during the day. So from midday till about six in the evening I would try to work while feeling like I was going through a hangover, doing the best I could, until I reached a moment when I felt able to say, 'OK, we've had a great day. Let's call it quits,' at which point I would drive back to the rented villa and hit the booze and coke again. I hardly slept at all. Of course I was trying my hardest to hide my drinking from everybody, unsuccessfully as it turned out. Nigel had got me a rental car, which didn't have a proper licence plate, so some of the crew, unbeknownst to me, had made a cardboard licence plate for the car, which said CAPTAIN SMIRNOFF.

In the months before Lori's baby was due to be born, I had come to realise that this was the one thing in my life that something good could come of, and I had been making some attempts to restore the relationship with her. On my return from recording in LA, I went to visit her in Milan a few times, and eventually, a few weeks before the birth, she returned to London, having told me that since I was English, she felt the baby should be born in England. I rented a mews house in Chelsea for her, where I used to visit her every day.

Conor was born on 21 August, 1986, at St Mary's, Paddington. As soon as I heard that Lori had gone into labour, I rushed to the hospital, determined to be in at the birth, though more than a little frightened of what I was going to experience. As it happened, he got stuck upside down, so they had to perform a last-minute Caesarean. They put a screen around the bed, and a nurse came and stood beside me. She told me that men often faint in these situations. I was determined to try to be present for this, I just had an incredible feeling that this was going to be the first real thing that had ever happened to me. Up till that moment, it seemed my life had been a series of episodes that had very little meaning. The only time it had seemed real was when I was challenging myself in some way with music. Everything else, the drinking, the tours, even my life with Pattie, it all had an air of artificiality to it. When the baby finally came out, they gave him to me to hold. I was spellbound, and I felt so proud, even though I had no idea how to hold a baby.

Lori spent a couple of days in the hospital. While she was there, I remember going down to Lord's to watch the cricket. The great English cricketer Ian 'Beefy' Botham was playing, who I knew through David English, the former president of the Robert

Stigwood Organisation, and after the match he raised a glass of champagne to me in honour of Conor's birth. By that time, it had begun to sink in that I was a father, and that it was time for me to grow up. I considered all my previous irrational behaviour to have been reasonably excusable, because it had been conducted with consenting adults. Whereas with this tiny child, so vulnerable as he was, I suddenly became aware that it was time to try to stop fucking around. But the question was how?

Conor's birth was commemorated with the release of the new album, which I called *August*, and which turned out to be my biggest-selling solo album to date. It had a hit single in 'It's In The Way You Use It', which was featured in the Paul Newman film *The Colour of Money*, and also included 'Holy Mother', which I had dedicated to Richard Manuel, the great keyboard player of the Band, who had hanged himself in March 1986. One song I decided not to include was 'Lady From Verona', which I had written specially for Lori. That might have been too much for Pattie to bear.

Lori returned to Italy soon after the birth, the idea being that I would go over and visit her and Conor for a few days whenever it was possible. The problem was that my drinking had become full-blown again, and I was finding it harder and harder to control. I really loved this little boy, and yet, when I went to visit him in Milan, I would sit and play with him in the daytime, and, every second of that time, all I could think about was how much longer it would be before Lori would arrive to feed him and take him away to bed so that I could have another drink. I never drank in his presence. I would stay white-knuckle sober all the time he was awake, but as soon as she had put him in his cot, I would get back to my normal consumption, drinking until I passed out. I would do this every night until I went back to England.

The trouble was that the company I was hanging out with

during this period did little to curb my excesses. Back in 1986, and throughout the summer of 1987, for example, I spent a lot of time with Beefy Botham and David English, and the three of us would go on mad sprees. David had been a friend since RSO days, and between us we had formed the EC XI (which later evolved into the Bunburys) a ragtag team of musicians and sportsmen who liked to play cricket for fun, and although some of us would take it fairly seriously, I for one treated it as another excuse for a grand piss-up. Sometimes I would just drive up to watch Beefy play for his county, Worcestershire. He's a wonderful man, very gregarious and generous, a great player and a natural leader, with a scaldingly cruel sense of humour. More often than not, poor David would be the recipient of our scornful attention, and would suffer extraordinary abuse at our hands, much in the same vein as Stiggy had with Ahmet and Earl. We were pretty merciless, but I just loved watching Beefy play, and drove all over the country to watch first-class county games. Drinking is a big part of the cricket social scene, and Beefy liked the odd quencher too, so I fitted right in.

This then was the pattern of my life over the next year, which reached its climax when I was touring Australia in the autumn of 1987. By then there had been such an erosion of my capabilities that I couldn't stop shaking. For the second time, I'd reached the point where I couldn't live without a drink and I couldn't live with one. I was a mess, and so far as my playing was concerned, I was just about scraping by. One day, cooped up in my hotel room, a long way from home, with nothing to think about but my own pain and misery, I suddenly knew that I had to go back into treatment. I thought to myself, 'This has got to stop.' I really did it for Conor, because I thought no matter what kind of human being I was, I couldn't stand being around him like that. I couldn't bear the idea that, as he experienced enough of life to form a picture of me, it would be a picture of the man I was then. I called

Roger and told him to book me into Hazelden again, and on 21 November, 1987, I went back into treatment.

My second visit to Hazelden was, on the face of it, much like the first, but on a deeper level it was very different. This time I had no reservations about why I was there, I had tried to control my drinking and failed, so there was no more debate, no more grey area for me. Also my life had become very complicated and completely unmanageable during my relapse. I now had two children, neither of whom I was really administering to, a broken marriage, assorted bewildered girlfriends and a career, which although it was still ticking over, had lost its direction. I was a mess.

My counsellor this time around, a great guy called Phil K, having first established a strong bond with me, employed a sort of ridicule method. It threw me completely. I had grown used to people treating me with a certain amount of reverence, maybe just out of fear, and here was this guy laughing at my pomposity and arrogance. I didn't know how to deal with it. It caught me off balance and helped me to see myself as others saw me, and it wasn't a pretty sight. I was captivated, and tried to engage him as much as I could, but he was rarely available, or made it seem that way. Like my half brother, Brian, he had something I wanted. More than that, it was something I knew I needed. I was like a blade of grass in the wind; one day I would be blown up, scornful and full of myself, the next, in a pit of despair. But I kept coming back to the thought of Conor, the reality of his life and what it required of me, and the horrible possibility that if I didn't get it right this time, history would probably repeat itself. The thought of him going through all that I had been through was what finally made the difference. I had to break the chain, and give him what I had never really had – a father.

Nevertheless, I stumbled through my month in treatment much as I had done the first time, just ticking off the days, hoping that something would change in me without me having to do much about it. Then one day, as my visit drew to an end, a panic hit me, and I realised that in fact nothing had changed in me, and I was going back out into the world again completely unprotected. The noise in my head was deafening, and drinking was in my thoughts all the time. It shocked me to realise that here I was in a treatment centre, a supposedly safe environment, and I was in serious danger. I was absolutely terrified, in complete despair. At that moment, almost of their own accord, my legs gave way and I fell to my knees. In the privacy of my room I begged for help. I had no notion who I thought I was talking to, I just knew that I had come to the end of my tether. I had nothing left to fight with. Then I remembered what I had heard about surrender, something I thought I could never do – my pride just wouldn't allow it – but I knew that on my own, I wasn't going to make it, so I asked for help and, getting down on my knees, I surrendered.

Within a few days I realised that something had happened for me. An atheist would probably say it was just a change of attitude, and to a certain extent, that's true, but there was much more to it than that. I had found a place to turn to, a place that I'd always known was there, but never really wanted, or needed, to believe in. From that day until this, I have never failed to pray in the morning, on my knees, asking for help, and at night, to express gratitude for my life and most of all, for my sobriety. I choose to kneel because I feel I need to humble myself when I pray, and with my ego, this is the most I can do. If you were to ask why I do all this, I will tell you . . . because it works, as simple as that. In all this time that I've been sober, I have never once seriously thought of taking a drink or a drug. I have no problem with religion, and I grew up with a strong curiosity about spiritual matters, but my searching took me away from church and community worship, to the internal journey. Before my recovery began, I found my God

257

in music and the arts, with writers like Herman Hesse and Khalin Gibran, and musicians like Muddy Waters, Howlin' Wolf and Little Walter. In some way, in some form, my God was always there, but now I have learned to talk to him.

I came home from Hazelden for Christmas, to Lori and Conor at Hurtwood. There was a lot to be done, a lot of wreckage to clear up, and Lori was very supportive. I think she knew intuitively that I was not ready to make a decision about our situation yet, and seemed reasonably content just to see where things would lead. Funnily enough the first person I wanted to see on my return was Pattie. We had parted on such bad terms, and I wanted to see if there was still a spark of something there, even if it was only friendship. We met for lunch, and it was great, I couldn't feel any enmity from her, and we were able to speak without manipulation, which for me was a miracle.

Shortly before the end of 1987, the phone lady contacted me again, saying she was about to be evicted from her flat and needed money. I made the mistake of sending her some cash. It was like opening Pandora's box. From that day on, for the next few years, she hounded me. It started in the press in the spring of 1988, with photos of her in the Sunday tabloids appearing to be several months pregnant, and dreadful headlines calling me every name under the sun. It went on for about a month, until someone, a girl who apparently worked for her, contacted the tabloids to say that it was all a hoax. The photos were taken with pillows, and there was no truth in any of it. The papers issued minuscule apologies, but I was badly shaken. There was, after all, the slim chance that she really was pregnant, and I was very confused about what my responsibilities would be, if that were the case. And all this took place in the first few months after I had come out of rehab for the second time. Talk about being thrown in at the deep end.

From time to time, over the next few years, the phone lady

would reappear, sometimes on the street, in broad daylight, screaming things like, 'You'll never get away from me,' and for a man who is naturally inclined to fear the opposite sex, this was sometimes more than I could bear. Gradually, though, she faded into the background, until one day I met up with her again in New York, with another guy, who she had obviously set up home with. I felt that I ought to straighten him out about who she was, and what she was capable of. In the end, I left it alone. They seemed very happy, and it looked pretty normal. I just didn't have the heart to rock their boat, and maybe he knew about it all anyway.

After coming out of Hazelden, there was work to throw myself back into, beginning with a continuation of something that had started in January 1986, when I had agreed to play six shows on successive nights at the Royal Albert Hall in London. It was to become a tradition, with the number of gigs increasing each year, until they would peak in 1991 with twenty-four. With a band that included Nathan East and Greg Phillinganes, from the *August* sessions, Steve Ferrone and Phil Collins on drums, and with the addition of Mark Knopfler on guitar, the gigs had gone so well that we had decided to try to make it a regular booking. I had always liked this venue, and had enjoyed going to see people play there. It's comfortable, has a great atmosphere, and the management has always made sure that it sounds good. It's also one of the few places to play where you can see all of the audience and actually feel that you're in amongst them. When you're on that stage, you've got them behind you, you've got them all around you in boxes, with standing up in the gods, and sometimes even in the stalls. The people at the front are right at your feet, so you really feel like you're in among the crowd. I remember when it was off-limits to rock music, and somehow the Mothers of Invention managed to get booked there. It was a fantastic show, and for an encore, Frank Zappa's keyboard player, Don Preston, known as

'Mother Don', broke into the organ keyboard, which was locked behind two glass doors, and played a raucous version of 'Louie Louie', which brought the house down.

The best times I had in those early years of sobriety were in the company of my son and his mother. It was the closest that things ever got to being normal for me. Conor was a good-looking boy with blond hair, much the same as mine at the same age, and brown eyes. I'd seen pictures of my Uncle Adrian as a little boy, playing in the Ripley woods with my mother, and he bore a strong resemblance to him. He was a beautiful child, with a wonderful, gentle nature, who was walking by the time he was a year old, and, as soon as he could talk, used to call me 'Papa'. But however deeply I loved this little boy, I had no idea where to begin with him, because I was a baby trying to look after a baby, so I just let Lori raise him, which she did brilliantly. She would come and stay with her sister, Paula, who also worked for her as her assistant, and occasionally their mother accompanied them, and, for a few weeks, we would live a very peaceful, family kind of life. I used to watch Conor's every move, and because I didn't really know much about how to be a father, I played with him in the way a sibling plays, kicking balls around on the terrace for hours and going for walks in the garden. He also got to know my mother and grandmother, and Roger too. Anyone that came into contact with him adored him. He was a little angel really, a very divine being.

In 1989, I began working on one of my own favourite albums, *Journeyman*. Produced by Russ Titleman, the album contained an interesting mixture of covers and originals, but mainly featured more of Jerry Williams' material. I really loved his writing. In fact musically I loved everything about him. He could be a bit overwhelming in person, but that was entirely forgivable given the scale of his talent. He was great to work with, a wonderful guy, very funny, very talented, and I knew we would be friends forever.

I had a lot of fun working on this album, which featured, amongst numerous musicians, playing by George Harrison, Cecil and Linda Womack and Robert Cray. Russ insisted I did a version of 'Hound Dog', which turned out to be a great idea, and a Ray Charles number, 'Hard Times', but my favourite track was 'Old Love', a moody blues song I wrote with Robert Cray, and on which we shared the guitar playing equally.

We took the album out on the road in 1990, first in the UK and Europe, and latterly across the USA. It was during the second half of this tour, at the end of August, that I lost a good friend and a musical hero. Stevie Ray Vaughan was a Texan guitarist and blues player, the younger brother of Jimmie Vaughan, who I knew pretty well from his group, the Fabulous Thunderbirds. In mid-1986, I had had a call to my office from Jimmie to say that Stevie Ray was in a drying-out clinic in London, and would I go and see him. I visited him, and told him that as someone who had been through all this before, I was there for him if he needed me. We became good friends, and during the following years, I saw him play a few times and we occasionally jammed together. At that time I would say he was one of the greatest electric blues guitarists in the world, with a style that was very reminiscent of Albert King, who was his hero.

On 26 August, we were playing at a ski resort in Wisconsin, in a venue called the Alpine Valley Music Theater, which is outside Chicago. Stevie Ray opened the show with his band Double Trouble, and watching him on the monitor in my dressing room, I remember thinking, 'Man, I've got to top the bill after this.' His playing was so fluid. It didn't seem like he was playing to emulate anybody; it just all came straight from him, seemingly played without any effort. It was very inventive, and his singing was great too. He really did have it all. I went on and did my thing, thinking that in the light of someone like Stevie Ray, I was a very eclectic musician, in that I didn't just play blues, I played ballads, reggae and all kinds of different things. The blues was in all of the things I did and the way I interpreted it. Also on the bill that night were Buddy Guy, Robert Cray and Jimmie Vaughan, and at the end of the show we all jammed together, Stevie Ray included, in a fifteen-minute version of the song 'Sweet Home Chicago'.

When the show was over, we all hugged goodbye and were rushed off to a series of helicopters that were waiting for us. They were the kind of choppers with big Perspex domes, and as soon as we got in I noticed the pilot using a merchandising t-shirt to clean the windscreen, which was covered in condensation. Outside, a thick wall of fog seemed to hover about ten feet above the ground, and I recall thinking to myself, 'This doesn't look right,' but I didn't want to say anything in case it promoted fear. After all, the last thing you want on a plane is a crazy person saying, 'We're all going to die,' so I just kept my mouth shut. At that moment, unbeknownst to me, Stevie Ray, who had been due to drive back to Chicago, had found a spare seat on one of the other choppers, along with two of my crew, Nigel Browne and Colin Smythe, and my agent, Bobby Brooks.

All four helicopters took off, flying up into a wall of fog. I remember thinking, 'I hate this sort of thing,' and then suddenly we were above the fog and it was a clear sky and you could see the stars. It was a short trip back to the hotel, and I went to bed and had a pretty good night's sleep. At about seven in the morning there was a call from Roger to say that Stevie Ray's helicopter hadn't come back, and no one yet knew what had happened to it. I went up to his room, where eventually we got the news that it had taken off, turned the wrong way and flown straight into an artificial ski slope. There were no survivors. Poor Jimmie had to go and identify his brother's body. The rest of the day was spent deliberating about whether or not we should carry on with the tour, or cancel it out of respect. The unanimous decision was to carry on, and though we went ahead and played that night's show in Kansas City in a state of shock, it was the best tribute to Stevie Ray we could have made.

During the *Journeyman* recording sessions, I was introduced to a pretty young Italian model, named Carla, who, by default, would become my next life teacher. Carla was introduced to me by a friend of Lori's, which in itself was a little odd, and caused a lot of problems for everyone over the next few months. Initially I wasn't overly interested, but she was clearly a music fan, and seemed quite taken with me. I was very flattered because she was only twenty-one, and very sexy, with long hair, a remarkable figure, and a young-looking face, which was slightly Asian, with high cheekbones and almond-shaped eyes. We began dating, and in a very short time I became obsessed with her.

I was living in New York while I made the record, and it served as a backdrop for our affair, very fast and very romantic. Carla took me to a great restaurant called Bilboquet, where I met and became friends with the proprietor Phillipe Delgrange. This place was the big hang-out for all the rich and fashionable Europeans in New York, and in my naivety, I believed I fitted right in. While it was still going strong, the Stones came through town on their Steel Wheels tour. Carla mentioned that she was a fan of theirs, and asked me if I would take her to see them. We went to the show, and afterwards I took her backstage to meet the guys. I remember saying to Jagger, 'Please Mick, not this one. I think I'm in love.' In the past he had made several unsuccessful passes at Pattie, and I knew Carla would appeal to his eye. For all my pleadings, it was only a matter of days before they started a clandestine affair. In the interim, I went to Africa to play a short tour, starting in Swaziland and going on to Botswana, Zimbabwe and Mozambique. The trip was supposed to reflect for the king of Swaziland what had been created in the UK for the Prince's Trust. I don't think it ever got off the ground, but it was a great excuse to have a look around Africa.

On my return, I visited Carla's family home in St Tropez, where I got a fairly chilly reception from Carla, but also got the chance to meet a couple of her previous boyfriends. They seemed like great guys, and they commiserated with me on my plight, implying that Carla tended to move through men quite quickly, sometimes quite ruthlessly. A short while later, after Carla had stood me up a couple of times, I got a call from the girl that had introduced us, telling me that Carla was definitely seeing Mick, and it was serious. I had heard rumours, and now apparently it was true. The obsession gripped me for the rest of that year, and took some grizzly turns when I found myself guesting with the Stones on a couple of shows, knowing that she was lurking somewhere in the background.

What did I learn from Carla? Not much at the time, but as time passed, I learned to differentiate between lust and love, and a little bit later, between pleasure and happiness. To her credit, once the seduction was complete, she didn't continue to lead me on, and at no time did she ever really express any deep feelings for me, but in my madness, I was able to convince myself that this was the love of my life. The deception involved in her affair with Jagger drove a deep wedge between me and him, and for a while I found it hard to think of him without malice. Later on, of course, I quietly felt both gratitude and compassion towards him, first for delivering me from certain doom, and second for apparently suffering such prolonged agony in her service.

Prompted by my obsession with Carla and Mick, I began to do some proper recovery work. For a start, it was deemed necessary by my sponsor that a fourth-step inventory be taken on the subject of my resentment toward them both. The fourth step is generally practised as an honest review of the past in order to identify the alcoholic's own contribution to his drinking problems. It can also be applied to specific situations in sobriety, where the lines of responsibility have become confused. It is

Rainbow concert.

At Carl Radle's house.

Me at Crystal Palace in the 70s.

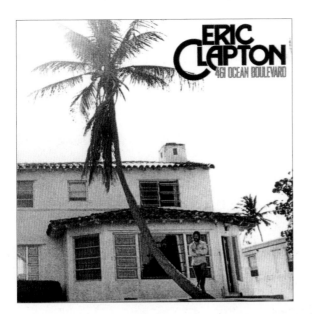

461 Ocean Boulevard
album cover.

George and me
at Friar Park.

Me enjoying a joint and a haircut on the set of *Tommy*.

Yvonne Elliman and me on tour.

70s touring picture.

70s conjunctivitis.

A polaroid of Pattie.

Me and Pattie
cutting the cake
on our wedding day.

Me and the wife heading off
to our honeymoon suite.

Our invitation to the
wedding party at Hurtwood.

HELLO

*Me and the Mrs. got married the other day, but that
was in America, so we've decided to have a bash in
my garden on Saturday May 19th about 3.00 p.m.
for all our mates here at home, if you are free, try
and make it, it's bound to be a laugh
.....see you then.....*

Eric and Pattie Clapton

R.S.V.P.
Hurtwood Edge,
Pitch Hill, Ewhurst,
Near Cranleigh, Surrey.
Telephone: Ewhurst 888

P.S.
You don't have to
bring any presents
if you don't
want to

Me at the house on Paradise Island.

Life on the beach at Paradise Island.
Left to right: Chrissie Wood, Pattie, Ronnie Wood and me.

Jack and Rose.

My mother Pat, me and Pattie.

Me and Muddy Waters
on his wedding day.

Me doing artwork for *One in Every Crowd*.

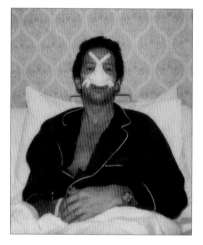

In hospital after surgery.

On tour in the 70s.

Members of the E.C.
Eleven. Left to right:
Phil Collins, Roger
Forrester and me.

Me and Beefy Botham relaxing on a fishing trip in Ballynahinch.

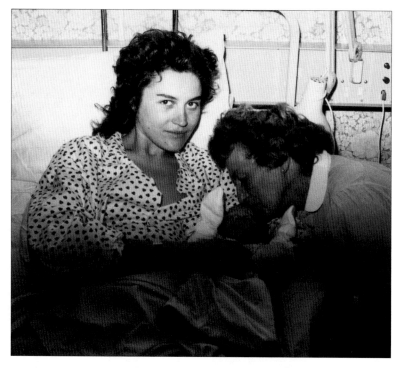

Lori and Conor in the hospital with Pat.

Left to right: Pat, me and Conor, Rose and Lori.

Backstage in the 80s.

The *Unplugged* album cover.

Left to right: Me, Pat, Rose, Sylvia and Adrian Clapton.

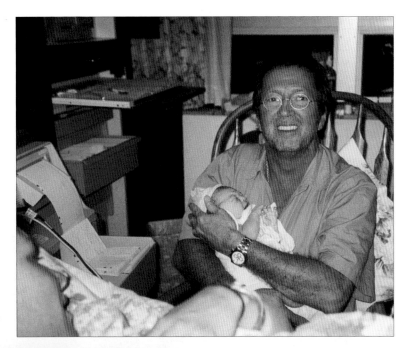

Me and Julie in
the hospital soon
after her birth.

Melia with Julie and Ella.

Me giving a guitar lesson to Julie.

Melia and I on our wedding day.

Me and Melia fishing
in Campbell River.

Giving a Ferrari-driving lesson to Julie on the driveway at Hurtwood.

generally symptomatic that alcoholics believe everything is being done to them, and that they are victims, with no control over their own lives. In terms of their ability to stop drinking, this is undoubtedly true, but in every other respect it can be changed or modified as they take more responsibility. This is part of what the steps are for. It came as a big surprise to me, therefore, to find out that I needn't have actually got into the relationship with Carla in the first place, I thought that it was something I had to do, and that I was compelled. What I found, as I worked through step four, was that I had chosen to do it, it was where I wanted to go and what I wanted to do. I didn't look at the reality of the situation at all, and with only two years of sobriety under my belt, I had very little notion of what was good for me.

I found a pattern in my behaviour that had been repeating itself for years, decades even. Bad choices were my speciality, and if something honest and decent came along, I would shun it or run the other way. It could be argued that my choices reflected the way I saw myself, that I thought I wasn't worthy of anything decent, so I could only choose partners who would ultimately abandon me, as I was convinced my mother had done, all those years ago.

I did not run away from Conor, even though there was to begin with a certain amount of fear involved in my relationship with him. I was, after all, a part-time father. Small children can be quite dismissive and unintentionally cruel, and I tended to take this very personally. However, as the time of my sobriety increased, I began to be more comfortable with him and to really look forward to seeing him. I was very much in this mood in March 1991, when I had arranged to see Conor in New York, where Lori and her new boyfriend, Sylvio, were planning to buy an apartment. On the evening of 19 March I went to the Galleria, an apartment block on West 57th Street where they were staying, to pick up Conor and take him to the circus on Long Island. It was the very first time I had taken him out on my own and I was both nervous and excited. It was a great night out. Conor never drew breath and was particularly excited at seeing the elephants. It made me realise for the first time what it meant to have a child and be a father. I remember telling Lori, when I took him back, that from then on, when I had Conor home on visits, I wanted to look after him all on my own.

The following morning I was up early, ready to walk crosstown from my hotel, the Mayfair Regent on Park and 64th Street, to pick up Lori and Conor to take them to the Central Park Zoo, followed by lunch at Bicé, my favourite Italian restaurant. At about 11.00 a.m. the phone rang, and it was Lori. She was hysterical, screaming that Conor was dead. I thought to myself, 'This is ridiculous. How can he be dead?' and I asked her the silliest question, 'Are you sure?' And then she told me that he'd fallen out of the window. She was beside herself. Screaming. I said, 'I'll be right there.'

I remember walking up Park Avenue, trying to convince myself that everything was really all right . . . as if anyone could make a mistake about something like that. When I got near the apartment building, I saw a police line and paramedics on the street, and I walked past the scene, lacking the courage to go in. Finally I went into the building, where I was asked a few questions by the police. I took the elevator upstairs to the apartment, which was on the fifty-third floor. Lori was out of her mind, and talking in a crazy way. By this time, I had become very calm and detached. I had stepped back within myself, and become one of those people who just attend to others.

By talking to the police and the doctors, I established what had happened without even having to go into the room. The main sitting room had windows down one side, which went from floor to ceiling, and they could be cantilevered open for the purpose of cleaning. There were no window guards, however, since the building was a condominium and escaped the normal building regulations. On this morning the janitor was cleaning the windows, and had temporarily left them open. Conor was racing about the apartment playing a game of hide and seek with his nanny and, while Lori was distracted by the janitor warning her about the danger, he simply ran into the room and straight out of the window. He then fell forty-nine floors before landing on the roof of an adjacent four-storey building.

There was no way that Lori was going to come down to the mortuary, so I had to go and identify him on my own. Whatever physical damage he had suffered in the fall, by the time I saw him they had restored his body to some normality. As I looked at his beautiful face in repose, I remember thinking, 'This isn't my son. It looks a bit like him, but he's gone.' I went to see him again at the funeral home, to say goodbye to him, and to apologise for not being a better father. A few days later, accompanied by various friends and family, Lori and I flew back to England with the coffin. We went back to Hurtwood, where the Italians all wailed, openly expressing their grief, while I remained quite detached, in a permanent daze.

Conor's funeral took place at St Mary Magdalene's church in Ripley on a cold, bleak March day shortly before my forty-sixth birthday. All the Ripleyites came and it was a very lovely service, but I was speechless. I looked up at his coffin, and I just couldn't talk. We laid him to rest in a plot right next to the wall of the church, and as his coffin was lowered into the ground his Italian grandmother became completely hysterical and tried to throw herself into the grave. I remember feeling a bit shocked by this, as I'm not very good at outward emotion. I just don't grieve that way. When we came out of the churchyard, we were faced with a wall of reporters and photographers, about fifty of them. The curious thing is that while a lot of other people were very upset and insulted by what they considered to be a lack of respect, it didn't impinge on my own grief in any way. I just didn't care. All I wanted was for it to be over.

After the funeral, when Lori's family had gone home and Hurtwood was quiet and it was just me alone with my thoughts, I found a letter from Conor that he had written for me from Milan, telling me how much he missed me and was looking forward to seeing me in New York. He had written 'I love you.' Heartbreaking though it was, I looked upon it as a positive thing. There were thousands of letters for me to read, written from all over the world, from friends, from strangers, from people like the Kennedys and Prince Charles. It blew me away. One of the first I opened was from Keith Richards; it just said 'If there's anything I can do, just let me know.' I'll always be grateful for that.

I cannot deny that there was a moment when I did lose faith, and what saved my life was the unconditional love and understanding that I received from my friends, and my fellows in the twelve-step programme. I would go to a meeting and people would just quietly gather round and keep me company, buy me a coffee and let me talk about what had happened. I was asked to chair some meetings, and at one of these sessions, when I was doing a chair on the third step, which is about handing your will over to the care of God, I recounted the story of how, during my last stay in Hazelden, I had fallen upon my knees and asked for help to stay sober. I told the meeting that the fact that the compulsion had at that moment been taken away was, as far as I was concerned, physical evidence that my prayers had been answered. Having had that experience, I said, I knew I could get through this.

A woman came up to me after the meeting and said, 'You've just taken away my last excuse to have a drink.' I asked her what she meant. She said, 'I've always had this little corner of my mind which held the excuse, that if anything were to happen to my kids, then I'd be justified in getting drunk. You've shown me that's not true.' I was suddenly aware of the fact that there was a way to turn this dreadful tragedy into something positive. I really was in the position of being able to say, 'Well if I can go through this and stay sober, then anyone can.' At that moment I realised that there was no better way of honouring the memory of my son.

CHAPTER FOURTEEN
THE AFTERMATH

The first few months after Conor's death were a waking nightmare, but the condition of shock prevented me from completely breaking down. There were also work commitments that I had to deal with. To begin with, Russ Titleman was sitting in a studio with a pile of tapes from the twenty-four shows I had done at the Albert Hall in February and March. I couldn't engage with the music at all, and didn't really want to be there, until he played me the version of 'Wonderful Tonight'. For some reason, listening to that song had a very calming effect on me, and I went into a deep sleep. I hadn't slept for weeks until then, so it was a very healing experience. I think it was because the song took me back to a reasonably sane and uncomplicated point in my past, where all I had to worry about was that my partner was late getting ready for dinner.

Back in the present, I bought a house in London, and built a house in Antigua. I couldn't stand sitting alone in Hurtwood after what had happened, so I asked one of my oldest friends, Vivien Gibson, to come round every day to answer the mail. Viv and I had been friends for many years, having started out when we had an affair during the eighties, and she was now working full-time as my secretary. She was also one of the only people that I wanted to have around me at this time. Somehow she understood my grief and was not afraid of it. It's amazing how many so-called friends disappear in the face of this kind of tragedy. She is a truly courageous person with tremendous compassion, and a lifelong friend. I also felt I needed a complete change of scenery. So with Roger in tow, I drove around London looking at houses until I found a beautiful house in Chelsea. Set back off the road in a side street, it was perfect. It had a courtyard to park in, and a small walled garden.

At the same time, with the help of Leo Hagerman, a developer in Antigua, and Colin Peterson, his friend, and an architect, I set about designing and building a villa within the grounds of a small resort hotel on Galleon Beach in English Harbour, on the south coast of Antigua. What was I doing? I was running in several directions at once. In fact, until Roger put a raging stop to it, I almost bought another country house, with the intention of selling Hurtwood altogether. Ostensibly, the London option made sense, the general consensus being that I should be around people for a while, and Hurtwood had so many memories. As for Antigua, I had been going on holiday there for years, and had brought Lori and Conor there many times. There was a flourishing community of crazy people in English Harbour, and I felt like I fitted right in. The governing factor in all of this though, was motion – keep moving, under no circumstances stay still and feel the feelings; that would have been unbearable.

I was three years sober, with just enough recovery to stay afloat, but no real experience or knowledge to be able to deal with grief on this scale. Many people might have thought it was dangerous for me to be alone, that I would ultimately drink, but I had the fellowship, and I had my guitar. It was, as it always had been, my salvation. Over the next two or three months, in England and Antigua, I stayed alone, going to meetings and playing the guitar. To begin with, I just played, with no objectives, then songs began to evolve. The first to take shape was 'The Circus Left Town' about the night that Conor and I went to the circus, our last night together. Later, in Antigua, I wrote a song linking the loss of Conor with the mystery surrounding the life of my father, called 'My Father's Eyes'. In it I tried to describe the parallel between looking into the eyes of my son, and seeing the eyes of the father that I never met, through the chain of our blood.

A few years later, in 1998, a Canadian journalist, Michael Woloschuk, was to take it upon himself to track down my real father, only to find out when his search was done that the man he was supposed to be, Edward Fryer, had died back in 1985. I suppose it shamed me into setting about a search of my own, or at least an attempt to authenticate his findings. I didn't get very far. The trail was muddy and I was never really convinced that this man was really my dad. At best all I could do was to verify what the reporter had already found out. All through my life, people had asked about my father, to the point where I had taken an 'I don't want to know' stance just to close the subject down. Consequently I had always resisted any impulse to find out the real truth, and by the time I did try, it was, it seemed, too late.

The most powerful of the new songs was 'Tears In Heaven'. Musically, I had always been haunted by Jimmy Cliff's song, 'Many Rivers to Cross', and wanted to borrow from that chord progression, but essentially I wrote this one to ask the question I had been asking myself ever since my grandfather had died. Will we really meet again? It's difficult to talk about these songs in depth, that's why they're songs. Their birth and development is what kept me alive through the darkest period of my life. When I try to take myself back to that time, to recall the terrible numbness that I lived in, I recoil in fear, I never want to go through anything like that again. Originally, these songs were never meant for publication or public consumption, they were just what

I did to stop from going mad. I played them to myself, over and over, constantly changing or refining them until they were part of my being.

Towards the end of my stay in Antigua, I chartered a boat for a two-week trip around the islands with Roger and his wife. I have always loved being by or on the sea, and although I have no ambitions to be a sailor, I find the scale of the ocean very calming and revitalising. To begin with, however, it wasn't a great success. Roger and I were at loggerheads over various things, and the atmosphere was chilly. During the trip we were joined, first by Russ Titleman, and then by Yvonne Kelly and my six-year-old daughter, who she had named Ruth. This lifted the mood, and the cruise took an upward turn.

Amongst the letters that had come in about Conor had been one from Yvonne, in which, to help me in my loss, she had offered me the opportunity to become fully acquainted with Ruth, as her father. It was an incredibly generous act, and gave me some direction until the fog cleared. This little sea cruise was in fact the first of many small visitations that took place to test the water for this idea, and it worked. It was great to be in the company of a child again, my child. I will always be grateful to Yvonne for having given me this second chance. It was a lifeline in a sea of bewilderment and confusion. Over the next couple of years, I visited them in Montserrat, slowly establishing a rapport with my daughter, until Yvonne decided that in order for Ruth to get a proper education, and spend more time with me, they would come home to Doncaster, the Yorkshire town where Yvonne had been brought up.

So far as helping me cope with the death of Conor, developing a relationship with Ruth was, to begin with, no more than a Band-Aid solution, and it wasn't until the pity was taken out of the equation, and we started to have fun, that it became a real thing for me. It took time, because first I had a lot of work to do repairing myself, and until that was done, my ability to be emotionally intimate with my daughter was seriously limited. As for discipline, I had a lot to learn, and was very unsure of my entitlements with her, but slowly, bit by bit we got to know one another, and I learned through therapy how to express my disapproval when it was necessary. Looking back on those years, I realise what a profound effect she had on my well-being as a whole. Her presence in my life was absolutely vital to my recovery. In her I had found again something real to be concerned about, and that was very instrumental in my becoming an active human being again.

In the early summer, I took a trip to New York to look at a film being made by a woman called Lili Zanuck, wife of the American movie producer Richard Zanuck. It was called *Rush* and was based on a true story about a female undercover narcotics agent, who becomes an addict herself. Lili was a big fan, and wanted me to do the score for the film. I had never taken on an entire project like this before, most of the film work I had done up until then having been supervised by the American arranger and composer Michael Kamen. We had got together to do music for an English thriller TV series called *Edge of Darkness*, and then the *Lethal Weapon* films, which had followed from that. In all honesty, from what I had seen thus far, I had no great love for the movie industry. I love film, and am a real movie buff, but being behind the scenes left me cold.

Nevertheless, I took the job, mainly because I liked Lili. She was outrageously funny, and I loved and identified with her views, be it on movies, music or just life. At the end of the summer I took up residence in LA and started working on the film. Lili assigned a guy called Randy Kirber to be my assistant, and he was fantastic. He showed me the ropes, and created beautiful musical pastiches for me to compose over. We were a great team, and I hope one day we can do it again. I remember at some point playing 'Tears In Heaven' to Lili, and her insistence that we put it in the movie. I was very reluctant. After all, I was still unsure about whether or not it should ever be made public, but her argument was that it might in some way help somebody, and that got my vote.

The song was released as a single, and was a massive hit, my only self-penned number one as far as I can remember. The film didn't do so well, although it deserved to. It was a controversial subject, and some scenes were quite harrowing to watch, but I thought it was sensitive and true to its purpose. It's since become something of a cult hit, and I'm extremely proud of the music.

I finished up the year by touring Japan with George Harrison. He and Olivia had been really kind to me over the last few months, and I wanted to express my gratitude. During the trip, Lori showed up out of the blue, and just checked into our hotel. Her boyfriend Sylvio had faxed me, warning me that she was coming to see me. They had broken up, and he was worried about her sanity. I couldn't handle it. I was just about holding myself together, and there was work to do. Curiously enough, George stepped in and took control. They travelled around together, and he seemed to have a calming influence on her. I felt very guilty about not being able to comfort her, but I was experiencing tremendous feelings of anger and sadness, with no real idea of how to cope with that and her at the same time.

By Christmas I had moved into London, and was enjoying being back in Chelsea after a twenty-year absence. The neighbourhood at the World's End hadn't really changed much at all, although the King's Road east of the town hall was almost unrecognisable. In the sixties there had literally been only three, maybe four boutiques in the whole of Chelsea, and now the Sloane Square end was wall-to-wall clothes shops, mostly rubbish. But I loved being back, and pictured a new era of bachelorhood dawning. I still thought that diversion was the solution for my grief, and that dating would take my mind off the loss of my son, as if it really worked like that.

Part of the reason for moving into London was to stop myself from being isolated, and to try and develop new friendships. Although London is a notoriously lonely town, I found within a few months I had met and become friends with quite a few people. My oldest friendships to this date, apart from my school friends, come from these days in Chelsea, Jack English, who is a great photographer, Chip Somers, who now runs a successful rehab called Focus, Paul Wassif, a great guitar player and counsellor, Emma Turner, who now works for Goldman Sachs and sits on the Crossroads board, and Richard and Chris Steele, who ran the rehab section of the London Priory for a number of years. Over the next decade in London, my life began to fill up with all kinds of interesting people, many of whom also happened to be in recovery.

I got a big kick out of watching Monster restore and furnish my new house with beautiful antiques and, inspired by his passion, I started buying art for the walls. I had just stumbled on to the work of Sandro Chia, and Carlo Maria Mariani, and began filling up the house with their canvases. It was the first time I had spent big money on art, and I remember showing Roger a Richter I had just bought in an auction for £40,000. It was grey brushstrokes from top to bottom. Roger couldn't believe it. I wish I had a picture of his face when I told him how much it had cost. Over the next couple of years I built up quite a respectable collection of contemporary painters, and became deeply interested in art all over again.

1991 was a horrendous year on the face of it, but some precious seeds were sown. My recovery from alcoholism had taken on a new meaning. It really was the most important thing in my life now, and had given me direction when I thought I had none. I had also been shown how fragile life really was and, strangely enough, had somehow been cheered by this, as if my powerlessness had become a source of relief for me. The music too took on a new energy. I had a need to perform these new songs about my son, and I really believed that they were meant to help, not just me, but anybody who had or would suffer such extraordinary loss. The opportunity to showcase them came in the guise of an *Unplugged* TV show for VH1. I had been approached to do it, and wasn't sure, but now it seemed like the ideal platform. I sat in my house in Chelsea and worked out a repertoire for the show that would allow me to revisit my roots, and present these new songs in a safe and careful environment.

The show was great. Andy Fairweather-Low and me did quite a lot of bare acoustic work on the Robert Johnson and Broonzy material, and we performed 'Tears In Heaven' and 'Circus Left Town', although I later vetoed 'Circus' on the grounds that it was too shaky. I also enjoyed going back and playing the old stuff like 'Nobody Knows You', which was how it all started in Kingston so long ago. Russ produced the album of the show, and Roger was like an expectant father hovering over the project, while I was fairly dismissive, saying that I thought we ought to put it out as a limited edition. I just wasn't that enamoured with it, and as much as I'd enjoyed playing all the songs, I didn't think it was that great to listen to. When it came out, it was the biggest-selling album of my entire career, which goes to show what I know about marketing. It was also the cheapest to produce, and required the least amount of preparation and work. But if you really want to know what it actually cost me, go to Ripley, and visit the grave of my son. I think that's also why it was such a popular record, I believe people wanted to show their support for me, and those that couldn't find any other way, bought the album.

The American summer tour that year, however, threw this particular phenomenon back in my face. 'Tears In Heaven' was high in the charts, and I was trying to open the show with it, in front of crowds of people who were screaming their heads off, with the result that I couldn't hear myself think, let alone play. I would come off stage every night, heartbroken and angry that they weren't listening. I felt I couldn't do the song justice, and with no stagecraft to fall back on, I had absolutely no idea what to do about it. How do you tell 20,000 people to curb their enthusiasm? It was a no-win situation. It eventually did calm down, however, and I found that putting the acoustic songs in the middle of the set gave the audience a chance to settle down before the big hit was launched on them.

The end of the year saw the birth of what has become an annual event for me – the New Year's Eve sober dance at the leisure centre in Woking. It had started the year before as a disco in Merrow, suggested by my friend Danny, as a recourse for people who don't want to drink on New Year's Eve. It was a great success, and marked my first ever attempt at sober dancing. But when we held the post-mortem meeting the day after the dance, some bright spark asked why we couldn't have live music in future, seeing as how there was such an abundance of talent in the fellowship. The dance has been going strong ever since, and I play every year, except in emergencies. I always look forward to it because it's fun, it's very relaxed and I can play anything I want. On top of that, I know that it has also kept a few people from drinking who otherwise would have succumbed to the pressure of the various festivities.

Meanwhile, dating was going full strength, but I was trying to restrict my attentions to women in recovery, the theory being that they would be safer, or saner, than my previous girlfriends. I obviously still had a lot to learn. One woman in particular had a profound effect on me. She lived in New York, and was quite self-possessed, enough not to be manipulated by me anyhow. This manifested itself in her views on smoking, or at least my smoking. I was not allowed to smoke in her apartment for one thing, and it made me very angry. But I liked her, and I thought it might be going somewhere, so at a dinner party a few months later, when I was introduced to a hypnotherapist named Charlie, I took the plunge. I had been smoking heavily ever since my twenty-first birthday party, and now I was smoking at least forty a day, sometimes sixty.

I went to see Charlie on a Monday morning on my way to rehearsals, and knew, deep down, that if I got to bed that night without a cigarette, then it was over. It was tough to begin with, and for the first month, from time to time I did feel like I had taken some bad acid. Overall, however, I was beside myself with joy for having beaten such a disgusting addiction. I have spoken to hundreds of people since then about the way they gave up smoking, and have been quite astonished at how many of them still miss it. For myself, stopping smoking was like giving up alcohol. I have never missed it, and not even in the darkest moments of my life have I ever felt like lighting up a cigarette, or taking a drink. Lucky fellow, you may say, but I really believe it is about spiritual application, no matter how poverty-stricken I feel my application may be.

Could it be, then, that without nicotine in my system I was emotionally vulnerable to the next woman that came along? Without a shadow of a doubt. That, coupled with the fact that she was quite fond of drugs and booze, was very vivacious and was totally unavailable, made her probably the most dangerous woman I would ever meet. But it takes two, and I was in a very illusory period of my life. I was swollen with success and feeling very sure of myself, although just under the surface there were caverns of grief, which weren't really being dealt with at all. I was definitely heading for a fall.

The woman in question was another Italian, named Francesca. She was a fine-looking girl, with dark hair and a slim, but at the same time voluptuous figure, with a face slightly reminiscent of Sophia Loren. Her mother worked for Giorgio

Armani. Giorgio and I had become friends over the last few years, and I was seeing quite a lot of him, going to his shows and socialising. I think he's an amazing man and a great designer, and I felt very proud and flattered that he would want to get to know me. When, through him, I was introduced to this young girl, I had no inkling of how much she would come to mean to me, I just thought she was interesting and refreshingly bright, that's all. Within months I was on my knees.

Our affair lasted for three years, but at no time did we actually live together. I think it's important to acknowledge this, because it should serve to illustrate how temporary and shaky the whole thing was. It would wobble along for a few days, and then the wheels would fall off, and it would be back to square one again. Francesca was a Gemini, totally unpredictable, and prone to violent outbursts of temper. On the other hand she could be as sweet as honey, and totally beguiling. The problem was, you never knew which one you were going to get. I think we broke up nine or ten times in that whole period, and I was addicted to her throughout.

Unhappy though I was, and despite the warnings of my friends, who could see no future for me in this relationship, I went crawling back for more, time after time. One day, while I was entertaining my friends Chris and Richard Steele in Antigua, I confided in them about my troubles, and showed Chris a letter I had written to Francesca to get her opinion. She looked at me as if I had landed from another planet. 'Why are you giving this woman all your power?' she asked. I had no idea what she was talking about, but I was intrigued. Chris was at that time director of the alcohol and addiction unit of the Priory psychiatric clinic in Roehampton, but I had heard that she also conducted one-to-one private counselling sessions. I asked if she would see me, and she said yes. For a while, I didn't really know what I was getting into. I thought that I could pick her brains to find ways to control

Francesca, but I was to find myself going in a very different direction altogether.

Chris' first question to me, at our very first session was, 'Tell me who you are,' a very simple question you would think, but I felt the blood rush up to my face, and I wanted to yell at her, 'How dare you, don't you know who I am ?' Of course I had no idea who I was, and I was ashamed to admit it. I wanted to appear that I was ten years sober, and fully mature, when in fact I was only ten years old, emotionally speaking, and starting from scratch. Her attitude to the relationship was pretty novel too. While everyone was saying get out, and that the girl was no good for me, her view was that my troubles were nothing to do with Francesca. In fact she liked her. What I needed to address, according to Chris, was what I was doing there in the first place. In short, her counsel was that I should stay there, until either I'd had enough, or learned whatever it was I needed to learn.

The essence of this period of my life was that the recovery work I was doing balanced up the chaos in my personal life. The crazier it got with Francesca, the deeper I delved into recovery, especially therapy. Along with Paul Wassif, who I had met through Francesca, I began doing peer-support work at the Priory, which involved taking a short training course, and among other things allowed us to sit in on group therapy sessions with clients at the beginning of their day. I loved it, it gave me a sense of real responsibility, and at times it was like living theatre; you never knew what would happen next, and the results could be so positive, sometimes miraculous. I also began working with a therapist who specialised in John Bradshaw's methods, in particular looking at family history as a guide to undoing present dysfunctional behaviour. My mum and my uncle were definitely suitable cases for treatment, and my past was riddled with weird scenarios. No wonder I was living it all out again in the present.

As much as I was engaged on a voyage of personal self-discovery, I was also rediscovering my roots. Having opened the door to my true musical tastes with *Unplugged*, I decided it was time to say thank you to the blues, and to the players and singers who had inspired me so much throughout my life, people like Elmore James, Muddy Waters, Jimmy Rogers and Robert Johnson. I went into the studio with the approach that everything would be recorded live, and having chosen the songs, we would play them as much like the original versions as possible, even down to the key they were played in. It was great fun, and I loved every minute of it. It was what I had always wanted to do. Unfortunately Roger didn't agree. I think he felt that having scored so strongly with *Unplugged*, I was squandering a golden opportunity. I don't know what else he had in mind, I was too busy marching to my own drummer, but it marked the beginning of the end for us.

My absorption with the blues project also blindsided me to the whole revolution that was taking place in the English music scene. Britpop and DJs, jungle and drum and bass, it was all going on and I had no idea. Plus, from what I could gather from Francesca, who was deep into all of this stuff, the culture was heavily fuelled by Ecstasy, and various other 'designer' drugs. I felt very much the same feelings as when punk burst on the scene in the eighties: scared and threatened, because even though I didn't view myself as 'the Establishment', I was fully aware that they did.

From the Cradle, which was what I called the new album, did very well, going to the top of the charts in the States, which was pretty good for a no-frills blues record. I toured on the strength of this for nearly two years, playing nothing but the blues all over the world, blissfully unaware of the way the music industry was changing. It was while I was on the American leg of this tour that I got the call from Francesca, telling me she had gone back to her old boyfriend and that it was finally over between us. I was devastated, and poured my heart out to anyone who would listen, and by this time that list had got quite short. In fact the whole weary business dragged on for another year, but the real heart had gone out of it, for both of us. To give her credit, like Carla several years earlier, Francesca had tried to make it clear right from the start that she didn't really want a full-time relationship. I just didn't want to hear her.

The end of the affair, when it finally came, coincided with an electrical fire in my London house, which seemed like an omen to me. I also saw it as an opportunity to wipe the slate clean, and start again from scratch, so I emptied the house, sold all the contents and began again. Now that Francesca was out of my life, I started to investigate the culture that she was so much a part of. I listened to everything I could get my hands on, and I woke up to what was happening with street fashion too. It was weird, because a lot of it tied in with the old fifties and sixties street look that I would wear in the Yardbirds – Levi's and windbreakers, hoods and sneakers – but there was a new angle on it. I started looking at graffiti art, and began collecting it. It was like a whole new world had opened up to me, the only problem was, I felt I was too old to be getting into this. I hated the idea that I was this old guy, trying to come across as a hip young street dude, but the culture was drawing me in, it was powerful and I felt like I understood it. What could I do? I was hooked again.

I began designing things once more, I had always been interested in great design, whether it be furniture, cars or clothes it didn't matter, and as much as design does not really recognise fashion, I felt it was OK for a guy my age to be interested in these things. I met a couple of ex-skaters called Simon and William who had a head shop called Fly in the King's Road, and we started a label called Choke. With me sharing most of the design duties, we made some very nice stuff for a couple of years, until the business end of it became unmanageable. Then, through Simon and his friend Michael Koppleman, I met Hiroshi Fujiwara and Hiroki Nakamura, and over the last few years we have become friends. Hiroshi is a great designer, among other things, and has influence over a very large area of the modern street culture. When I first met him, he was involved with a label called Goodenough, and was starting some other labels, the most prominent one now being Head Porter Plus. Hiroki designed for Gravis when I first met him, and now has his own label, Visvim; these are the clothes I wear every day, they are simple and beautifully designed. I also became very close to the graffiti writer Crash, and bought a lot of his work. So Francesca, for all her obstreperousness, indirectly turned me on to a whole new lifestyle, and also, accidentally, was involved in the founding of Crossroads Antigua. Not bad for someone who I literally wanted to strangle every time I saw her.

CHAPTER FIFTEEN
CROSSROADS

One day, during the summer of 1994, I got word from her family that Alice, who had disappeared for a while in France, had shown up again in England and was seriously ill in hospital in Shrewsbury. This didn't come as a great surprise to me since over the years I had heard that she was still getting pretty messed up. Now that I knew where she was, and that she appeared to have hit a rock bottom, it occurred to me that it might be the right time to try to get her some help. I talked to Chris and Richard about her, knowing how good they were at dealing with situations like this, and they very kindly went up to see her and talked her into coming back to the Priory with them.

Because of our past together, it was considered ethically inappropriate for me to work with Alice in group therapy, but at one point Chris called me in to tell me that there was a lot of anger still hanging about from our relationship. They needed to address this in order for her to be able to move on, and had come to the conclusion that it would be beneficial for her to be able to confront me with these feelings. They warned me that it could be quite a traumatic experience, but there would be a counsellor present, and I felt I could handle it. When the day came, she ranted at me for about an hour without stopping, regurgitating all the scenarios from our fractured past with absolute clarity. It was terrifying to realise the damage I had done to this poor girl, but I had to stay silent and just absorb it. It was a humbling experience, and at times I could hardly believe the things she said that I had done. It was as if she was talking about somebody else. The saddest part for me was knowing that she had held on to all this poisonous stuff for over twenty years, in order to fuel her need for oblivion.

Alice stayed in the Priory for the entire course of treatment, and on a couple of occasions I bumped into her and asked how she was doing. 'It's going great,' she would say, so I was fairly hopeful that it was going to work. I knew it would take a long time once she got out of the clinic, and that she would have to find something to do to regain her self-esteem, but the fact that she had stayed put was, in itself, a fantastic achievement. The next thing I heard was that she had gone into a halfway house in Bournemouth, a facility that I'd visited once, and remembered as being a really good place, so I was confident that she was making progress, and anticipated that she would soon be on the road to a full and complete recovery.

I went off on tour to America, and the next time I saw Alice was at my grandmother's funeral. Though Rose had been ill for some years with emphysema, it was cancer that took her in the end. Her death, just before Christmas 1994, was a huge blow to me. She had always been the one constant figure in my life, encouraging me in all my endeavours, and loving me uncon-ditionally to the very end. Her house was always a refuge, and at weekends, when I was home, it had become a tradition to go there for delicious Sunday lunches. Until my drinking kept us apart, we had had a wonderful life, and some very funny times together. All in all, up until that point, she had been the single most influential person in my life.

In the last few years, encouraged by Chris in my counselling sessions, I had spent a lot more time with both Rose and my mother, in the hope that we could heal the wounds that had for so long prevailed in our collective relationship. My mother in particular was quite sick, and had become fairly dependent on prescription drugs. She became very jealous, even of me, which made life very complicated. At one point her and Rose had a dreadful rivalry going in which they would use my visits against one another. So when it came to calling on them, I would have to take turns as to who I would see first, one week my mother, the next week my grandmother, and so on. It was exhausting, and so when Rose died, as much as I really missed her and grieved for her, there was a certain relief in the fact that I didn't have to play that awful game any more.

Four months after Rose's death I heard the news that Alice had also died. She had checked herself out of the Bournemouth halfway house and moved into a bedsit where at some point she had injected herself with a massive dose of heroin. The post-mortem also revealed that she had been drinking heavily. She died alone, and her body was not discovered for several days. I was gutted and could scarcely take it in. I really had thought that she had a chance, and then something that Chris had told me came back to me. When Alice was still in the Priory, she had said to Chris that she couldn't stand the pain of being sober. That only emphasised to me how fortunate I was in that, through all my years of drinking and drugging, I still had music. It had always been my salvation. It made me want to live. Even if I wasn't playing, just listening would pull me through.

My own work in the Priory, and my relationship with Chris, now led to one of the most significant periods of my life. On my recent trips to my house on Galleon Beach in Antigua, I had become increasingly disillusioned with the number of addicts and drunks that were springing up, or maybe it was just that I was noticing them more now. There were, for instance, a couple of places I liked to hang out in English Harbour, in particular a bar owned by a friend of mine called Dougie. I used to go in there to play pool, and sometimes just people-watch, but when I came out I'd get hit on by some of these guys, who were quite frightening, and it began to wear me out.

Coming home from one trip there, I confided in Chris and Richard about this dilemma, saying that I was thinking of selling up, and not going back again, and they both said, 'Well, why don't you take the programme to Antigua?' I asked how I would do that, and Chris said, with a twinkle in her eye, 'You've got the money, build a treatment centre.' She also said, if I were to do that, then she would advise me. My immediate reply was, 'Well, I'll build a treatment centre if you come and run it.' This was not such a crazy idea, as I knew that Chris was experiencing some difficulties with the way the Priory was run. But it was the way she ran the rehab that impressed me. I really believed in her philosophy of treatment, and how it could be applied, collectively and individually. It really hinged on the need to always come back to focusing on the individual, so the scheduling had to be flexible in order to achieve that aim. A tall order, but that was the ideal I wanted the new clinic to be founded on.

I was introduced to the head of the Priory group from America, who turned out to be a music fan, and I told him what I had in mind. To my surprise he seemed quite interested in the idea. In fact he was so enthusiastic that I felt vaguely suspicious. My intuition was telling me that things were not what they seemed. Nevertheless I forged ahead, explaining that I was happy to provide much of the finance and the experience I had of recovery, but that I needed help in creating an infrastructure, and that was where the Priory group would come in. The object would be to build the clinic in Antigua, with a view to servicing the entire Caribbean area. It was accepted that few clients would initially come in from the local communities, and that we would need to promote the centre elsewhere, drawing on people from America and Europe who would pay to come there and thus fund scholarship beds for the locals who couldn't afford it. It was a Robin Hood scheme really; take from the rich to feed the poor. Finally, we had to headhunt somebody to be the chief clinician, and the person we found was a lady called Anne Vance, who came from the Betty Ford Clinic in California.

The more I considered it, the more excited I became by the project, to which we gave the name the Crossroads Centre. It seemed like the perfect antidote to the toxicity of my love life, and I was excited by the idea of doing something to pay back for all the good times and spiritual healing that I'd got in Antigua. It really has been one of the only places on earth I've found where I can completely discard the pressures of my life, and blend into the landscape. The villa that we had built in English Harbour, however, had become a bit of a tourist landmark, and I had asked Leo to find something a bit more remote. He showed me a piece of land jutting out into the sea, just around the coast from Falmouth, that was absolutely beautiful. I bought it on the spot, and eventually extended back until I owned almost the whole peninsula, and set about building a house on the very end of it. As for the treatment centre, the next step was to make it all legal, so hundreds of documents were drawn up, and the wrangling between Roger and the Americans began. It got a bit heated from time to time, and I wondered every now and then if we were all in it for the same reason, but it was early days and I had nothing to guide me but my intuition.

Of course, we also had to sell the idea to the Antiguan government, and that's where it got really funny. The Cabinet of the day invited us to show them what we had in mind, and at the end of our presentation, during which I gave a shortened version of my drinking and recovery history, the health minister asked if it would be OK for him to visit the centre sometimes, whenever he felt he needed to lose some weight. They obviously had no idea of what we had been talking about, and it dawned on me then that we would be facing similar responses in every direction we turned. There was absolutely no notion of what recovery was in the Caribbean. Alcoholism was still regarded as immoral or sinful behaviour, with gaol time and social ostracism being the only practised solutions. In order to set up a treatment centre here, we were going to have to educate, and to a certain extent emancipate the entire community. At this point I needed to ask myself some very deep soul-searching questions: what business was this of mine? What right did I have to try to bring these kind of changes to a community that, on the face of it, wanted just to be left alone? The answer was always the same. In order to keep what I had, I had to give it away. In order to stay sober, I had to help others to get sober. That is the main principle which still governs my life today, and I had to apply it to this situation. I was in no doubt, however, that if I was wrong, or if it was simply not meant to be, I would soon find out, when the whole thing came crashing down around my ears.

Even though it was quite clear that they simply didn't get it, we decided to go ahead anyway. Then, about a third of the way into the building, I got word from Roger that the head of the Priory conglomerate in America had decided to sell his share of the Crossroads project to another healthcare corporation that had no interest in building a rehab in Antigua. They were either going to scrap it, or sell it to me. Roger wasted no time in telling me to cut and run, because the alternative was picking up the whole thing myself, which would cost an enormous amount of money that I would probably never see again.

While I knew there was no choice but for me to go ahead, I don't think Roger ever really understood the kind of commitment I felt for this. To start with, I had given my word, if only to myself, that I would finish what I had started. If I abandoned everything, it would probably mean that I would never be able to return to Antigua, and by this time, we had cleared ground, and were already starting to lay foundations. In fact, we'd got quite a long way into the construction, and the word was out. The other thing was I really believed in the project, I had seen enough people who were, on the face of it, hopeless cases, turned round to start a new life as happy human beings. I knew that it was worth it, and my reasoning was that if only one person came out of there sober, and managed to stay sober, then the whole thing would have been worth it.

I turned away from Roger, and in one fell swoop became the sole owner of a half-built treatment centre that nobody but me wanted. A lot of money had already been spent, and it looked like quite a lot more would follow when we found out that they'd cut corners with the building, and had not really laid the foundations correctly. Even though it wasn't completely built, walls were cracking and doorways were warping, so I called in Leo, who was helping me build my house in Indian Creek, and asked him to have a look at it. He gave me a full report, and said it was shockingly done, but it wasn't beyond hope, so we set him up as the building manager, and gave him the job of putting it back in shape.

I felt let down by Roger, which was symptomatic of a general decline in our relationship. Over the course of a year, we had disagreed on just about everything, a lot of it being to do with my growing need to take responsibility for myself. Now that I was actually a thinking human being again, with a modicum of self-respect and pride in what I was able to do, I wanted to become more involved in the decision-making process of my business, and the more this became clear, the more it set Roger and I at odds. A perfect example of this, which happened while we were in the middle of all the problems in Antigua, was when I got a direct call on my home phone from Luciano Pavarotti, asking me if I would play at his annual concert in Modena to benefit children affected by war. I said I'd love to, and thanked him for asking me.

Speaking to him directly was wonderful and a brand-new thing for me, because for so long I'd been kept away from any kind of contact like that. I then called Roger and told him that I had been asked, and had accepted the invitation to play at Pavarotti's event. I passed on the phone number of Pavarotti's agent, asking if he would attend to the business end of things. It seemed like a reasonable request to me, but I could feel a bristling at the other end of the line. This was not the way he wanted to work it.

Deciding to go ahead with the treatment centre was one of the first decisions I had made for myself, and it felt great. It took my mind off the disastrous goings-on with Francesca, and gave me cause to feel good about myself. But I had written some songs that needed to be finished and realised these had to be done before I could feel completely at peace with myself. For this I turned for help to Simon Climie. We had met at Olympic Studios, and though I knew him best as a songwriter and one half of the group Climie Fisher, I also knew he was producing modern R&B records, so it seemed for me like a natural progression. We also had a lot of musical tastes in common. In fact our relationship as collaborators began as my affair with Francesca limped into oblivion, as he was one of the few who would still listen to my tale of woe. I would go round to his house, and he'd make me tea and provide a sympathetic ear, and then we would play. It was power-ful stuff. Most of it was done on his computer, using Pro Tools, with me jamming away or writing melodies on top.

We managed to persuade Giorgio Armani to let us do the music for one of his fashion shows, and took that and turned it into an album called *Retail Therapy*. We called ourselves TDF which stood for Totally Dysfunctional Family, and launched our music on to the club scene, with twelve-inch singles and radical remixes. We decided that we would remain totally anonymous, in the hope that the music, on its own merit, would provide our credibility. Sound familiar? It was totally ignored, until someone got wind that I was somehow involved, and then the whole thing became completely untouchable. It was a shame really, because it was a good album. In truth, however, it was just a warm-up for *Pilgrim*.

I had told my friend, the legendary drummer Steve Gadd, that I wanted to make the saddest record of all time. He said that he could identify with that. It was a dangerous ambition, but in the aftermath of Francesca, one that I felt I could accomplish. We booked the studio, and made the whole album up as we went along. The only prewritten songs I had ready were 'Circus' and 'Father's Eyes', neither of which seemed to have found their right incarnation yet. For almost a year, we worked day and night, sometimes just perfecting little guitar motifs, or honing and reshaping tracks with the Pro Tools system that Simon is a master of. The result was one of my favourite albums; I poured my soul into this one, and I believe you can hear that.

Every now and then Roger would come to visit us in the studio, and I knew he was not happy, I don't think he liked the music much, and we were running up incredible studio costs. I could see his point, but I was convinced there was no other way to make this record. It had to bleed out of me until there was nothing left to be said or done, however long it took. The situation with Roger and me had been getting more and more strained and tenuous over the last two years, and there was very little we did agree on any more. I was becoming more interested in the overall direction of my career, and had almost entirely stopped asking Roger for advice. Also I no longer felt the need to have hits, or be overly concerned with what was expected of me, either from my audience or the record company. It was borderline arrogance, but

I needed to spread my wings. Artistic integrity became more and more important to me, and in a distorted way it all started to resemble my last days with Giorgio Gomelsky and the Yardbirds.

Then one day I received a letter from Roger in which he told me that I might not have been aware of it, but when he was working on my behalf, I sold this amount of records and made that amount of money. He then proceeded to list all the areas in which he was in disagreement with me regarding the way I was now running things for myself, and the mistakes I was making, and they were numerous, everything from the way I made my albums to audience seating at concerts; I found it really insulting and offensive. I thought it was time for a showdown.

I had been collecting Tibetan Dzi beads for quite a while. These are rare stones that are sometimes found in the earth in Tibet and are thought by local people to have been dropped from heaven. They are supposed to be pre-Buddha, and to have great power and meaning. I put together a string of them and wearing them round my neck tucked underneath my t-shirt, I went to Roger's office to dissolve our partnership. Since he had always claimed that contracts meant nothing, I didn't expect there to be any serious legal ramifications, but I was totally unprepared for how badly he took it. He was visibly shaken, even though I had taken great care not to lay criticism at his door. I simply thanked him for all he had done for me over the years, and told him I had learned everything I could from him, but now it was time to fly the nest. He was quiet for a minute, and then said, 'Well, I thought there was going to be something like this, but I thought you were just going to ask me to stay out of your private life, and would still want me to handle the money and the business.' He then offered to find me a new manager. 'If I need a new manager, Roger,' I told him, 'I'm quite capable of finding one myself.' Looking faintly amused, he wished me luck, though I don't think he meant it. I remember coming out of the office and walking back towards Chelsea, and feeling three feet off the ground. Roger's contract officially ended three months later, although my financial obligation is still tailing off today. I haven't set eyes on Roger since that day, and that saddens me. The humour and fun we shared were phenomenal, even after I'd stopped drinking. We had an incredible journey together, and he successfully restarted a career that was as good as over. Maybe we will meet again and laugh at our memories one day. I hope so. They were precious times.

Of course I had made contingency plans for this day, and the first was to make my solicitor, Michael Eaton, aware of what I was about to do, and to tell him what I had prepared for the aftermath. In truth I was abysmally unprepared for the reality of breaking up with Roger, and I knew that the only way to play it out was to follow my heart. This I did by asking two of the closest people who already worked for me to come in closer and help re-establish my business situation. They were Vivien and Graham Court. Graham came into my life on the recommendation of my production manager, Mick Double. At the time I was being stalked by yet another crazy woman, who was convinced that I had stolen all my songs from her, through the ether. It sounds mildly funny, but she was deadly serious, following me around the world, and once even showing up at the gates of Hurtwood. The final straw came one day when she turned up at a gig, and when she was searched, a gun was found in her handbag. Enough was enough, and it was deemed I needed proper protection. Graham has been at my side almost ever since. He is a brilliant companion and exceedingly reassuring to have around. So these were the people I wanted to help me manage my life from now on. For a little while it was Amateur City, and at Vivien's urging, I asked Michael to become my business manager, thereby putting some structure into the company, and he has been at the helm ever since, adding the much-needed ingredients of sanity and reason to the equation.

By the time Roger and I had parted company, the Crossroads Centre had opened its doors, and was up and running, with Anne Vance at the helm and a weekly programme, based on the twelve steps, in place. When Anne started to talk about promotion, however, I became nervous because I saw a dichotomy that might prove hard to resolve. While a treatment centre depends for its existence on being quite vocal and self-promoting, the twelve-step fellowship relies on anonymity and secrecy. Yet we needed promotion and it had to be honest.

I got an idea from an event I had attended just before Christmas 1998, when Bobby Shriver, whose mother, Eunice, is the founder of the Special Olympics, invited me to play in front of the Clintons at a concert at the White House to celebrate the thirtieth anniversary of the SO. The event, which was hosted by Whoopi Goldberg, consisted of the artists involved, who included Mary J. Blige, Sheryl Crow, Jon Bon Jovi and Tracy Chapman, performing Christmas songs like 'Santa Claus Is Coming To Town' and 'Merry Christmas Baby'. It took place in a marquee on the White House lawn. I remember being desperate to pee, but since finding a toilet would have meant having to go through complicated security and back into the main building, I decided to sneak out and have a pee on the lawn. I opened a flap in the tent and walked out into the darkness and had just undone my flies when I heard 'Don't move!' and there was a SWAT man there, all in black and camouflage pointing an M16 at me. The event made a huge amount of money for the SO through the release of an album of the show, and it occurred to me that this was the kind of road we should go down.

This was a busy and exciting time for me. Having let go of Roger, I was travelling all over the place to try to round up my business, spending time in New York, and visiting LA to talk to record companies. I'd bought a house in Venice, California, and I was footloose and fancy free, beginning to really enjoy life again.

In LA, I talked to Lili Zanuck about the White House concert and about what she thought might be the best way to promote Crossroads. She suggested that we should do something in Hollywood, and came up with the idea of a concert combined with a guitar auction. It sounded a great idea.

In early March, I got a call from my sisters, Cheryl and Heather, to say that my mother, who had moved to Canada after my grandmother's death, was dying. She had been ill for a while, and they had been keeping me aware of the growing uncertainty of her condition, so it didn't come as much of a shock. I flew up to Toronto to be with them. I still had such mixed feelings about Pat. The last few years of her life had inspired a lot of disturbance in my own. Even though I was in my mid-fifties, it seemed like I was still looking for someone to take her place. I tried to kid myself that all my girlfriends since Pattie had been different from one another, all originals, and on the face of it, you could be fooled into thinking that. But in one or two essential elements, they had all been the same: always unavailable, sometimes unstable, and in terms of my sobriety, even dangerous. Were these the conditions that had governed my feelings about my mother, and was I still unconsciously trying to replicate that relationship? I think so. My low self-esteem had dictated all my choices. I had chosen what I knew and was comfortable with, but they had all been unworkable situations. I had done a lot of family-of-origin work in my recovery, but it seemed like I would never be able to break the mould.

My mother's passing was difficult, for everyone. There was a dreadful dilemma, created by the fact that it wasn't really clear amongst any of the family whether she was truly aware of her plight, and that she might be going to die. I went looking for a counsellor in the hospital, to see if this had been broached with her. When I was told that the subject had not been discussed, I said I thought it was important that we did talk to her about it. I

299

tried to instigate a discussion, with the counsellor present, but she didn't want to know. As much as we tried to introduce the reality of her situation to her, she clung on to the notion that she was going to get better. So I went along with it. After I had returned to my hotel, a call came to say that she'd had another attack, and had gone into a coma. We all went back to the hospital, and they told us that she'd signed papers saying that if things became bad, then she did not wish to be resuscitated. We were all sitting there with her when she died, but it was very traumatic, because I don't think she was fully aware of her predicament, and at the last minute she resisted. She didn't want to let go. It was very painful, and it left me, and I think my sisters too, angry and frustrated. I am still haunted by the sadness and loneliness of her last minutes. I really believe it's important for people, at that stage of their departure, to know exactly what is going on, but what we have had to honour and accept was, whatever her reasons, that was the way she wanted it. I flew back to the West Coast and went into a sort of emotional blackout.

For a while I was mooching around in a state of shock until the necessity of organising the Crossroads fundraiser with Lili snapped me out of it. The idea was that I would donate a number of guitars – 100, to be precise – from my lifetime's collection, to an auction at Christie's, New York. First of all, however, there would be a preview of forty of them at a gala evening in Hollywood to be thrown by Giorgio Armani, who was a master party-giver. The event took place at Quixote Studios in West Hollywood on 12 June. It's an enormous space, and they had converted it into a vast Moroccan tent. It was a fantastic party. Moroccan food was served, and the guest list of 500 was sprinkled with movie stars. The evening included a concert given by Jimmie Vaughan and his band, with me jamming, as ever.

I had gone to the party with two dates, a couple of glamorous West Coast ladies, who I didn't know very well, and was feeling very detached and numb, which is the way I usually feel at big gatherings anyway. Suddenly a very beautiful girl came up to me with her friend, and asked if she could have her picture taken with me. She said her name was Melia, and her friend was called Satsuki, and they were part of the Armani staff, helping show people to their tables. It was clearly against the rules, as they'd been given instructions not to fraternise with any of the guests, but there was something about Melia that got me right away. I think it was her smile, which was totally open and genuine, so I said I'd have my picture taken with them if I could take them both out to dinner the following night. They giggled and said yes, and we made a date. I left alone a little while later, and looked back to see if I could see Melia in the crowd. I found her, our eyes locked, and there was that smile again. I can think of many times when this has happened in my life, but there was always some kind of device employed, seduction, aloof indifference, some act, some angle. This was different. It just felt honest, and great.

CHAPTER SIXTEEN
MELIA

The following day, I dropped round the Emporio Armani store in LA, where Melia and Satsuki worked, and took them to lunch, and after that the three of us dated, for about a month, and had fun. We went to restaurants and openings together and were generally seen around town, and tongues soon began to wag, for good reason I suppose, since both these ladies were half my age. There was nothing sexual in it yet, however. We were just having the time of our lives. I didn't care much what people thought. It wasn't supposed to be serious, and anyway I would be leaving town soon, to perform at a Crossroads benefit concert in New York, and that would probably be the end of it.

In the meantime there was the guitar auction to think about. I had picked out 100 guitars to sell from my collection, together with several amplifiers and a number of Versace guitar straps. The guitars, predominantly Martins, Fenders and Gibsons, were all good vintage instruments, not necessarily collector's items, they were just guitars that I particularly liked to play, and which I had picked up over the course of my career, often in junk shops, pawn shops and second-hand shops. Christie's had put together a fantastic catalogue in which they had made a point of highlighting their careers. It was a brilliant idea because what made the collection intrinsically pretty valuable was the fact that each guitar had been used on something fairly significant. So, for example, a 1958 Gibson Explorer which had been used on the ARMS tour fetched $120,000, the 1974 'Rodeo Man' Martin, which had been my main guitar during the seventies, fetched $155,000, a 1954 Sunburst Stratocaster, which had accompanied me on numerous tours including the Behind the Sun tour, went for $190,000, while my 1956 Fender 'Tobacco Sunburst' Strat, known as 'Brownie' and on which I played 'Layla', fetched an astonishing $450,000.

Sadly I wasn't able to attend the sale as I was rehearsing in LA, so I watched it on a live feed on the internet. Brownie was the last guitar to be sold and when it was brought out on to the revolving rostrum, they played 'Layla' over the PA and the whole audience stood up. It really was an extraordinary event, raising $4,452,000 for the Crossroads Centre, a sum that was beyond my wildest dreams. It also hugely raised the awareness of what we were trying to do in Antigua, as did a documentary featuring the centre made by *Sixty Minutes*, the US TV show. Ed Bradley, the celebrated journalist, came down and spent a week researching and interviewing myself, and different members of staff. It came out very well, and I revealed a great deal about my own journey, taking as much care as I could to protect my own anonymity. Whether or not I did that successfully, I cannot say, but the feature was brilliantly done, and has brought hundreds of clients to the centre, people who would not have known anything about it otherwise, and many of them are still sober. I will never be able to express my gratitude enough to the people who made that programme, they helped save a lot of lives.

A week later, I took Melia and Satsuki to New York where I was to host and perform in a Crossroads benefit concert at Madison Square Garden. The show was called Eric Clapton and

Friends and was put together by myself, Peter Jackson and Scooter Weintraub. I had met Scooter back in the eighties when he was organising commercial sponsorship for high-level artists like Michael Jackson, and we had been friends ever since. He is a big music fan and loves the blues, so we get on like a house on fire. The line-up for the concert was Mary J. Blige, Sheryl Crow and Bob Dylan, all guesting with my band. The music was fantastic, and was preserved on a DVD that continues to rake in money for the centre. It was during these few days that I first began to take a serious interest in Melia. She just seemed so natural, a beautiful girl with a big heart, and no agenda or ambition, and I had the feeling she was getting serious about me too. After the concert, I flew home to England for a break, but couldn't get her out of my mind. I knew I would have to go back to LA soon to finish up working on a film score, and I couldn't wait to see her again. Unfortunately, when I eventually returned there, a couple of months later, Melia was out of town visiting with her family in Columbus, Ohio, so I dated Satsuki until she came back. At that point we hadn't really talked about breaking up the threesome, but I knew I couldn't put off making a choice any longer, and when Melia returned from Ohio, I asked her if she would like to come back to England with me. She said yes without hesitation, but she had no passport. There was a last-minute scramble for her to get one, and next thing I knew, we were on the plane home to England.

The big obstacle for any woman I had started to get close to up until then was Hurtwood. I loved this house, I had been there for a good part of my life and it would be an important requirement for any woman that came into my life, that she felt comfortable there too. Without fail, almost all the girls I had brought there in the past had found it overwhelming, even threatening. Maybe the atmosphere, with its memories, was too daunting, who knows? But from the very start, Melia was fine.

She loved it, and we had a great time there together. In the early days, the question of our age difference was a little bit of a problem for me, though only in terms of how it was viewed by others, for as much as I like to pretend that I don't care what people think, I really do. I am a chronic, recovering, people-pleaser. But that soon passed, the strength of our mutual attraction far outweighed anything as superfluous as age, and if she didn't care, why should I?

When we started to live together, it suddenly felt as if a huge weight had been taken off my shoulders. All the competitiveness and comparative thinking that I had experienced in the past just disappeared. I suddenly found myself with a friend and a lover, and the two things were actually compatible. I didn't have to look around any more. My age or her youth seemed pretty irrelevant, because the fundamental ingredients were right. We enjoyed one another's company, respected each other's feelings, and shared very distinct similarities in our tastes. Most importantly we were drawn to each other through love and friendship. Imagine how this felt for me, having just lost the one woman I could never get close to. I had finally found someone who was not only available, but also seemed to have my best interests at heart. The mould was finally broken. Maybe it had broken when my mother died, I don't know. The important thing was, at the age of fifty-four, I had probably made the first healthy choice in a partner in my entire life.

I was happy for the first time in as long as I could remember, and I didn't really have a plan, work-wise or domestically, I just wanted to live in the moment for a while without any resolution. I sensed, however, that Melia wanted, or maybe needed, to know where our life was going. We would talk about it, and I would evade the issue to a certain extent. I had become used to living on my own, and in the years of recovery, had learned to enjoy my own company. A full-time relationship, at this point in my life, would mean giving up an awful lot of territory, as well as time that I had only just learned to cherish. I also knew, intuitively, that this was as good as it was ever going to get for me, so really my choice wasn't too difficult. I had had a good run, if you can call it that, and I was happy to know that my life was entering a new, fuller phase. I had achieved as much as I could on my own, and now I had a chance to find out what a real partnership was like; it would be pure insanity to walk away from this.

Musically, life was full too. Over thirty years since we had first jammed together at the Café Au Go Go, I finally cut the album with B. B. King that he and I had been talking about for a long time. We called it *Riding With the King*. Working with B. B. was a dream come true, and I put together a band that I felt could rise to the occasion. Remembering the Atlantic session with Aretha that I had played on where there were wall-to-wall guitar players, I thought I'd like to give that concept a try. On bass it was Nathan East as usual, Steve Gadd on drums, Tim Carmen and Joe Sample on keyboards, and Doyle Bramhall, Andy Fairweather-Low and myself on guitars. On one track Jimmie Vaughan joined us, and it worked so well, I kind of wished I'd asked him to do the whole thing.

All this time I was living in LA with Melia, in the house I had bought a year earlier, when I thought that I might move to LA. It was a beautiful modern construction built by the Japanese architect, Isozaki. Situated one block back from the mellow end of Venice Beach, it was a perfect bachelor pad and I loved it. But now that life had taken a more domestic turn, I began to question my reasons for living there. Maybe because Melia was American, I continued to entertain thoughts of staying in California, and we began to look for places up north, maybe somewhere like Santa Barbara, but I knew we would never find anything to beat Hurtwood, and finally giving in to homesickness, we went back to England for good.

The next album I made in this period was *Reptile*, which was inspired by the death of my Uncle Adrian. He passed away in 2000, and at his funeral, Melia got her first taste of what was left of my crazy, wonderful family. It also hit me between the eyes how big an influence he had been in my life, and how much he had shaped, just by example, my view of the world. After the funeral, hosts of memories came flooding back: movies we had seen together, music he listened to, his whole stance haunted me for days. I also felt dreadful remorse that I hadn't found a way to step in with regard to his drinking, which had become a problem. My principle has always been to mind my own business unless I am asked to help, but I now wonder if this wouldn't have been an exception to that rule.

I wanted to make the *Reptile* album with the same concept as the B.B. album, but there were two major additions: one was Billy Preston, and the other the Impressions. Billy had been part of my musical experience from the day I first saw him play with Little Richard, when we were both in our early teens, and I finally got to play with him when he signed with Apple and we recorded the album *Encouraging Words* back in 1970. Now he was at a loose end, and I asked if he would like to play on the album and join my touring band. I was delighted when he said yes. He had been my favourite keyboard player for as long as I could remember, and now we could finally play together. I had also been a lifelong fan of Curtis Mayfield, and had the honour of being invited to sing with the Impressions at his memorial service in LA. I asked if they would come and sing on the album, and was over the moon when they said yes too.

There was a short break in the middle of the recording schedule, and Melia and I flew up to Vancouver for some fishing. Melia had never picked up a rod before, and took to it right away. We were fishing for pink salmon, and she caught far more than me. She was a natural. The place we were staying in wasn't too luxurious, and I knew from the fact that she didn't complain that she was the girl for me. She didn't mind at all, in fact, she seemed to quite like roughing it, and I do too.

In the autumn of 2000, Melia and I were on holiday in Antigua when she told me she was pregnant. At first I was a bit taken back. We had talked about kids and I had said I wasn't sure if it was a good idea because of my age. I didn't know if I would have the energy for such a huge commitment. But as I let the idea wash over me, I realised it was exactly what I needed, and I was overjoyed. The following year I began a world tour which had been planned before I knew of Melia's condition. It was a little difficult, but all we needed to do was arrange the dates around the predicted birth date, so that I could be there.

The band for the tour was Billy Preston, David Sancious from Bruce Springsteen's E Street Band, Andy Fairweather-Low, Nathan East and Steve Gadd. It was a great outfit, and benefited greatly from Billy's presence. He was a natural leader himself, so for me it was almost like guesting with Billy. It was very tight and very creative. By the time we got to the States Melia had gone back to Columbus to be with her folks for the approaching birth date. She wanted to establish a rapport with the local medical people well in advance. From my side, I enlisted Graham and Nigel to set up a home base for us, so that when the baby was born we would have somewhere of our own to stay until it was time to go home. I was getting very excited. I had been present at Conor's birth and that was miraculous, but this was different. For one thing I was sober.

Peter Jackson, my tour manager, had arranged the dates so that I could stay with Melia during the day in Columbus, and then commute to the shows in the evening by plane. Though it was a bit gruelling overall, it was a good arrangement, in that it meant I could provide support and attend pre-birth counselling etc. Then one day we went to see the doctor to finalise Melia's hospital schedule, and she said she thought Melia ought to go in right away. I panicked. I wasn't ready now that it was actually about to happen. I got scared. Ridiculous really, because there would be very little expected of me. I would be on the sidelines, but I just couldn't handle the unknown of it all.

We went straight into hospital, and our daughter, Julie, was born that night, 15 June, 2001, around ten o'clock. The bliss we felt on her arrival was slightly marred by some minor difficulties that we weren't really prepared for. It has always been my understanding that babies feed on their mother's breast on impulse, straight away, without any coaching, just pure instinct. That wasn't the case with Julie. She seemed confused, and didn't want to feed at all. We later found out, when we got back to England, that having entered the world from the womb, the bones in her head didn't completely decompress, which made it difficult for her to swallow when she tried to feed, and she would gag. It was nothing serious, just an alignment issue with some of her bone joints, but we didn't know that then, and we were really worried. After getting some advice from a friend, we quickly got her to a sacro-cranial therapist who, after some fairly traumatic realignment sessions, managed to get her back on track. But for the first three months of her life she suffered from dreadful colic, which, unbeknownst to us, was directly related to this problem, and it was fairly normal for one of us to be carrying her around screaming in agony, without thinking there was anything unusual about it. Gradually, in fact quite quickly after getting her treatment, she turned the corner and became the joy of our lives, and I wondered how I could have ever envisioned my life without this divine creature in it.

Once Julie arrived, we had to start arranging our lives to fit this new reality. There was no doubt in either of our minds that Hurtwood was the best place to begin raising children, but we hadn't really decided on how to approach the family-help situation. Melia began interviewing nannies, because although we wanted as much direct involvement as possible, it was clearly going to be necessary to have someone standing by if one of us got sick, or if I had to go off to work. We had no idea how difficult this was going to be, or how complicated. It transpired during one interview, for instance, that in an emergency situation, probably because of insurance requirements, a properly trained nanny would have responsibility priorities over both parents. A ridiculous scenario, and totally unacceptable, if legally, I suppose, understandable. We finally found a wonderful lady named Annie, who has been with us ever since, and to supplement the situation when necessary, Melia's sister Maile has occasionally stepped in. In addition, we had one other source of help – a great book given to us by Lili Zanuck, called *The Baby Whisperer*. Written by a British child-care expert, Tracy Hogg, it was really invaluable to us, and helped us in every department, especially with sleep patterns, and I thoroughly recommend it to anybody who's starting a family.

I had to work out the rest of the year on the road, coming back to Columbus when I could, and on one visit to New York, I went into a jeweller's and bought a ring, a modern design by the Roman jewellery designers, Buccellati. It was a spontaneous action, but I had obviously been subconsciously working up to it. When I got back to Columbus, I went round to see Melia's dad, and asked for her hand in marriage. It was an emotional moment, and he was very gracious, making me feel like I really belonged in his family. Half an hour later, I was on one knee in front of Melia, asking if she would marry me. It was a fantastic moment in my life, and cynical old bastard though I am, I really believe that this is where it all began to change for me, as if the sun had finally decided to shine.

The final leg of the tour was in Japan, and Melia and Julie joined me for part of this. We really didn't like being apart at this time, especially as we were both learning so much about being parents. Graham was a great help to us, as he has always been. He is tremendous around kids, firm but loving, and ours think the world of him. It was tough for me, trying to do both roles, and I knew it wasn't a pattern I would want to repeat again too often, though of course we have done it since many times. Maybe it was just that Julie was so young, and we were so green.

Halfway through the Japan tour, during a long stint at the Budokan, I got the news that George Harrison had died of cancer on 29 November. I had been following his condition through one of our closest mutual friends, Brian Roylance, who had been spending more and more time with him as his health gradually failed. The last time I had seen him was in late 1999, shortly after he had been attacked so brutally at Friar Park. The three of us had sat in his kitchen as he relived the night that the crazy guy, Michael Abram, had come after him with a knife. George was still very disturbed, and didn't seem to know where to go with his life. I could only use my own predicament with addiction as a reference, encouraging the possible use of some kind of support system, although maybe that's how he saw us. I know that with Brian, he had the best friend a man could ever have. I only wish I could have been more help. There had been an opportunity back in 1991, when Olivia and Brian had seen the possibility of rekindling his interest in performing live. We had put together a package, using all my existing touring paraphernalia, and toured Japan. It was a fine show, well rehearsed with great songs and tremendous musicianship, but I knew his heart wasn't in it. He didn't really seem to like playing live, so it did nothing for him, except maybe he saw how much he was loved, both by his fans, and by us.

Back home from Japan in December, Melia and I arranged with Chris Ellson, the Ripley parson, for Julie to be christened. We had also been talking to him for the last few months about the different ways we could get married. It was really important for us to be able to have as private a function as we could, since Julie's birth had already made us a target for the paparazzi, so the normal wedding processes, putting up the banns etc., were completely out of the question. Chris had an idea, which we both loved, even though it would take careful planning. We invited our closest family members and a select little group of friends to come to Julie's christening service, and on New Year's Day, 2002, we gathered in the church of St Mary Magdelene in Ripley, which already held so many memories for me, and baptised our six-month-old baby girl.

Melia's mum and dad were there, and my Auntie Sylvia, and the godmothers and godfathers. It was a simple moving service, and at the end Chris announced, 'At this point, there is usually a closing prayer, but the parents have asked for something different,' and started, 'Dearly beloved, we are gathered here together, to join the hand of this man, and this woman, in holy matrimony.' You can hear a pin drop anyway in that ancient old building, but this was like 2,000 pins dropping. It was fantastic. I looked around at the shocked and stunned faces of my in-laws, family and friends, and realised that they had no idea what was happening. We had succeeded in keeping it a complete secret from everybody. It was a perfect way to do it, and so romantic, we couldn't have planned it better, and not a journalist in sight. Having posed for Chip, a dear friend of ours who took our wedding photos outside the church, we drove home to Hurtwood, listening to Stevie Wonder singing: 'Bridge Over Troubled Water'; our new life had begun.

Several months before, a new man had come to work at Hurtwood, his name was Cedric Paine, and we had been friends for a very long time. Cedric had done odd jobs for me and quite a few other musicians over the years, and up until now had been freelance, then I heard a rumour that he was looking for a 'steady job', for one boss, and I snapped him up. He is a good man and we needed somebody really trustworthy to take over the job of caretaker. The former one, Ron Mapstone, had expressed a desire for retirement, and he would be a hard man to replace. Ron had been with me since the seventies, having taken over from the original family, Arthur and Iris Eggby and their son Kevin. Throughout my career there has been a steady wave of 'loonies' showing a fairly unhealthy interest in my private life, and to have someone with good resolve and a bit of authority up at the gatehouse is essential. Cedric more than fits the bill, having been a policeman in one of his incarnations. I don't think he ever arrested anybody, but it gives him a bit of grit. All in all he is a lovely man, and a comforting presence to have around.

In the spring of 2002, Brian came round for dinner and we talked about George. I wanted to know how it had been for him during his illness. Brian assured me that George was fully aware of his circumstances, and that he had been calm and happy. I ventured the remark that it was sad that there would be no memorial for George, at least in a musical sense, and Brian said, 'Not unless you do something.' The trap was sprung, and I happily walked into it.

It was a labour of love, which I threw myself into. Over the next few months Olivia, Brian and I planned the event, discussing who we would ask and what songs we would play. Olivia master-minded the whole thing, and I planned and assembled the rock part of the programme. Ravi Shankar and his daughter Anoushka were writing music specially for the show, and it was decided that that was how the gig ought to begin. I thought the band that regularly played the New Year's Eve gig would be ideal as a nucleus, and invited them. This was Henry Spinetti, Andy Fairweather-Low, Dave Bronze and Gary Brooker. We then asked people who had been special in George's life to come and sing a song. All went well, and we managed to get the Albert Hall for the night of 29 November, which was a year to the day that George died. The only minor difficulty arose over who should sing 'Something'. Olivia thought I should sing it. Paul McCartney had been doing it on the ukelele in his shows, and wanted to do it that way, and I wanted Paul to sing 'All Things Must Pass', which I considered to be the key song of the whole event. In the end we compromised and Paul and I did 'Something' as a duet, and later in the show, he performed a brilliantly soulful version of 'All Things'. It was a great night, and everybody that was there or has seen the DVD agrees that it was the perfect send-off for a man we all loved, and who, throughout his life, gave us so much beautiful music.

During this year, Graham decided that he needed to be back in the States with his family, so we needed to find his replacement. He had helped me through a sticky patch, and although his days in the office were over, I knew that we would get together again soon.

As long as I had been living in Chelsea, we had been doing quite a lot of business with the local Mercedes dealer, and had got to know their sales manager pretty well. His name was Cecil Offley, and the first time I actually met him, he had run from his office to help me push a Ferrari that had broken down. I knew from this little incident that he had a good heart, and with Graham's blessing, I asked him on board. He has been with me ever since, and has proved to be an absolute godsend in every way imaginable.

At home it was a period of settled domestic bliss for me and Melia, made even happier by the arrival of a second daughter, Ella Mae, born on 14 January, 2003. I was now determined to stay at home and learn how to be a father. I had learned a little from my experience with Ruth, but she had already been semi-raised by the time we met. As for Conor, I never really had a chance, and now I wanted to start from scratch. I honestly don't believe I could have been a proper father before. I just didn't have the wherewithal. It has taken twenty years of non-stop sobriety for me to acquire any kind of maturity, and to be able to enjoy wearing the mantle of responsibility that parenthood requires. A lot of the time, in my day-to-day relationship with the kids, I have had to learn to just stay in the background and support Melia, even if I don't agree with what's going on, because I have found, on reflection, that she is usually right, and also, being an only child, I have had very little experience of healthy family life. My wife's intuitive knowledge often astounds me, and in the occasional difficult family situation that arises, just being there and staying there is sometimes all that's required from me, and that in itself is a big one.

CHAPTER SEVENTEEN
A FAMILY MAN

After a while it was time to start on another album, and I knew I needed to write about the great things that were going on in my life. It is not an easy thing to do, writing songs about happiness, but I wanted to bear witness to how radically my life had changed. To begin with I addressed the basics, and started dropping round to Simon Climie's house every day for a couple of hours, where we would experiment with different rhythmic ideas, trying to lay foundations for me to write on. It was slow, arduous work, and lyrics just weren't coming, but I knew there was no sense in trying to force it. They would come when the time was right. We did have studio time booked, however, and the usual suspects were standing by – Andy Fairweather-Low, Billy Preston, Steve Gadd, Doyle Bramhall and Nathan East. When the day arrived to begin recording, however, it was clear to everyone that there was not enough material to work with, and with the level of proficiency that we had within the musicians, we would soon run out of things to do. So I came up with the idea that whenever there was a lull in the proceedings, instead of getting frustrated, or trying to force something through, we would play a Robert Johnson song, to relieve the tension and just have some fun. There was no agenda in place as such, but for some reason his influence had resurfaced in my consciousness. It was interesting, too, to see what players like Billy Preston and Steve Gadd would make of his music, and how they would interpret it. As usual, I tried not to steer the proceedings, and just let everybody play the way they felt it. It was amazing. Within two weeks we had a complete Robert Johnson tribute album, *Me and Mr Johnson*, without ever having had any intention to do anything of the kind. It just grew out of necessity, from nothing.

My whole life I had intended to make this album, but until now, just like with my children, I had not been ready. It was a good record I thought, with great work from everybody, and I really loved doing it. It was representational but not derivative, and the songs came to life because of the way they were played. Tom Whalley, the head of my record company, Reprise, seemed happy with it too. Over the years, my relationship with Warner Brothers, with whom I had been for so long, had become pretty disjointed, as one executive after another either left or was fired. I had originally signed with Mo Ostin back in the seventies, and the team that they had in place back then was pretty awe-inspiring: Larry Waronker, Ted Templeman and, of course, Russ Titleman. But everything had changed, and some of those guys, along with Robbie Robertson, had gone to Dreamworks. Today, what has evolved from my original agreement is that I deal with Tom over projects and ideas, while I retain Rich Fitzgerald, who had been my 'inside man' at Warners and had been laid off, as a sort of independent record man, who monitors what is going on with the record company on a day-to-day basis. Over the years, he has become a good friend, and in an industry which abounds with hustlers and faceless corporate entities, he stands out as a decent, honest man, with a passion for music and boundless energy, who really cares about what he is doing. I wish there were more like him.

With the completion and delivery of the Robert Johnson record, the other compositional album was put on hold, to give me time to come up with more songs, and try to make a decent record of what was going on in my life, without rushing it. I asked Hiroshi Fujiwara if he would be interested in directing a video for the Robert Johnson project, more for fun than to promote it. He said he liked the idea, but asked to bring in a friend of his, who had more experience of this kind of thing, Stephen Schible, the co-producer of *Lost In Translation*, a film I really loved. As soon as these two came on board, the whole project quickly transformed into something else, and what started out as a simple video quickly became a fully fledged documentary.

Stephen and Hiroshi thought we ought to examine my preoccupation with Robert Johnson, and explain, if possible, what it was that had kept his music fresh for me. I saw it as an opportunity to finally express my gratitude to this great musician. It was also pretty interesting to watch these two guys, who on the face of it were quite modern men, quickly fall under the spell of Johnson's music, and also be equally captivated by the mystery surrounding his life and death, just as I had been, all those years ago. It helped confirm what I and many others had always believed about Robert Johnson. He really was the one. *Sessions For Robert J* became a DVD, and included interviews, and some decent live versions of some of the songs from the album, plus solo performances of me playing 'Crossroads' and 'Love In Vain'. All in all, a very worthy effort I think, and I finally felt like my debt was paid.

The album was released in March 2004, and at the latter end of the year, I went into the studio to finish the 'family' album. I had written four songs that talked directly about my new role as a family man, 'So Tired', 'Run Home', 'One Tracked Mind' and 'Back Home', and I was very proud of them. I also wanted to pay tribute to Syreeta Wright, who had passed away in July, with

'Going Left', and to George with 'Love Comes To Everyone', which I had originally played on. I recorded a couple of Doyle Bramhall's songs too, 'Lost And Found' and 'Piece Of My Heart' and did a cover of a Detroit Spinners song I had always loved called 'Love Don't Love Nobody'. I called the album *Back Home*, and the title song summed up exactly how I felt about my new life. It felt like a good album, and I couldn't wait to play it on the road.

Another thing that I'd always wanted to do was to put on a music festival. Maybe it was to make up for the fact that through being drunk, I had missed the first one I ever attended, at the ripe old age of fourteen. That summer of 2004, I put this to rights by staging the Crossroads Guitar Festival in Dallas. With the help of Michael Eaton, Peter Jackson and Scooter Weintraub, plus the rest of my domestic and road crew, we put together a two-day event and invited a fantastic array of musicians to play, including B. B. King, Buddy Guy, Carlos Santana, Jimmie Vaughan and J. J. Cale, all of whom graciously donated their instruments for a second auction, which Christie's was to hold in New York. In order to try to reduce logistical problems, we combined the festival with the beginning of an American tour. I thought the family would enjoy being there, so we all flew into Dallas at the beginning of June for rehearsals, only to find that we had landed smack in the middle of a series of electrical storms. For the next week, while we struggled to assemble the festival, storms raged all around, sending down sheet lightning and rain like I had never seen before. Strangely enough, my sweet little girls slept soundly each night through the most savage conditions, while I was quaking with fear, on my knees, praying for the weather to move on and spare our festival.

The day before the first show, the rain stopped, and the event was a great success. I spent the whole day welcoming and listening to all of my favourite musicians. I was like a kid in a sweet shop. At some point in the proceedings I asked J. J. Cale if he would consider making an album with me. In fact, what I asked was for him to produce my next album. I have always been a huge fan of his recorded sound. He has a unique approach to recording and I wanted to avail myself of that. He kindly said yes, and we made a plan to meet up in a year's time and do it. If nothing else came from the festival but that, I would have been happy, but in fact it was a tremendous experience, and the subsequent auction raised a lot of money for the centre. This was when I finally parted with 'Blackie', and the cherry red Gibson ES335 that I had had since the Yardbirds. It was the first serious guitar I had ever owned, and the day before the festival, I went to see them both on display, and bid them farewell. It was hard. We had travelled a lot of miles together, and I knew I would never find another instrument that could take the place of either of these. The sums they fetched defied belief. Blackie went for $959,500, creating a world auction record for a guitar, while the Cherry Red fetched $847,500, the highest price ever for a Gibson. Altogether, eighty-eight guitars were sold, which raised $7,438,624 for Crossroads.

The tour of America took me through to the autumn, and then on my return to England, I delved into a new hobby which was to become an equal obsession to fishing as the years went by. My friend Phillip Walford, who is the river keeper on the stretch of the river Test that I fish, had always said that I should take up game shooting, if only for the logical reason that the shooting season starts when the fishing season ends. I had always avoided the subject, simply because I intuitively knew that shooting was an intensely social pastime, as opposed to fly fishing, which is almost entirely solitary. To balance up the amount of time my business requires me to be in the public eye, I have always steered towards activities which allow a certain amount of solitude, and fly fishing has always provided me with that.

In fact it was pigeons roosting in the eaves of our house, cooing in the evenings, and waking the kids up at five in the morning, that tipped the balance. I went out and bought a shot-gun, and one thing just led to another. I am a deep-end person, and it was only a short amount of time before I was ordering braces of fine English guns, and driving all over the country to shoot on different estates, gradually improving my skill, and having the time of my life. Ethically it was never a problem for me, and it is the same with fishing. My family and I eat what I catch and shoot. It is fresh and healthy and we love it. I believe it is in my genes to hunt, and I am quite comfortable with that. I also support a lot of other countryside pursuits, quite simply because I believe they are an important part of our culture and heritage, and need protecting, usually from people, or movements of people who have little understanding of the delicate economic balance of countryside communities, and who have watched too many Disney movies.

I soon began to bump into old friends who had also taken up the sport, like Paul Cummins, who had been the co-manager of Dire Straits. He introduced me to a man called Jamie Lee, who runs a shoot called Rushmoor, in Dorset. Jamie is said to be one of the best game shots in the world, though it's usually him that's saying it, and his shoot, a private syndicate, is the best run I have ever been on. In addition, the guys in the syndicate are some of the most interesting people you could ever hope to meet, even though one or two of them are borderline psychotic. Gary Brooker, Steve Winwood, Roger Waters, Nick Mason and Mark Knopfler are also keen shots, so it's almost like coming full circle, meeting up again with all my old chums from the sixties music world in another, completely different sphere.

During the time that I wasn't shooting, I was hatching a plot for the following year. For some time I had been thinking about a reunion of Cream. It had been almost forty years since the creation of the band, and given the fact that we were all still capable of playing together, I thought it would be fitting to pay tribute to ourselves while we still could. I was also very aware that I had always been the reluctant one on this score, so, cap in hand, I made some delicate enquiries as to whether Jack and Ginger would be interested. They came back with a fairly positive response, and we decided to put on a week of shows at the Albert Hall, which of course was where we played our farewell concert. The dates were set for May 2005, with a month of rehearsals preceding. Realising that it was likely to be an experience I'd need to recover from, I also chartered a great boat, a motor yacht called *Va Bene,* to take Melia and the kids on a cruise through the Aegean when it was all over. She had never been to Greece, and the idea was dreamed up when we were watching the Athens Olympics on TV and I was regaling her with the whole story of my escapades with the Glands all those years ago.

On 1 February, 2005, my fourth daughter Sophie was born. I had given up hoping for a son by this time. In fact I had been quietly hoping for another girl, because so far my girls had all been such wonderful loving creatures, and I was dreading the possibility of a boy coming into our midst and causing guaranteed havoc. Sophie was born with bright red hair and, just like the other two girls before her, was constantly sick with one thing or another, and whatever it was, I would catch it, as would her sisters. But her spirit shone through, and because she is the youngest, she is probably the toughest and most assertive. I love all my girls equally, but it amazes me how different their characters are, and how, in turn, I respond to their various needs and manipulations. With the pace increased a notch, we soon realised that as well as Annie, we needed another pair of hands, and my friend, Jane Ormsby-Gore, Alice's older sister, suggested we offer the post to her daughter, and my god-daughter, Ramona. It seemed like a splendid idea, and she spent the next year with us.

I turned sixty this year, and to celebrate, Melia organised a massive bash at Banqueting House in Whitehall. We invited just about everyone I have ever known, even the members of the Glands band, some of whom I hadn't seen in forty years. It was a fantastic night, Jimmie Vaughan flew in to play, along with Robert Randolph and Steve Winwood, and I had the time of my life. The highlight of the evening for me was listening to my plucky wife make an impromptu speech about me, which brought tears to my eyes. A few other people had wanted to get to the microphone to say something, but she fought them all off to have her say, and I loved her for it. It was a truly great night, and I felt very happy and proud.

Cream rehearsals began in April and went on for almost a month. We needed a lot of preparation because we were reaching a long way back, and also Jack had just recovered from major surgery and complications, and was still convalescing. Ginger was also suffering from back problems, but for the moment I was in good health, and gloating. For the first couple of days we would only play two or three songs, trying to find our feet, but as the days went by we quickly found our pace again and it started to sound really good. I was tremendously relieved, I wasn't sure how it would go, and I knew that some of the old resentments were right there under the surface waiting to be rekindled. But after a minor skirmish right at the beginning, we all got on very well, and actually started to have fun. It was great, because it took me straight back to the times when being in Cream really was a fantastic place to be. As luck would have it, the day before the first gig at the Albert, I came down with a serious flu virus, and for the first three shows I was completely out of it. So much for my gloating. I started on antibiotics, and thank God recovered enough to be on form for the last couple of shows. It was a great experience, and I'm so glad we did it. I'll never forget the standing ovation we got when we first walked on stage. It went on and on, and on, for at least two or three minutes. It was tremendously moving, and made it all worthwhile. If only we'd left it there.

The offer, when it came, was too good to refuse. Ginger did refuse, because he had no desire to go back to America for a myriad of reasons. But we persuaded him, and agreed to play Madison Square Garden for a lot of money. We had played the Albert for love, and now we were cashing in, but who could really blame us? It just seemed like the logical thing to do. First of all, however, I was going on holiday.

I had recently bought a house in the South of France, and, with the shows over, I drove down there with my dear friend Brian Roylance, who was going through a rough time with his marriage and needed a break. There we met Melia and the kids and my in-laws, Mac and Laurie, and spent a few days getting ready, before getting on the boat in Cannes. I had booked it for the whole of June, which was a huge gamble, not knowing whether the girls would like it, or if they would get seasick, and if that was the case I had no contingency plan whatever. Thank goodness everyone loved the boat right away, and I breathed a huge sigh of relief. Only on a couple of occasions, when the weather was quite rough, did the kids experience any ill-effects, so on the whole it was a great success, and we were set for a fantastic holiday.

Our captain, Nick Line, had put together a fairly flexible plan to sail around Corsica and Sardinia, with the option of going on to Sicily, depending on weather and whatever preferences developed as the trip went on. To begin with, we weren't really sure what we wanted from our cruise, but there were lots of options in terms of things to see, and it quickly transpired that soft sandy beaches were the simplest solution for the kids. I personally loved Corsica. The landscape and rugged architecture were magnificent, so were the beaches, and every port we sailed into had a different charm. I had never been there before, and fell in love at first sight. It being early summer, the weather was still quite cool with strong winds, which made the water almost too cold to swim in, so we kept moving, and sailed down to Sardinia where, though the weather was warmer, the atmosphere was drastically different. From the sea, all the buildings looked like they belonged in a Flintstones movie. They were like caricatures of ancient buildings, obviously built quite recently from flimsy materials, and were, to my eye, very silly-looking. I couldn't wait to sail back to Corsica.

Melia's folks left after a week, and Richard and Chris Steele took their place, with Brian staying on for a few more days. During the trip, I was only speaking to the captain occasionally, usually to discuss our sailing plans, but I noticed that Richard was spending a lot of time up on the bridge, and kept coming back to us with little snippets of inside information. A couple of days into their stay, he came back looking very excited, with the news that the ship was for sale, and there was a curious gleam in his eye. 'You can't be serious?' I said, but he was not to be put off, and kept coming back with more and more information. Finally I gave in to my curiosity, and broached the subject directly with the skipper. Yes, it was for sale, and for a price that seemed quite reasonable. I asked around a lot, and spoke to my business manager, Michael Eaton, who to my surprise was very encouraging, unlike most of the other people I spoke to, who were fairly negative about the whole business. Funnily enough, the people whose advice I normally value the most leaned to the positive side, the general attitude being 'You can't take it with you.' So, after not much deliberation, I took the plunge and made an offer. What I said to the captain, and anybody else who needed to know, was that I was not really interested in buying a boat as such, but I wanted this boat. It is a seriously beautiful thing, and leagues ahead of anything else I have seen on the water.

For the first time in my life, I had to borrow money to pay for something, and I wasn't very comfortable with that. Throughout my life I had always bought everything outright, probably a reaction to my childhood, where everything was paid for on instalments, 'the never-never' as it was known back then. Luckily I had a tour coming up, the 'tour to end all tours' in fact, as it would cover the entire world, and hopefully that would establish, for a little while at least, some semblance of solvency. The tour would start in April 2006 and go on until April 2007, and I was quietly quite excited about it. It was a long time since I had toured at that level, and it would probably be the last time too.

Towards the end of our holiday, Brian came back on board for a few more days, and it was great to see him relaxing and having fun. We were sailing around the south coast of Corsica, and had fallen in love with the port of Bonifacio, and every other day we would go shopping for clothes in the local boutique, buying trendy things that were much too young for us. Also, little Ella had fallen in love with him, calling him 'my friend Frian', and for that short sweet time they became very close. It was a magical time for all of us. Sicily never saw us. It had no beaches apparently, so for the rest of our holiday, we lurked around Corsica until it was time to go back to port in Cannes. On the way there, we stopped off in Elba, where crowds of Italian holiday-makers would gather in the evening on the quay, and stare at the boat, sometimes ten people deep. I knew how they felt. It was dream-inspiring, and soon it would be mine.

Through the summer of this year, we started making preparations for Vivien's retirement. This was a big one, she had been with me for fifteen years, was always supportive, totally loyal and one of my closest friends. Vivien probably knew me better than anyone else on earth, and had never turned away from me, even when I was at my worst. Cecil had recommended a previous workmate of his named Nici, and after a couple of short meetings, I knew she was as good as we could hope to get, as replacing Vivi was not going to be easy. After a couple of months of overlapping, with Vivi providing coaching in the niceties of what is an extremely difficult job, Nici finally took over and has been doing an outstanding job ever since; like Cecil, she is totally pragmatic, and gets things done faster than I can think of them. Vivien finally left, with plans to start anew in France. I shall miss her.

I fished in Iceland for the first week in July, as I do every year if possible, and then after another week at home, set off for the States, where I was due to start recording with John 'J. J.' Cale. He had sent me a collection of songs for my approval, and initially three of them jumped out. The more I listened, however, the more I liked them all, and I knew that we would have to use them because, with all that was going on in my life, I had had no time to write anything myself. Once we got to America, Melia and the girls set up camp in Columbus, Ohio, and I went on to LA. Melia's parents lived in Columbus and we had bought a house near them the year before, so that we could visit her family and yet still have some space of our own. I really liked it there too. It was very countrified, and exactly the way I imagined the Midwest to be, plus, I could tool around in my hot rod without getting a second look; the ideal situation in fact, quiet and anonymous. It was also going to be our home base while I was touring the following year. We needed to get Julie started in full-time school, and it made more sense for Melia and the girls to be near her folks while I was away, although we planned to visit one another whenever we could.

I moved in with JJ for a week before we went into the studio, to go over the material, and get to know one another. He has a modest little house in the hills just outside Escondido, and we had a great time, listening to music, talking about the old days, and just generally hanging out. Not a lot of work got done, but that wasn't the point. We were getting ready to play. His idea was to bring in a lot of musicians, and try to record as much 'live' as we could, overdubbing only when we needed to. This was fine with me – that's the way I like to work too – but I thought we might have a problem now and then, capturing the groove that I heard on his demos, which is usually created with drum machines etc., and is such an important part of his sound.

I had decided to change my band line-up for the forthcoming tour, and wanted to use the Cale sessions as a 'get to know you' process with the new rhythm section, and with Derek Trucks, guitarist nephew of the Allman Brothers Band drummer, Butch Trucks, who I had asked to join the front line with me and Doyle. I had met Steve Jordan many years ago, when I had sat in with the David Letterman house band, and he was their drummer. We had also played together, back in 1986, on the Chuck Berry tribute *Hail! Hail! Rock 'n' Roll*, and I liked him a lot. He can play the way drummers played on early blues and R&B records, and is clearly a student of the real history of rock 'n' roll. Aside from that, he plays from the heart, a real 'feel' player. I didn't think I'd ever met Willie Weeks, but he claims we met on one of George Harrison's sessions, and I'm sure he's right. I was probably so drunk that I just don't remember it. Willie is one of the superheroes of rock. His legendary work with Donny Hathaway set the standard for everyone that followed, and hearing them play together on the JJ sessions was a delight. Along with Derek and Doyle and Billy Preston, I knew we were in good shape for the tour. Derek's playing was stunning, like nothing I had ever heard before. He has clearly grown up listening to many different forms of music, and all of them come through in his expression. He seems to have no limit. The other guys on the sessions were, for the most part, old friends of John's, great players all of them, even though many of them were now in retirement, enjoying a laid-back life. My guys were Doyle and Billy. Both these men had become indispensable to me now, and I totally trusted their musical intuition, in any situation.

The album, *The Road to Escondido*, was done and dusted

within the month, but it had changed shape. Rather than just another EC record, with John producing, it was now a duet album, owing to the fact that I wanted John's contribution to be larger. Overall I thought it improved the album, and, if nothing else, it made it more memorable for me. My friend Simon Climie was on board as an associate producer, and it was really good to see him behind the glass along with our other team member, Alan Douglas, who was in charge of the engineering. Mixing it all would spin out over the next six months, but as long as John had the last say, I felt confident that it would remain pure.

We clambered back on to the boat in September for a last-minute cruise, this time around the Greek Islands and Turkey. Hiroshi and his girlfriend Ayumi, plus his business associate Nobu Yoshida, joined us for the first week and Michael Eaton and his wife Ally came for the second. I thought it was important that Michael saw where all the money was going, and I couldn't wait to show off my new toy to Hiroshi. Now that the boat was actually mine, it really did feel different. It was strange. I couldn't quite believe it, and kept mentally pinching myself, as if I was dreaming. Did I really have the right to own something like this, a toerag from Ripley, with no idea how to make money, and no real respect for it either, cruising around in a 150 ft floating palace? It seemed unbelievable. I was on cloud nine, and had to keep telling myself, 'Yes, you do deserve this.' Our brief to the skipper had now become quite fixed: soft, sandy beaches, no sightseeing. My excuse was the little ones, who love to play in the sand, and who were also just getting used to being near the water, but in fact this was what I wanted too. I liked nothing more than sitting in a beach chair, watching the children play in the shallows, and occasionally glancing out across the water, to where our beautiful boat was anchored. It was like a dream.

While we were on the beach one day, I got a call from Cathy Roylance, Brian's daughter telling me her father had died from a heart attack. It felt like someone had punched me in the stomach. I had no idea it was coming. When he had been on the boat only a month earlier, he had looked better than I had seen him look for a long time. Now he was gone, at least from this world. He was my closest friend, and had done more to help me get sober, and stay sober, than anybody I had known. I was devastated. Looking back, I realised it had been ten years since he had had a quad-ruple heart bypass. I confess I experienced feelings of anger and guilt, that maybe he hadn't been looking after himself properly of late, and that I should have done more to keep an eye on him, but really I think that was just self-pity for my own loss. In truth I had lost track of the intricacies of Brian's private life in the last couple of years, owing to the growing needs in mine. All things must pass, and I had to let him go, but it was difficult. For well over twenty years we had watched each other's backs, and now it was over.

The shooting season began, and for a while it took my mind off my loss. I was invited to join Jamie's syndicate, and began driving down to Dorset every weekend, to shoot on one of the most difficult shoots in the country. The lay of the land, the wind direction, and the skilful management of very high pheasants, all conspire to make it an exciting and demanding shoot. The interesting thing about situations like this for me, is that the people I am shooting with have little or no grasp of what I do for a living. Consequently, I am starting out on the ground floor, and that makes me try even harder, and is good for my humility.

In October, I caught a plane to New York, where Cream had agreed to perform three shows at Madison Square Garden. In many ways I wish we had left it at the Albert Hall, but the offer we were made was too good to refuse. We walked into a rehearsal room the day before the first show, and did a meagre two-hour run-through without breaking a sweat. Logistically speaking, it made sense. We didn't want to cut into our lovely fee by spending too much on accommodation and rehearsal time, and of course we didn't need to practise too much. We were above that. In that short amount of time, our mindset had gone back to the sixties, and once again we were flying high on our egos. As a result, and this of course is just my opinion, the New York shows were a pale shadow of what we sounded like in London. Lack of rehearsal was one thing, but it reflected something else. The arrogance was back. Also Madison Square Garden is a big place, and we sounded small and tinny in there. I repeat, I am only stating my opinion, but for me the heart had gone out of it, and also a certain amount of animosity had crept back in. Maybe it was the money, who knows, but I did know that enough was enough, and I would probably not be passing this way again.

I got word in November that Billy Preston had been taken seriously ill, and had fallen into a coma. It came as a huge shock, because, just like Brian, he had seemed so well when I last saw him. In truth he had been very ill on and off for the last five years, suffering from failed kidneys, and having dialysis two or three times a week, even on the road. But comparatively speaking, he had looked and played well on the *Escondido* sessions, so it was dreadful news, and from what I could gather, things did not look very good for him. I planned to go and see him as soon as Christmas was over.

Christmas was very welcome when it came. With all that had happened through the autumn, I needed some light and laughter, and these days, because of the kids, Christmas was becoming exciting again, just like when I was a kid myself. We now had three children to buy presents for and entertain, and it was fantastic, just the way it is supposed to be. Also I had got hold of a Santa Claus outfit, and at a set time, just after dinner on Christmas Eve, I, or a suitable volunteer, would make a fleeting appearance as Father Christmas, strolling across the garden just outside the window. The kids would be alerted to this by Melia, and would go crazy, talking about it for days on end. It was so heart-warming to be able to do these little special things for my family, and I felt blessed.

On Boxing Day, I flew to Arizona to see Billy. He was in a private clinic, still in a coma, and it was thought that the chances of his recovery were slim. His manager, Joyce Moore, had been in contact with me throughout his illness, and was hoping that a visit from some of his friends might help to pull him back from wherever he had gone. When I saw him, however, my heart sank. He looked so old, and his eyes were open and staring off to the side, not what I had expected at all. I thought he would just look like he was asleep, and it shocked me. I talked to him a lot, whispering in his ear, telling him that I loved and missed him, and that we all wanted him to get well and come back to us, but I have to admit that I thought it was a lost cause. I don't have much experience of these things, but it seemed that he had already left us. For that reason, I said my goodbyes to him before I left to come home. It may have been premature if he recovered, but I needed to do it for both us, as I really didn't believe that I would see him again in this life.

The year ended with a sad but sober gig at the Guildford leisure centre, with Brian's image projected above the stage. He was well loved, and would be sadly missed by the Guildford recovering community, and we gave him a splendid send-off. His children Cathy and Nick attended and his good friend Pat made a heart-wrenching speech. I for one will never forget him, and what he did, so selflessly, for so many of us.

CHAPTER EIGHTEEN
A YEAR ON THE ROAD

The year of the world tour began quietly enough, although there were a lot of preparations to make, but we chose to get on the boat and have a short cruise around the Caribbean before the workload took me away. The sea around Antigua and the neighbouring islands was a lot rougher than the Mediterranean, and the kids sometimes had a tough time of it, but it was great for me to be able to show my family around places that I been before, many years ago. Ruth and her boyfriend Derek came out to join us for a week, and it was good to see Ruth, who was born in Montserrat, back in her element. Not much had changed in the Caribbean. New designer boutiques had sprung up here and there, but for the most part, many of the islands were just as they were thirty years ago. We spent the first part of the holiday in the house that I had built in Antigua. It has had so many additions over the years, guest cottages for the most part, that it actually now resembles a small village. It is a beautiful house, made entirely of local stone, and it is totally hurricane-proof, but because it was planned and built in my bachelor days, I have had to do a lot of work making it safe for the family. For a start, it stands on the top of a cliff, overlooking a breathtaking view of Indian Creek, and the drop is terrifying, so I am always a bit apprehensive when I'm there with my children. I long to spend more time there, and I know we will one day, but it is a harsh environment, and the girls will have to grow up a little bit more before I can feel completely assured about their safety there.

In April, I went off to France to begin rehearsals for the tour. The new band was very exciting, fresh and strong, and in some respects very reminiscent of the Dominos, perhaps because of Derek's presence. We began the tour in Europe, playing as many songs from *Back Home* as we could, and including a sit-down section where we picked up acoustic instruments. For the first time ever, I played 'I Am Yours' from the *Layla* album. Maybe it was this in itself that awoke in me a new love for the old Dominos stuff, but it was certainly helped on by Derek's and Doyle's insistence that we give those songs another airing. Over the course of the year, the set changed to the point where the whole of the first half was entirely from *Layla*, and then broke down into tunes from different eras, ending up with the song 'Layla' itself. It felt like a great show, and when we played to audiences who were old enough to remember the original album, we went down very well. In fact, even when we played to crowds who weren't so familiar with the songs, it didn't really matter, as we were having such a good time playing them.

Halfway through the European tour we had a break to avoid the World Cup. We had seen the preparations for it building in Germany, where it was being hosted, and knew that it was going to be next to impossible to get hotels, or conduct normal business until the whole thing was over. We got on the boat with Jamie Lee and Paul Cummins and their families, and trolled around Corsica for a couple of weeks. It was good fun trying to find bars that were showing the qualifying games for the cup, and watching the locals get into heated disputes. I'm convinced it's all rigged anyway. I tend towards conspiracy phobia in all things of this nature, including politics. With the amount of money that's at stake, I don't believe the likes of Rupert Murdoch or George Bush are inclined to leave very much to chance. Call me cynical, but every other week someone gets caught, or spills the beans.

We started up the tour again in Verona, and as luck would have it, the Italians were playing France in the final. The game was played the night before our first show, and we were invited by our hotel manager to watch it on a big-screen TV in the lounge. The famous Zidane foul stole the show, reminding me a lot of Cantona's equally infamous drop kick, a strange phenomenon, totally riveting, and yet utterly repellent and horrifying at the same time. When the final whistle blew, we were smack in the middle of all the World Cup madness we had hoped to avoid, and the whole of Italy went totally berserk. The fact that their victory was decided by a dismal penalty shoot-out didn't seem to quell their enthusiasm. I felt strangely detached from it all, my attitude towards national sporting events being slightly ambivalent. I tend to support any team that I think is playing creatively and fairly, and with character, and through the course of this particular event, there wasn't much of any of that to be seen. We moved on, back into Germany and up through Scandinavia, and at the end of the European leg we took another, longer break. The family and I met up in France, and a few days later flew on to Columbus.

The last half of August and a good part of September were spent just lolling around the house, swimming and relaxing in the sun, my idea of heaven. Julie and Ella were now proficient swimmers, inasmuch as they were confident and comfortable in the water, and Sophie, who had been walking for quite a while, wasn't far behind. This is exactly what I had been working for, the ability to be able to sit and play with my family in the sun, basically doing nothing, just having fun.

Our summer sojourn was broken in half by the need to take photos with JJ for the *Escondido* album, and the agreement was that I would travel to LA, meet John there – he hates to fly – spend a couple of days taking pictures, and meet with Tom Whalley to catch up on business while I was in town. Hanging out with JJ is one of my favourite pastimes. He is a great character with a brilliant sense of humour. I would say, from having got to know him, that he has been misunderstood by most people, often being referred to as a recluse, when in fact he is a very sociable man, open and charismatic. He just prefers his own company. As far as I know, JJ has never even been nominated for the Rock 'n' Roll Hall of Fame, while I have been inducted three times. In my humble opinion, he is one of the most important artists in the history of rock, quietly representing the greatest asset his country has ever had, and a lot of people in Europe have never even heard of him.

Travelling back to Columbus, because I had a one-way ticket I was a prime suspect for blowing up the plane, and the security people joyfully took me apart as usual. I swore quietly to myself, for the hundredth time, that I would never come back to this country again. Of course it's the same everywhere now, but for some reason it just feels worse in America. When we tour, we always charter a small aeroplane, which has been common practice for people in this business for a long time, but it tends to make me forget how grim it is trying to get around these days. I used to love travelling. I've always felt it was in my blood, but I can't stomach it any more, and literally dread going to an airport. The interesting thing about this tour has been the quiet, and sometimes happy knowledge that I may be going to some of these places, places I have been visiting all my life, for the very last time.

We began the American tour by commuting out of Columbus for a few days to maximise family time, starting in St Paul, and working our way across to the eastern seaboard. About a week in, just before I left home to hit the hotels, I caught a bug which completely laid me out. It turned into a chest infection, which forced us to cancel a gig in Detroit, and remained with me off and on for the rest of the tour. I have only cancelled two or three times in my whole career, and I am proud of that. I take it very hard when I can't show up, as I feel like I've let everybody down. Nevertheless, once I'd recovered, the shows continued to pick up momentum, and we hit our groove early on. This was a great band, one of the best I've ever gone out with, and I knew we had tons more to give.

After another shorter break in Columbus, listening to my kids' new American accents, I headed west, to meet JJ again, and launch our album. We were scheduled to do a three-day intensive press junket, after which I would travel on to Tokyo, to begin the Japanese tour. I really don't know if this promotion stuff serves any real purpose. I've always been resistant to it, and it's not unusual for me to do a week of promoting, and then meet someone on the street who will ask, 'Are you still making records?' The best part of this particular affair was to be sitting next to John, feeling him bristle as his patience wore thin from being asked the same ridiculous questions over and over again.

I was really looking forward to Japan. I have a lot of friends there, and a very loyal following. The morning after I arrived in Tokyo, Hiroshi came over to the hotel on his new Cinelli track bike, to give me a sample of some jackets he was designing for the Japanese division of the Levi's company. He is a great designer, taking classic or military designs and just adding one or two distinguishing features to make something new and unique. He is still a leading pioneer in street culture, hence the Cinelli. Track-bike riding is taking over from skateboarding in Japan, and Hiroshi is in the avant-garde as usual. I have caught the obsession of course. He is very infectious, and I have begun buying vintage road bikes, not to ride, but because I have always loved the equipment of cycling, especially the stuff from the sixties. My magpie tendencies have led me into a lot of different territories over the years: cars, guitars, clothes, art, watches and most recently western belt buckles. The watch collection was a dangerous excursion, and I became really obsessed, particularly with rare Patek Philippes. I couldn't believe the prices some of their chronographs would reach at auction, and it was as if I was testing myself to see if I had the nerve to buy these things. I was spending vast amounts of money at one point, on pieces that were arguably only of interest to someone like me. I found that out when the boat issue came up, and I tried to sell some of these priceless pieces to pay off my debt, the interest wasn't half as great as I had been led to believe. But no matter. I have educated myself enough to know that what I have is good, and I love these things. They are so beautifully made.

We stayed in Japan about two weeks too long, playing eighteen shows, twelve of which were at the Budokan. I didn't really mind, because I love being in Japan, but I was intensely homesick, I had been away from home for almost seven months and was really missing my family. The music was great, and the fans there know their rock history, so the Dominos stuff was well received. The highlight of the tour, as it is every time, is hanging out with Aki and Tak, and their boss Mr Udo. Tak is usually the tour producer when we're there, sharing management respon-sibilities with Peter and Doc, and Aki looks after me, driving me around, and taking care of my every need. They are great guys, and we have become close friends over the years.

Seijiro Udo has been promoting concerts in Japan and the Far East for fifty or sixty years, and has promoted every tour I've done in Japan since 19⁻3. The first thing I do when I arrive in Tokyo, without fail, is to meet Mr Udo at the Hama steakhouse for Kobe beef. I will go to my hotel, drop my bags and go straight to the restaurant, and I have been doing that for the last thirty-four years. I love Japanese food, and while I am there, I will probably eat with Mr Udo about three times a week, the finest food that you can imagine. He is Samurai, and that says it all. His sense of honour and integrity are peerless, and along with that he has an outrageous sense of humour. We laugh and tease a lot. I love him and think the world of him, he is one of a kind.

After travelling to Osaka and a couple of other cities, I was ready to go home. I'd had enough of hotels with pillows that collapsed into nothing when I put my head on them, and people endlessly asking to have their picture taken with me. I was worn out, and Christmas was around the corner. I was already making CD compilations of Christmas carols and hymns, and had bought toys and clothes for Melia and the kids. The plan was to meet up at Hurtwood, spend a week getting over the jet lag, and then get the house ready for Christmas and New Year. After that we would have to split up again, with Melia and the kids returning to Columbus, while I toured Indonesia and Australia. But for now, I was going home, and I just couldn't wait.

Thank God for the computer. When I am away from the family for long periods of time like this, we use it a lot, sometimes just to say goodnight when it's the kids' bedtime, but also generally to try to stay current. I honestly can't imagine life now without I-Chat and I-Sight, especially travelling and trying to raise a young family at the same time. Computer culture is another thing I caught from Hiroshi. I remember seeing him fooling around with a beautiful little Sony laptop, shortly after we met, and thinking, 'I have to have one of those things,' even though I had been curmudgeonly and contemptuous of the whole technology craze from day one. Since then I have managed to teach myself basic skills, and although I can still only type with one finger, I surf constantly, and have a massive library of music, which I constantly convert into playlists and CDs for the car. I

343

have become very dependent on it over the last couple of years, but it has been invaluable on this tour, with all the travelling I have had to do.

Getting off the plane at Heathrow was like stepping into a warm bath. I was so glad to be home. Melia and the girls were already at Hurtwood and I couldn't wait to see them. I complain so much about England once I'm safely ensconced there, but there really is no place like home, and there is nothing to compare with arriving home and seeing those little faces creased with happiness, and to hear their shrieks of joy when I get out of the car. They all want to show me their new toys, and they're talking all at the same time. It's absolute mayhem and I love it. It was great to see the Christmas decorations too, and to know for a few days I could bathe in the happiness of being really at home, with nothing else to do but indulge myself.

Not much had changed at the house, although some repainting had been done, and the overall style of the house was going through another transition. I had asked Jane Ormsby-Gore to help put the house into a Georgian mode, from having been modern Italian for the last ten years. She has a great eye, and I totally trust her judgement. The only family plan we had was some shooting between Christmas and New Year, this time with Melia in attendance. She had been taking lessons and was ready to enter the field. Needless to say, she was a fast learner, and is rapidly becoming a good shot. I'm so happy I have a wife I can share these things with, not only because it helps our friendship, but because she can then understand my passion for them too.

Ruth and Derek were coming down on Christmas Eve, and I had received an email from Derek a few days earlier, asking to speak to me about something urgent. It seemed that he and Ruth were thinking of getting engaged, and he wanted to do the proper thing, by asking me for her hand. I was a little shocked, because although Ruth had talked about getting engaged a long time ago,

I now knew that she was seriously considering a career in music, and I thought there might be a conflict between the two different directions. My God, everything was becoming so normal in my life. It was hard to believe that I was having to consider things like this, and that life was unfolding in this way, for me, and for all of us.

Christmas was wonderful. Richard and Chris, and Ruth and Derek came down the night before, and after dinner, Richard did the honours with the Santa Claus outfit. Julie has suddenly been expressing a certain amount of scepticism about the whole thing, and she's only five years old, and it's sad to think that the bubble will probably burst quite soon. We all had a great time. Melia cooked a delicious lunch, and all day we opened presents. My favourite was a white, Mexican Stratocaster, with a gold anodised scratchplate, that Melia had seen me eyeing up in a local guitar store. On the back of the guitar she had written a lovely dedication, and all the girls had signed their names. It's the best present I've ever had.

On Boxing Day I went out for a drive with Derek, and we talked about his prospects for Ruth and himself. I thought he was a really good guy, and they had been seeing each other for a couple of years, so I had no real objections to their marriage, and happily gave my consent. I asked him if he wanted me to make a formal announcement before we all parted company, but he said he had not actually proposed yet, and wanted to bide his time. I was impressed by his sense of prudence. After lunch we said goodbye to everybody, and drove down to Jamie Lee's to set up camp for our shooting spree. Jamie and his wife Lydia have two lovely girls, Jessica and Georgia, who are a bit older than ours, and get on famously with them, also Paul Cummins was coming down later with his wife Janice, and their little boy Jamie, so we were all excited and looking forward to the next few days.

We shot at three different venues, back to back, all high and difficult birds, and had a great time. Melia shot really well, with Alan Rose, the famous instructor from the West London Shooting School, standing beside her, giving her tips, and the occasional word of encouragement. The company was good, the weather was fine, and the shooting was great. I was really pleased that Melia actually enjoyed the day, and that shooting game, and not clay pigeons didn't put her off. It's obviously not everybody's favourite sport, and some people can get quite worked up about it. I remember a few years earlier, with trout fishing, I actually hit a kind of brick wall myself. I was fishing down on the Test, when I suddenly stopped and thought, 'Why am I doing this?' I had caught a couple of fish, killed them, and put them in my bag, and I thought, 'This is not right.' I was confused because I really enjoyed fishing, but it seemed that if I couldn't justify it to myself, at that exact moment, then I was going to have to stop. That's when I decided that from then on, I was going to eat everything I caught, and that catching large numbers of fish was no longer really an option. I have tried to apply the same principle to shooting, which is all well and good, but it's a tall order, trying to eat all the pheasant and partridge I shoot. Nevertheless we try.

The Christmas break had been a welcome rest from touring, and all in all, the horizon looked good. What had seemed like an impossible mountain to climb was, for the most part, now behind us, with three more months to go. The only bad news to come in over the holidays, and unfortunately it was equally as devastating as last year's loss, was that Ahmet Ertegun had passed away, after having been in a coma for several weeks after a fall at a Rolling Stones concert at the Beacon Theater in New York City. Shortly before that, his colleague and companion from the early days of Atlantic records, Arif Marden, had also died. It was a massive loss to the music world. These two men had been just as active and inspiring in recent years as they had been right from the start of their careers. They were also friends and colleagues, I had worked and collaborated with them both many times over the years, and Ahmet was the first heavy hitter in the business who truly saw and understood what I was trying to do, way back then. It was a terrible shock. I had Ahmet's old number in New York, and on the off chance, called to see if Mica, his wife, would answer. To my surprise, she answered herself straight away, and we talked briefly. It was so good to be able to share her grief, and to tell her how much he had meant to me. There are not that many people left from those days that I would be able to express that to. I offered my services, if she should need them, and I hope I was able to ease her burden for a moment or two.

January signalled the final ascent on the tour; we would start in Singapore, and head north into China via Thailand. Most of it was familiar territory, but it was everyone's first time in Shanghai, and we were all excited about that. Melia and the girls left for Columbus just before me, so that Julie could begin school on time, allowing for a couple of days of jet lag. This was going to be another long leg, like Japan, and we would be depending on the computer for family support. I was also carrying the complete manuscript of my book so far, with the intention of doing a thorough correction check whenever there was time in my schedule.

The first week in Indonesia was like a blur for me. It seems my ability to transcend jet lag has completely disappeared in my old age, and my natural curiosity has also diminished a great deal, so that venturing out of my room had become a highly debatable occupation. The change in climate was also a shock to the system. Having left an average English winter, we were suddenly planted in extreme tropical conditions, and it did nothing to boost my energy, leaving me limp like an old lettuce leaf. Fortunately we needed little rehearsal, and quickly climbed back into a confident stride with the music. Our daily schedule had quite a few decent holes, so I was able to get my teeth into my book quite early on.

By the time we reached mainland China, I was pretty well hooked, and it was all I could do to stop writing, pecking away with my one finger like a demented chicken. I have always enjoyed the different aspects of English literature, ever since I was a little boy, and spelling and grammar have been a source of great fascination for me. The only classes I did well in at school, other than art, were English and English literature, though that doesn't necessarily qualify me to write this and assume that it will be interesting to others.

With all the expectations I had about Shanghai, it was a huge disappointment. Flying in through the smog and blinking lights atop the bizarre array of new skyscrapers, it felt like I was entering a real-life version of the movie *Blade Runner*, and for some reason, I was instantly on my guard. That feeling never really left for the next few days, and I was always on edge, from the fractious stare-down with the immigration officer when I arrived, to the constant sidestepping of street hustlers, selling knock-offs of everything from DVDs to Mont Blanc pens. Thanks to Hiroshi, who was emailing street support, and a heads-up to where all the 'underground' stores were on my travels, I met some interesting people here. Tommy Chung was the man in Shanghai, he ran the only store to stock Visvim, my favourite shoe, and I thank him for his great hospitality while we were in his town. Overall though, I was pleased to be moving on.

New Zealand and Australia were a big surprise. I loved it there, and I had had huge trepidations, all for nothing. It proved beyond doubt that my attitude and state of mind would always govern my impressions of people, places and things. Meeting up with Beefy Botham in Melbourne was an example of the same principle. I had spent half of my last year of drinking with him, back in 1987, and so have always been a bit nervous of him ever since. We have met up a few times since then, and it's been fine, but in a way our friendship has been limited by the fact that he still likes a drink. This time was different. We really connected, perhaps because I have grown up a bit more, and realise that his choice to drink is none of my business, and that anyway, I really love the guy a lot. We have a lot in common and he has a heart of gold, and best of all, we can make one another laugh. So now I look forward to spending a lot more time with him, further on up the road.

It was summertime while we were down under, and I got brown and healthy, while back in Ohio I knew they were in deep winter, and getting snowed in. We had made a plan to meet in Hawaii, where Melia was born, for our next break, but had abandoned it, because the travelling involved would be so convoluted that by the time we all got there, and had recovered from our respective jet lag, it would be time to leave again, so I was going back to Columbus for ten days. For the next twenty-four hours, I flew from eighty-five degrees of perfect weather, to five below zero and blizzards. In fact, it was skin-of-the-teeth stuff getting into Columbus, because the weather was so bad. While we were taxiing in, I saw them de-icing the wings of another plane that was getting ready to take off, and said a silent prayer under my breath, as well as another vow to stop all this wandering around.

I got instantly sick during this break, the climate change was pretty drastic, and it was the first time I had experienced an Ohio winter, I couldn't believe how severe it was. That, coupled with the fact that I have a phobia about air conditioning, far preferring radiators for heating, left me feeling pretty low and physically vulnerable. All that aside, though, it was great to spend some time with the girls again, even though we were pent-up inside the house most of the time because of the cold. They were excited to see me too, and there was a lot of fighting over who was going to sit next to me at mealtimes. I loved it, and needed it too, being out on the road for months at a time, without any direct affection from another human being was having a pretty detrimental effect on my psyche, causing me to isolate myself in my room. The contrast between the empty hotel room and the roaring crowd in the auditorium can cause a lot of emotional confusion too, but for the moment that world could wait, I was safe with my loved ones again.

Picking up the thread again in Dallas, it was exciting for me to think that this was the last stretch, only one more month to go, and the tour would be over. Not that it had been a misery, in fact it had been a tremendous success on every level, I had thoroughly enjoyed the music and the companionship, but the travelling itself had taxed me far more than I had ever imagined. When me and Peter Jackson had planned this venture, back in 2005, it seemed fairly straightforward, and I was more than a little blasé about it, but after only two months in Europe I had begun to fully realise what I had let myself in for.

From Texas we went on to California, and commuted to a lot of shows around the West Coast from LA. I had been looking forward to this part of the tour because I planned on flying the girls in for a few days of much-needed sunshine, plus I would be able to look up a couple of old friends. Nigel Carroll still works for me, and he has two sons, who are fully grown now. They are both extremely artistic kids with a lot of flair, who've grown into fine young men, and I know he's very proud of them. I had also asked Nigel to trace Stephen Bishop, who had been a close friend during the seventies, and whom I regard as one of the great singer-songwriters. I felt compelled to look him up again, because as I have grown older, I think a lot about the friends I no longer see, and it worries me that we have all drifted so far apart. In Stephen's case, it was easy. When we met up it was as if time had stood still, and we were picking up where we left off. So for two weeks or so, the tour hit a warm patch; the family came in, old friends were around and life was good until, that is, we went north.

At the end of every leg of the tour so far, we had all agreed that it had been perhaps a week too long. In the case of this last leg, it was more like two weeks. The weather had got colder, the hotels were getting noisier, and I was running out of stamina. The amount of planning and day-to-day strategy involved in ensuring that I had enough energy for the gig in the evening, was getting ridiculous. At this stage it was absolutely necessary for me to have an hour's nap in the afternoon, and in order to get that hour, I had to create three hours of vacuum – not as easy as it might seem. We were also now travelling on show days a lot, and that was wearing me out. In short, it was getting really tough. Another aspect that had stretched all of us was that Derek Trucks had had to leave the tour to fulfil a prior commitment with the Allman Brothers halfway through this leg. We had all known this was coming, and there was nothing we could do about it, but it was hard to watch him go. It had a been a great journey playing with him through the year, and had altered and influenced the way we all played together. Thank goodness his absence was not as problematic musically as I had thought it would be. In fact Doyle and me really enjoyed playing more directly with one another. But in terms of pure energy, it was draining me unbelievably, and seemed to add more weight to the lead I felt in my legs.

In Canada, I got to see my half-sister Cheryl and her family. We don't see much of one another, and I felt poorly equipped to socialise, plus we were moving on right after the show, so time was short. It had been the same for my other half-sister, Heather, in Toronto the year before, and I realised that times have changed. In the old days I would have made time to visit with them the day before, or the day after the show, but now I was having to rest every chance I got. By the time we got to Fargo on my birthday, I was exhausted, and had had enough, but Melia and the girls came to visit, and that did a lot to restore my equilibrium. We had a big party before the gig and I got some wonderful presents from the band and crew. I found it really moving to have everyone in the same room together, and when I tried to speak to say thank you, I started choking up. I really believe this crew of techs and managers, from the riggers to the computer boffins, are the best in the business. They have been with me for ever, and I rarely give them enough credit. Funnily enough the only present I can remember getting is a pair of ghastly pink Crocs (rubber sandals with holes in), that Michele and Sharon had given me. Thanks for the memory, girls.

The last week was a nightmare, I was only getting about three hours' sleep a night, and in Kansas City, over the course of a three-day visit, I changed hotels four times. The noise was unbelievable. It was either construction outside, roaring elevator shafts inside, or people throwing things around their rooms. I was shattered. The only thing that made it bearable was the music we would make in the evening, which was always brilliant. Even so, I was praying for the end, and counting the minutes. By the end, however, every gig was memorable, the only thing that could rattle us, or me in particular, being bad acoustics, and it seemed we had left those places behind us. Luckily the last show in Columbus was a great one. It had needed to be, as my entire American family was there.

Brief goodbyes were said, but we knew that, apart from Steve Jordan, we would all be together again in Chicago in July at the next Crossroads Guitar Festival. As for Jordan, I was going to see him in a couple of weeks at a tribute evening in memory of Ahmet Ertegun, which was to take place in New York, and of which he would be the musical director. It was still snowing in Columbus, which gave me the opportunity to sit and practise the songs I wanted to play for Ahmet. He had always loved the song 'Please Send Me Someone To Love' by Percy Mayfield, and in the bad old days, when we would get smashed together, he would sing the opening lines to me with a twinkle in his eye – 'Heaven please send to all mankind, understanding and peace of mind. But if it's not asking too much, please send me someone to love.' I think for him it summed up the simple irony that the blues so often embodies. He never pressured me to record it. He just loved to sing it to me in that cracked old voice of his, and that's my fondest memory of him. The other song was called 'Wine Spo-Dee-O-Dee', which was apparently the first record officially released on the Atlantic label.

Time passed slowly in Ohio, and when I wasn't practising Ahmet's songs, I was watching cricket on TV. Amazingly enough, my brother-in-law, Steve, had managed to get the World Cup cricket tournament on cable, and it became my drug for the next two weeks. It also helped with my cravings for England and home, giving me something I could identify with until we finally made the trip. I loved our house in Columbus, and the family are a superb gang of people, but I was yearning for England, and with still one more gig to do, I felt like I was in limbo. I was also finding it hard to believe that the tour was finally over, and I went into a bit of a decline. It always happens, but my experience over the years has helped me prepare for this, and I know how to deal with it, although I'm sure my family and friends must find it very confusing. I had been looking forward to the last stretch for as long as I could remember, and now that it was a reality, I was depressed. It seems completely illogical, and can be mis-interpreted very easily, but it is, in my experience, almost unavoidable. It's part of the process, and always passes, but it takes a lot of patience and understanding from everyone involved.

Ahmet's tribute evening was to be held at the Lincoln Jazz Center in New York. I had played there in 2003 with Wynton Marsalis, who had helped establish it, and thought it was the perfect venue. As we were also moving home as a family unit, the plan was to stop in NYC for the tribute, allowing time for rehearsals and sightseeing, and then travel on the following day.

There are no direct flights from Columbus to London, and with the strong possibility of losing luggage and just general wear and tear, it has become our routine to break the journey in half, by staying the night in Manhattan. It also gives me the chance to visit friends, shop, and of course the kids love to play in Central Park. Unfortunately the weather turned nasty, and torrential rain kept us cooped up in our room, just as the snow had in Ohio. By now, after all the hotel rooms and general bad weather, I was craving fresh air and outdoor life, but we would have to wait a few more days.

The celebration for Ahmet was a great success, well staged and very well attended. The evening was mostly given over to speakers like Henry Kissinger, Oscar De La Renta, David Geffen and Mick Jagger, all of whom spoke with love and eloquence, while a few others, including Ben E. King, Phil Collins, Stevie Nicks, Crosby, Stills, Nash and Young, Bette Midler and myself, provided the music. Melia was with me, and I thought it was great for her to see just how much this man had meant to all of us. Mick was incredibly funny, telling great stories, and referring to Ahmet as his 'wicked uncle', but as entertaining and emotionally stirring as it was, I still felt that, had Ahmet been there in the flesh, he would have said something like, 'Let's get out of here and find the real shit.'

After the show, Melia and I went to the after-party for a few minutes, where we bumped into Robbie Robertson. He's always great fun to be with, and earlier in the day we had been listening to some music we had written back in the nineties, with a notion to finishing it off. I had always wanted to collaborate with Robbie, he has a great ear and brilliant writing skills, and maybe, finally, this would lead us there, but that's another story. All in all, our reason for getting together, to pay tribute to an amazing man, had resulted in a great event, and it was extraordinary to see all the different people he had touched in his life, all together in one place, for one moment in time. A perfect send-off for a remarkable man.

The following day we got on the plane and flew home, everyone was really excited, and I personally couldn't wait to crash on the big couch in our front room and have a nap. I had been watching the weather on my computer, and while everywhere else in the world seemed to be having snow and rain and stormy weather, England was enjoying a warm and sunny spring. Needless to say, I had already planned to go fishing the first Saturday after we got home, along with doing absolutely nothing, or at least trying to. It was what I had been dreaming of all year. The trip was painless and uneventful, the kids slept throughout the flight, no luggage was lost, and Cedric and Cecil were there to meet us and drive us home.

There is something about the drive to our house in Surrey that never fails to move me. I'm sure everyone feels that way about going home after a long trip, but this is really special. The last mile is spectacular, going through the beautiful Surrey Hills, finally resolving in a short drive through high rhododendron bushes, before the house itself appears. There's no doubt that Hurtwood itself is imposing, but not in a frightening way. It just seems to have a personality of its own, so that it welcomes you, even when it is empty. That's exactly how it was on that day. We walked through the door, and a great weight seemed to be lifted from us, as if to say, the time for rest had begun. In a short while our English nanny, Annie, was cooking lunch, Melia and the kids were in the playroom, rediscovering their toys, and I was upstairs, hurriedly unpacking, desperately trying to put the road, and its various duties, behind me.

I'm so glad that my family loves it here as much as I do. It provides the foundation for our life together in the physical sense. I know we can find a way to be happy wherever we are, but this place seems to have special meaning for all of us, and I hope it will always be this way. I have no intention of going anywhere for a little while, and can't wait for my home life to re-establish its normal routines, like going for walks up in the hills, feeding Gordon the pig, and just generally lolling around.

I have been retiring all my life, constantly vowing to give up the road and just stay at home, and maybe one day I will be forced to do that for one reason or another. For now I will leave the door open, and maybe that will make it easier for me to stay inside, a kind of reverse psychology, but who knows. All I know is, right now I don't want to go anywhere, and that's not bad for someone who always used to run.

EPILOGUE

The last ten years have been the best of my life. They have been filled with love and a deep sense of satisfaction, not because of what I feel I have achieved, but more because of what has been bestowed on me. I have a loving family at my side, a past I am no longer ashamed of and a future that promises to be full of love and laughter. I feel really fortunate to be able to say this, for I'm fully aware that, for a lot of people, approaching old age represents the end of all things pleasurable, the gradual onset of infirmity and senility, and regret for a life unfulfilled. Maybe I will eventually feel the grip of fear as I view my final years, but right now I am very happy, and I feel that way a lot of the time. The only time I get really disgruntled is when I'm working and don't feel I have the capacity to deliver the goods, usually because I'm ill or overtired. That's the perfectionist in me and it's always been like that. If I have any real qualms about the future, it is for my children. It grieves me to think that they may lose their father while they are still young.

As I write this, I am sixty-two years old, twenty years sober and busier than I have ever been. I have just completed a big world tour, and even if it is sometimes gruelling, I like the pace. I am virtually deaf, but refuse to wear a hearing aid because I like the way things sound naturally, even if I can hardly hear them. I am lazy, refusing to do any exercise, and as a result, am completely unfit. I am a complete curmudgeon and proud of it. I know who I am these days, and I know that if there is nothing much going on at any given time, I will start something, not out of boredom, but because I need movement. I have a rhythmic nature. That's not to say that I don't know how to relax. I like nothing better than doing nothing, but after a while I will need to be on the move again.

It is 2007, and this summer I will help stage another Crossroads Guitar Festival, which I'm really looking forward to. Some great musicians are coming out to play, and I value the chance to hear them more and more as time goes by. Last year I had to say goodbye to Billy Preston, who was, aside from Ray Charles and Chris Stainton, the greatest keyboard player, that I have ever heard, as well as to Ahmet Ertegun and Arif Marden, giants of the music world who knew more about music and how to create it than anyone they have left behind. It seems like I've been saying goodbye all my life to great players and friends, and it never ends. Thank God there are plenty left. I have, for instance, been playing on this tour with Doyle Bramhall and Derek Trucks, two fine guitar players who prove that the real thing is still alive and kicking. Playing with them keeps me young, and pushes me far beyond my normal limitations.

My family continue to bring me joy and happiness on a daily basis, and if I were anything but an alcoholic, I would gladly say that they are the number-one priority in my life. But this cannot be, because I know I would lose it all if I did not put my sobriety at the top of that list. I continue to attend twelve-step meetings, and stay in touch with as many recovering people as I can. Staying sober, and helping others to achieve sobriety, will always be the single most important proposition of my life.

But let's stay real here too. I have been out on the road all my life, and at the end of every tour, I swear it will be my last. Nothing has changed in that regard. 'It's a goddamned impossible life,' as my friend Robbie Robertson once said, and this recent tour, as great as it has been musically, has also been very taxing on me. I can't sleep well away from home any more, hotels are not what they used to be, and I miss my family so much. I also suffer from physical complaints a lot more than I used to in my youth, such as bad back pain, and digestion disorders. It all adds up, and going on stage under par is my worst-case scenario. So, as much as I love to play, touring on the grand scale has, I think, seen the last of me; I will work as long as I live, but I will have to find another approach that isn't quite so taxing.

Looking back, my journey has brought me into proximity with some of the great masters of my profession, and all of them took the time to show me something of their craft, even if they weren't aware of it. Perhaps the most rewarding relationship I have had with any of these great players has been with Buddy Guy. In all the years that I have known him, he has never really changed, and we have always remained great friends. In the musical sense, it was he who showed me the way forward, by example. The combination of wildness and finesse that his playing encompasses is totally unique, and has allowed players from the rock genre to approach the blues from an unfettered perspective. In other words, he plays free, from the heart, acknowledging no boundaries.

I never really knew Stevie Ray Vaughan well. We played together only a couple of times, but it was enough to be able to link him with Jimi Hendrix in terms of their skills and style. They both played out of their skin, every time they picked up their instruments, as if there was no tomorrow, and the level of commitment they both showed to their art was identical. Listening to him on the night of his last performance here on earth was almost more than I could stand, and made me feel like there was nothing left to say. He had said it all. His brother, Jimmie, is one of my closest friends, and is, in my opinion, in the same league as Buddy, totally unique in style and free as a bird. We have been pals and collaborators since the sixties, and as much as anything musical, I owe him a debt of gratitude for turning me on to the hot-rod culture. I have three cars, all custom-built by Roy Brizio, with two more on the way. Robert Cray is another friend who has my total admiration too. His singing has always reminded me of Bobby Bland, but his guitar style is all his own, although if you know your blues history, you can hear just about everyone in his playing. There are so many players I have admired and imitated from John Lee Hooker to Hubert Sumlin, but the real king is BB. He is without a doubt the most important artist the blues has ever produced, and the most humble and genuine man you would ever wish to meet. In terms of scale or stature, I believe that if Robert Johnson was reincarnated, he is probably B. B. King.

While I am talking about heroes and musicians that have moved me, I would have to put Little Walter near the top of my list. He played harmonica with Muddy Waters in the early days, before going solo, and he was the master of his instrument. He was also one of the most soulful singers I have ever heard, and while I am talking about singers, I have to say that I have only one regret in this department, and that is I never had the good fortune to play with Ray Charles. He was, in my opinion, the greatest singer of all time, and he was also a blues singer. The historical definition of the blues is that it is a style of music born out of the union between African and European folk cultures, conceived in slavery and fostered in the Mississippi delta. It has its own scale, its own laws and traditions and its own language. In my view it's a celebration of triumph over adversity, full of humour, double entendre and irony, and very rarely, if ever, depressing to listen to. It can be, and usually is, the most uplifting music you will ever hear. Ray Charles took that essence, and injected it into every style of music he played, from gospel to jazz, R&B, and country and western. Whatever the occasion, whatever the format, he always sang the blues. I had the privilege of playing on an album of his in the eighties, but it was overdubbed, and he wasn't actually there. I would have loved to have been able to sit in a room accompanying him while he sang and played, just to have had that experience.

The one man I have left out so far is Muddy Waters, the reason being that for me, he represented something much more fundamental. He was the first of the truly great bluesmen that I met and played with, and the first to show me real encouragement and kindness. Long before we ever met, he was the most powerful of all the modern blues players I had heard on record, and the sheer strength of his musical character had a profound effect on me as a green young scholar listening my way forward. Later on, right up until the day he died, he was very much a part of my life, touring with me, counselling me and generally acting as the father figure I never really had. I was even present, along with Roger, at his wedding ceremony, when he married his last wife Marva.

Towards the end of our last times together, Muddy began speaking to me in earnest about carrying on the legacy of the blues, calling me his adopted son, and I assured him that I would do my best to honour this responsibility. It was almost an overwhelming thing to fully take in, but I took him at his word, and as much as this kind of thing is humorously disregarded these days, I am absolutely certain that he meant it. One of the few regrets I have in my life is that my drinking was at its peak during the years that we spent together, thereby preventing me from having a truly intimate relationship with him. Alcohol would have always come first in those days. It was also highly illuminating to me that many years after Muddy's death, I read an interview that was done when he was very young, where he named Leroy Carr as his first real influence. I had always felt the same way about Leroy Carr, but had never met anyone who shared that. To me the connection felt logical, and gave me affirmation that I did really belong in this precious thing, which I suppose you could call the blues family, and, apart from at home with my kids, there's no other place I'd rather be.

The musicians I have had the honour and pleasure to play with over the years are far too many to mention, but all have been unforgettable for one reason or another. Most of them have also been philosophers too, in an unspoken way. There seems to be a silent acknowledgement amongst most players that we have a certain responsibility as teachers or healers, and although we all have different ways of honouring this commitment, it is certainly something we are all aware of. For myself, I have tried to steer clear of social or political comment in my approach to writing and playing, except in the vaguest possible way, simply for the reason that I don't want to gather any moss, so to speak, or be associated with any movement that would detract from my mission as regards blues music, or music as a whole. I have always believed that music in itself is a powerful enough agent to cause change, and that sometimes words, or agendas, can get in the way.

The music scene as I look at it today is little different from when I was growing up. The percentages are roughly the same – 95 per cent rubbish, 5 per cent pure. However, the systems of marketing and distribution are in the middle of a huge shift, and by the end of this decade, I think it's unlikely that any of the existing record companies will still be in business. With the greatest respect to all involved, that would be no great loss. Music will always find its way to us, with or without business, politics, religion or any other bullshit attached. Music survives everything, and like God, it is always present. It needs no help, and suffers no hindrance. It has always found me, and with God's blessing and permission, it always will.

Picture credits

Chapter Opening Pictures

Eric Clapton in a field of long grass with his guitar © Terry O'Neill/Getty Images

1. Eric playing with his dog and toy guitar
2. Student identification card picture
3. John Mayall and the Bluesbreakers © Michael Ochs/Getty Images
4. Cream © Pattie Boyd
5. Blind Faith
6. Derek and the Dominos with kind permission from Robert Stigwood Organisation
7. At Hurtwood
8. On stage © Michael Putland/Retna Pictures
9. Eric Clapton and Pattie Boyd
10. In hospital
11. Fishing
12. Eric Clapton and Phil Collins © Pattie Boyd
13. Conor
14. Ruth
15. Eric Clapton outside the Crossroads Rehabilitation Centre,

Antigua © Stuart Clarke/Rex Features
16. Eric and Melia on their wedding day © Chip Somers
17. Ruth, Eric, Julie, Sophie, Ella and Melia © Jack English
18. On tour © AP/PA Photos
Playing guitar in the grounds of Hurtwood © Christopher Simon Sykes

Plate section 1
Page 4 © Getty Images
Page 5 © David Wedgbury
Page 7, top left and bottom © Getty Images
Page 7, top right: Cream album artwork with kind permission of Universal Music Group.
Page 10 both © Dezzo Hoffman/Rex Features
Page 11, top © Ray Stevenson/Rex Features
Page 11, bottom: Blind Faith album artwork with kind permission from Universal Music Group.
Page 12, top © Christopher Simon Sykes
Page 12, bottom © Getty Images
Page 13, top left © PA Photos
Page 16 both © Getty Images

Plate Section 2
Page 1, top © Getty Images
Page 3, top: 461 Ocean Boulevard album artwork with kind permission of Universal Music Group
Page 3, bottom © Spa Press/Rex Features
Page 4 © Johnny Dewe Mathews
Page 6, top © Getty Images
Page 8, top © Pattie Boyd
Page 10, top © Getty Images
Page 10, bottom right © Getty Images

Page 11, top © Eric Ellington
Page 13, top © Getty Images
Page 13, bottom: Eric Clapton Unplugged artwork with kind permission of Warner

All other photographs are from Eric Clapton's private collection

Index